HCNA Networking Study Guide

Huawei Technologies Co., Ltd.

HCNA Networking Study Guide

Huawei Technologies Co., Ltd.
Shenzhen
China

ISBN 978-981-10-9384-5   ISBN 978-981-10-1554-0   (eBook)
DOI 10.1007/978-981-10-1554-0

Printed on acid-free paper

This Springer imprint is published by Springer Nature
The registered company is Springer Science+Business Media Singapore Pte Ltd.

Foreword

Huawei is one of the leading ICT solution providers worldwide. Our vision is to enrich life through communication, and it is with this vision that we are able to leverage our ICT technologies and experience to help everyone bridge the digital divide and become a part of the information society so that all may enjoy the benefits of ICT services. We endeavor to popularize ICT, facilitate education, and cultivate ICT talents, providing people with the tools necessary to build a fully connected world.

This book is a study guide for Huawei HCNA certification. It is the culmination of efforts by Dr. Yonghong Jiang and his writing team. Dr. Jiang is a senior technical expert in Huawei and has worked with us for over 10 years. Before joining Huawei, Dr. Jiang gained many years of teaching experience in both domestic and international universities. He therefore has a deep understanding of how knowledge can be taught and mastered. Logic is important for explaining principles, as too is the accuracy of information—the very essence of this is embodied in *HCNA Networking Study Guide*. I truly believe it is a must-have book for those who intend to learn HCNA network technologies.

March 2016

Wenjie Tu
Director of Global Training and Certification Department
Huawei Enterprise Business Group

Preface

Declaration

This book is the study guide for Huawei HCNA certification. It is crafted to help understand the principles of network technologies. Apart from the knowledge offered in this book, HCNA also covers other knowledge, such as RSTP, MSTP, DNS, FTP, VRRP, NAC, 802.1x, SSH, xDSL, HDLC, FR, GRE, IPSec, WLAN, VoIP, data center, cloud computing, 3G/4G, and IPv6. If you want a solid foundation for preparing for the HCNA exam, you will also have to learn those concepts.

Organization of This Book

This book is divided up into 14 chapters. Chapters 1 and 2 are preparations for the network technologies discussed in Chaps. 3–13. The last chapter, Chap. 14, is the Appendix and provides answers to all review questions contained in the preceding chapters.

Chapter 1 Network Communication Fundamentals

The OSI and TCP/IP models are vital to understanding network communication. This chapter describes and compares the two models. It further introduces and describes typical network topologies, LAN and WAN, transmission media, and methods of communication.

Chapter 2 VRP Basics

VRP is Huawei's network operating system that runs on network devices such as routers and switches. Knowledge of VRP is essential to understanding Huawei products and technologies, and many of the configuration examples provided in this book are based on VRP. This chapter systematically introduces how to use VRP.

Chapter 3 **Ethernet**

Ethernet is the most widely used type of LAN today, and as a result, the terms Ethernet and LAN are almost synonymous. We start this chapter by introducing Ethernet network interface cards on computers and switches and the differences between them. We then discuss MAC addresses, Ethernet frames, switch forwarding principles, MAC address tables, and ARP operating principles.

Chapter 4 **STP**

Layer 2 loops are a major problem on Ethernet networks covering both computers and switches. Loop prevention protocols, such as STP, RSTP, and MSTP, can be used on switches to prevent such loops. This chapter provides background information about STP and describes how STP is used to prevent Layer 2 loops.

Chapter 5 **VLAN**

Another problem showing on Ethernet networks is how to flexibly and efficiently classify Layer 2 broadcast domains. The solution to this problem is to use VLAN. This chapter describes the VLAN principles, the format and forwarding process of VLAN frames, and the link and port types used in VLAN. It also describes the functions of GVRP.

Chapter 6 **IP Basics**

Chapters 3–5 focus on the data link layer. Chapter 6 describes IP basics, including IP addressing, IP packet format, and IP forwarding. This chapter also addresses the concepts of Layer 2 communication, Layer 3 communication, and the Internet.

Chapter 7 **TCP and UDP**

This chapter introduces the two transport layer protocols: TCP and UDP. It focuses on the differences between connectionless and connection-oriented communication. It also demonstrates how a TCP session is created and terminated, and presents the acknowledgment and retransmission mechanisms of TCP.

Chapter 8 **Routing Protocol Basics**

Knowledge of routing and routing protocols is the basis to understand networking and its technologies. This chapter starts by introducing basic concepts, such as a route's composition, static and dynamic routes, and routing tables. It then describes RIP, the simplest routing protocol. This chapter also introduces the concepts of OSPF.

Chapter 9 Inter-VLAN Layer 3 Communication

Computers on different VLANs cannot communicate over Layer 2, but they can communicate over Layer 3. This chapter describes the working principles of inter-VLAN Layer 3 communication through a one-armed router, a multi-armed router, and a Layer 3 switch. It covers the contents of how a Layer 3 switch, a Layer 2 switch, and a conventional router forward data.

Chapter 10 Link Technologies

Link aggregation is a commonly used link technology that can flexibly increase bandwidth and improve connecting reliability among various network devices. This chapter includes the basic concepts, application scenarios, and working principles of link aggregation. It also involves two Huawei proprietary link technologies that can improve network link reliability: Smart Link and Monitor Link.

Chapter 11 DHCP and NAT

This chapter describes the basic concepts and working process of DHCP as well as DHCP relay. It also introduces the basic concepts, principles, and application scenarios of NAT.

Chapter 12 PPP and PPPoE

This chapter describes the basic concepts and working process of PPP, the format of PPP frames, and the different phases involved in PPP. It further elaborates the combination between PPP and Ethernet, known as PPPoE.

Chapter 13 Network Management and Security

Management and security are vital concerns in today's networks. This chapter concentrates on SMI, MIB, and SNMP used in network management and ACL used in network security.

Chapter 14 Appendix—Answers to Review Questions

Many sections in each chapter of this book include review questions for the readers to oversee the contents they have studied. The suggested answers to these review questions are provided throughly in this chapter.

Target Audience

This book is targeted to the readers preparing for Huawei HCNA certification. It covers the detailed basis of routing and switching technologies, which also makes it a valuable resource for ICT practitioners, university students, and network technology fans.

Important Notes

While reading this book, please be aware of the following:

1. This book may refer to some concepts which are beyond its scope. We advise you to research these concepts for the better understanding but doing so is not a requirement.
2. The Ethernet mentioned in this book only refers to the star-type Ethernet networks. This book does not include bus-type Ethernet or such related concepts as CSMA/CD and collision domain. Many resources are available to be traced by most of the search engines if you are interested in Ethernet's history and its development.
3. Unless otherwise specifically explained, IP in this book refers to IPv4. IPv6 is not covered in this book.
4. This book presents two data link layer technologies, Ethernet and PPP. Unless otherwise stated, network interface cards, network interfaces, interfaces, and ports specifically stand for Ethernet network interface cards, Ethernet network interfaces, Ethernet interfaces, and Ethernet ports, respectively, and frames refer to Ethernet frames.
5. In this book, the network interfaces on routers and computers are noted as interfaces and the network interfaces on switches are noted as ports.
6. Unless otherwise stated, switches in this book refer to Layer 2 Ethernet switches that do not support Layer 3 forwarding.
7. In Sect. 8.1.2, we state that the cost of a static route can be set to 0 or any desired value. This is true theoretically, but most network device vendors require the cost of a static route to be only 0 and do not allow it to be configured or changed. In addition, many such vendors set the minimum number of RIP hops as 0, meaning that there is no hop from a RIP router to its directly connected network. However, the Routing Information Protocol itself stipulates that there be a minimum of 1 hop from a RIP router to its directly connected network. This difference exists due to historical factors, but does not affect the deployment and functions of RIP. In Sects. 8.2.1–8.2.7, the minimum number of RIP hops is thus defined as 1. In Sect. 8.2.8, the minimum number of RIP hops is defined as 0.
8. If you have any feedback or suggestions regarding this book, please e-mail Huawei at Learning@huawei.com.

Icons in This Book

Router

Access
switch

Aggregation
switch

Core
switch

Server

PC

IP-DSLAM

HG

Network cloud

Internet

Ethernet or PPP link (Ethernet by
default)

Huawei Certification Overview

Huawei's training and certification system has a history of over 20 years, involving more than 3 million people in more than 160 countries. It is created to match the career development life cycle of the ICT industry and provides technical certification for associates, professionals, experts, and architects from single disciplines to ICT convergence. Huawei's Certification Solution covers all technical areas of ICT, making it one of a kind in the industry. Leveraging Huawei's Cloud-Pipe-Device convergence technology, the solution covers IP, IT, and CT as well as ICT convergence technology. Huawei offers field-specific knowledge and training solutions to different audiences and provides accurate assessments to gauge understanding at Huawei-provided training centers, Huawei-authorized training centers, and joint education projects with universities.

To learn more about Huawei training and certification, go to http://support. huawei.com/learning. For the latest news about Huawei certification, follow us on our microblog at http://e.weibo.com/hwcertification. Or, to discuss technical issues and share knowledge and experience, visit the Huawei Forum at http://support. huawei.com/ecommunity/bbs and click Huawei Certification. The following figure shows the hierarchy of Huawei's ICT career certification.

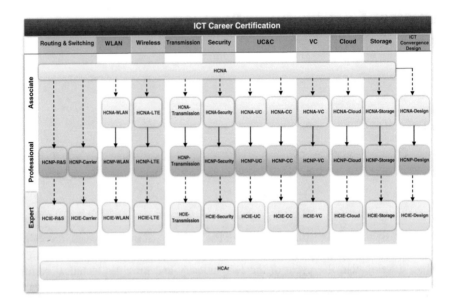

Authors of This Book

Chief editor is Yonghong Jiang.

Contributors of this book are as follows: Zhe Chen, Ping Wu, Yuanyuan Hu, Diya Huo, Jianhao Zhou, Chengxia Yao, Jie Bai, Huaiyi Liu, Linzhuo Wang, Huan Zhou, Pengfei Qi, Yue Zong, Chaowei Wang, Tao Ye, Zhangwei Qin, Ying Chen, Hai Fu, Xiaolu Wang, Meng Su, Mengshi Zhang, Zhenke Wang, Fangfang Zhao, Jiguo Gao, Li Li, Yiqing Zhang, Chao Zhang, Qian Ma, Xiaofeng Tu, Yiming Xu, Yang Liu, Edward Chu, Rick Cheung, and Cher Tse.

Contents

Abbreviations

AAA	Authentication, Authorization, and Accounting
ABR	Area Border Router
AC	Access Concentrator
ACL	Access Control List
ADSL	Asymmetric Digital Subscriber Line
AP	Alternate Port
ARP	Address Resolution Protocol
ARPANET	Advanced Research Projects Agency Network
AS	Autonomous System
ASBR	Autonomous System Boundary Router
ATM	Asynchronous Transfer Mode
BDR	Backup Designated Router
BGP	Border Gateway Protocol
BIA	Burned-In Address
BID	Bridge Identifier
BOOTP	Bootstrap Protocol
BPDU	Bridge Protocol Data Unit
CHAP	Challenge-Handshake Authentication Protocol
CIDR	Classless Inter-Domain Routing
CLNP	Connectionless-mode Network Protocol
CMIS	Common Management Information Service
CRC	Cyclic Redundancy Check
CSMA/CD	Carrier Sense Multiple Access with Collision Detection
CU	Control Unit
DD	Database Description
DHCP	Dynamic Host Configuration Protocol
DNS	Domain Name Service
DP	Designated Port
DQDB	Distributed Queue/Dual Bus
DR	Designated Router
DSAP	Destination Service Access Point

DSCP	Differentiated Services Code Point
DSLAM	Digital Subscriber Line Access Multiplexer
DV	Distance Vector
EIA	Electronic Industries Alliance
FC	Frame Collector
FCS	Frame Checksum
FD	Frame Distributor
FDDI	Fiber Distributed Data Interface
FE	Fast Ethernet
FR	Frame Relay
FTAM	File Transfer Access and Management
FTP	File Transfer Protocol
GARP	Generic Attribute Registration Protocol
GE	Gigabit Ethernet
GMRP	GARP Multicast Registration Protocol
GPS	Global Positioning System
GRE	Generic Routing Encapsulation
GVRP	GARP VLAN Registration Protocol
HCAr	Huawei Certified Architect
HCIE	Huawei Certified Internetwork Expert
HCNA	Huawei Certified Network Associate
HCNP	Huawei Certified Network Professional
HDLC	High-Level Data Link Control
HG	Home Gateway
HTTP	Hypertext Transfer Protocol
IB	Input Buffer
ICANN	Internet Corporation for Assigned Names and Numbers
ICMP	Internet Control Message Protocol
ICT	Information and Communication Technology
IEC	International Electrotechnical Commission
IEEE	Institute of Electrical and Electronics Engineers
IETF	Internet Engineering Task Force
IGMP	Internet Group Management Protocol
IGP	Interior Gateway Protocol
IP	Internet Protocol
IPCP	Internet Protocol Control Protocol
IPSec	IP Security
IPX	Internetwork Packet Exchange
ISDN	Integrated Services Digital Network
IS-IS	Intermediate System to Intermediate System
ITU	International Telecommunications Union
LACP	Link Aggregation Control Protocol
LAN	Local Area Network
LC	Line Coder
LCP	Link Control Protocol

LD	Line Decoder
LSA	Link State Advertisement
LSAck	Link State Acknowledgment
LSDB	Link State Database
LSR	Link State Request
LSU	Link State Update
MAC	Medium Access Control
MIB	Management Information Base
MRU	Maximum Receive Unit
MSTP	Multiple Spanning Tree Protocol
NAC	Network Access Control
NAPT	Network Address and Port Translation
NAT	Network Address Translation
NBMA	Non-Broadcast Multi-Access
NCP	Network Control Protocol
NIC	Network Interface Card
OB	Output Buffer
OSI	Open System Interconnection
OSPF	Open Shortest Path First
OTN	Optical Transport Network
OUI	Organizationally Unique Identifier
P2MP	Point to Multipoint
P2P	Point to Point
PADI	PPPoE Active Discovery Initiation
PADO	PPPoE Active Discovery Offer
PADR	PPPoE Active Discovery Request
PADS	PPPoE Active Discovery Session-Confirmation
PAP	Password Authentication Protocol
PDU	Protocol Data Unit
PID	Port Identifier
POP3	Post Office Protocol 3
PPP	Point-to-Point Protocol
PPPoE	Point-to-Point Protocol over Ethernet
PVID	Port VLAN Identifier
QoS	Quality of Service
RIP	Routing Information Protocol
ROM	Read-Only Memory
RP	Root Port
RPC	Root Path Cost
RSTP	Rapid Spanning Tree Protocol
RX	Receiver
SDH	Synchronous Digital Hierarchy
SMI	Structure of Management Information
SMTP	Simple Mail Transfer Protocol
SNMP	Simple Network Management Protocol

SPF	Shortest Path First
SPT	Shortest-Path Tree
SSAP	Source Service Access Point
SSH	Secure Shell
STP	Shielded Twisted Pair
STP	Signal Transfer Point
STP	Spanning Tree Protocol
TCN	Topology Change Notification
TCP	Transmission Control Protocol (TCP)
TFTP	Trivial File Transfer Protocol
ToS	Type of Service
TTL	Time To Live
TX	Transmitter
UDP	User Datagram Protocol
UTP	Unshielded Twisted Pair
VID	VLAN Identifier
VLAN	Virtual Local Area Network
VLSM	Variable Length Subnet Mask
VoIP	Voice over IP
VPN	Virtual Private Network
VRP	Versatile Routing Platform
VRRP	Virtual Router Redundancy Protocol
VTY	Virtual Type Terminal
WAN	Wide Area Network
WLAN	Wireless Local Area Network

Chapter 1
Network Communication Fundamentals

1.1 Communication and Networks

Communication has been around long before the human race existed, but has evolved dramatically. From smoke signals to snail mail to instant messaging, communication is the act of conveying meaning and transferring information from one person, place, or object to another. Without communication, humanity's progress would have been severely hampered, and extremely slow.

When talking about communication in its broad sense, it generally means telegrams, telephones, broadcasts, televisions, the Internet, and other modern communication technologies. However, in this book the term communication specifically refers to computer network communication, or network communication for short.

After completing this section, you should be able to:

- Understand the basic concepts of communication and its ultimate purpose.
- Understand some basic characteristics of network communication.
- Understand the reasons for encapsulation and decapsulation of information.
- Understand some common terminology used in network communication.

1.1.1 What Is Communication?

Communication is the act of transmitting and exchanging information between people, people and objects, and objects and objects through various media and actions. The ultimate purpose of communication technology is to help people communicate more efficiently and create better lives from it.

To help understand what technology assisted communication is, this section provides some basic examples of network communication.

© Springer Science+Business Media Singapore 2016
Huawei Technologies Co., Ltd., *HCNA Networking Study Guide*,
DOI 10.1007/978-981-10-1554-0_1

Fig. 1.1 File transfer
between two computers
through a network cable

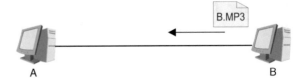

Fig. 1.2 File transfer
between multiple computers
through a router

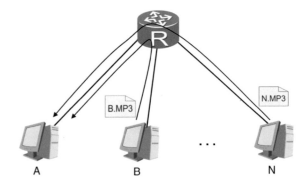

Fig. 1.3 File download from
the Internet

In Fig. 1.1, two computers connected through a single network cable form a simple network. For A to retrieve the file B.MP3, both A and B must be running appropriate file transmission software. Then, with a few clicks, A can obtain the file.

The network shown in Fig. 1.2 is slightly more complicated because it connects multiple computers through a router. In this kind of network, where the router acts as an intermediary, computers can freely transfer files between each other.

In Fig. 1.3, file A.MP3 is located at a certain web address. To download the file, A must first access the Internet.

The Internet is the largest computer network in the world. It is the successor to the Advanced Research Projects Agency Network (ARPANET), which was created in 1969. The Internet's widespread popularity and use is one of the major highlights of today's Information Age.

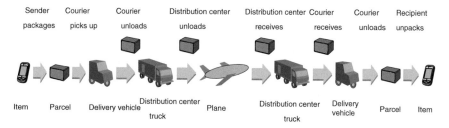

Fig. 1.4 Delivery process

1.1.2   Courier Deliveries and Network Communications

To help you visualize the virtual way in which information is transferred, look at it compared to something experienced on a daily basis: courier deliveries. Figure 1.4 illustrates how an item is delivered from one city to another.

Table 1.1 compares the information transfer process against the courier delivery process. It also introduces some common network communication terminology.

Table 1.2 describes the similarities between transport/transmission technology used in courier delivery and network communication.

This analogy of delivery services is helpful for understanding key characteristics of network communication, but due to the complexities of network communication, an accurate comparison is not possible.

1.1.3   Common Terminology

In Sect. 1.1.2, some common network communication terminology was introduced. Table 1.3 further explains these terms.

1.1.4   Review Questions

1. Which of the following are examples of network communication? (Choose all that apply)

   A. Using instant messaging software (such as WhatsApp) to communicate with friends
   B. Using a computer to stream videos online
   C. Downloading emails to your computer
   D. Using a landline to speak with your friend

Table 1.1 Comparison of courier delivery process and network communication process

No.	Courier delivery	Network communication
1	Sender prepares items for delivery	Application generates the information (or data) to be transferred
2	Sender packages the items	The application packages the data into the data payload
3	The sender places the package into the plastic bag provided by the courier, fills out the delivery slip, and sticks it to the bag to form a parcel The most important information on the delivery slip is the recipient's name and address	A header and trailer are respectively added to the front and end of the data payload, forming a datagram. The most important piece of information in the datagram header is the recipient's address information called a destination address When a new string of information is added to an existing unit of information, to form a new unit of information, this process is known as encapsulation
4	The courier accepts the items, loads them onto the delivery vehicle, and transports them along the highway to the distribution center The delivery vehicle contains many different parcels that are going to many different addresses; however, the vehicle is responsible only for delivering them to the distribution center. The distribution center handles the remaining transmission process	The datagram is sent to the computer's gateway through a network cable
5	When the delivery vehicle arrives at the distribution center, the parcels are unloaded. The distribution center sorts the parcels based on the delivery addresses so that all items destined for the same city are loaded onto a larger truck and sent to the airport	After receiving the datagram, the gateway performs decapsulation, reads the destination address of the datagram, performs encapsulation, and sends it to a router based on the destination address
6	At the airport, the parcels are unloaded from the truck. Those destined for the same city are loaded onto the same plane, ready for departure	After being transferred by the gateway and router, the datagram leaves the local network and is transferred across the internet pathway
7	When the plane lands at the target airport, the parcels are unloaded and sorted. All parcels destined for the same district are loaded onto a truck heading to the relevant distribution center	After the datagram is transferred across the internet, it arrives at the local network of the destination address. The local network gateway or router performs decapsulation and encapsulation, and sends the datagram to the next router along the path
8	Upon arrival, the distribution center sorts the parcels based on the target addresses. All parcels destined for the same building are placed on a single delivery vehicle	The datagram arrives at the network gateway of the target computer, undergoes decapsulation and encapsulation, and is sent to the appropriate computer
9	The courier delivers the parcel to the recipient's door. The recipient opens the plastic bag, removes the packaging, and accepts the delivery after confirming the item inside is undamaged. The delivery process is now complete	After receiving the datagram, the computer will perform datagram verification. Once verified, it accepts the datagram and sends the payload to the corresponding application for processing. The process of a one-way network communication is now complete

Table 1.2 Delivery and network communication similarities in transport and transmission technology

No.	Courier delivery	Network communication
1	Different transport modes such as road or air are required in the transmission process	Different transmission media such as a network cable or optical fiber are suitable for different communication scenarios
		However, changes in the transmission medium will not affect the information being transferred
2	The transmission process often requires the establishment of several transit stations, such as couriers, distribution centers, and airports, to relay transmissions. All transit stations can identify the destination of transmission based on the address written on the parcel	Long-distance network communications often require multiple network devices to complete relays and transfers. Based on the "destination address" indicated in the information, all network devices can accurately determine the next direction of transmission
3	In the delivery process, items are packaged and unpackaged, and parcels loaded and unloaded multiple times	There are two main purposes for repeated encapsulation and decapsulation: • It adds tags to the information so that network devices can accurately determine how to process and transport the information • To adapt to different transmission media and transmission protocols
4	Each transit station focuses on only its own part of the journey rather than the parcel's entire delivery process For example, a courier is only responsible for ensuring that the parcel is properly delivered to the distribution center, not what happens to it afterwards	Each network device is responsible only for correctly transmitting the information within a certain distance and ensuring that is delivered to the next device

Table 1.3 Explanations of common network communication terminology

Terminology	Definition and remarks
Data payload	In the analogy of delivery services, the data payload is the ultimate piece of information. In the layered network communication process, the unit of data (datagram) sent from an upper-layer protocol to a lower-layer protocol is known as the data payload for the lower-layer protocol
Datagram	A datagram is a unit of data that is switched and transferred within a network. It has a certain format and the structure is generally comprised as header + data payload + trailer. The datagram's format and contents may change during transmission
Header	To facilitate information delivery, a string of information, called a datagram header, is added to the front of the data payload during datagram assembly
Trailer	To facilitate information delivery, a string of information, called a datagram trailer, is added to the end of the data payload during datagram assembly. Note that many datagrams do not have trailers

(continued)

Table 1.3 (continued)

Terminology	Definition and remarks
Encapsulation	The process in which a new datagram is formed by adding headers and trailers to a data payload
Decapsulation	The reverse process of encapsulation. This process removes the header and trailer from a datagram to retrieve the data payload
Gateway	A gateway is a network point that acts as an entry point to other networks with different architectures or protocols. A network device is used for protocol conversion, route selection, data switching, and other functions. A gateway is defined by its position and function, rather than on a specific device
Router	A network device that selects a datagram delivery route. In subsequent sections, these devices are further explored

2. Which of the following are related to the purposes of encapsulation and decapsulation? (Choose all that apply)

    A. Faster communication
    B. Interaction between different networks
    C. Layering of communication protocols
    D. Shorter length of datagrams.

1.2 OSI Model and TCP/IP Model

The OSI model and TCP/IP model are two terms commonly used in the field of network communications and are vital to understanding network communication.

As you progress through this section, please pay attention to the following points:

- Definition and role of a network protocol
- Concept of network layering (layering of network functions and protocols)
- Differences between the OSI model and TCP/IP model.

After completing this section, you should be able to:

- List the names of several network protocols and well-known standards organizations.
- Describe the basic content of the OSI model and TCP/IP model.

1.2.1   Network Protocols and Standards Organizations

People use languages like English, French, and Chinese to communicate and exchange ideas. These languages are similar to communication protocols used in network communications. For example, a Frenchman might say to his Chinese friend, "ni hao" (meaning "hello" in Chinese), to which the friend replies "bonjour" (in French, again meaning "hello"), and both in turn may say "hey dude, what's up?" in English to their Irish friend. You can look at this exchange of words as Chinese, French, and English protocols. Some words like "dude" are considered as slang or a "sub-protocol" of the English protocol (other languages may also have slang words and so will have similar sub-protocols). For outsiders to understand all the communication exchanged in the group, they must understand Chinese, French, English, and slang.

In network communications, protocols are a series of defined rules and conventions in which network devices, like computers, switches, and routers, must comply in order to communicate. Hyper Text Transfer Protocol (HTTP), File Transfer Protocol (FTP), Transmission Control Protocol (TCP), IPv4, IEEE 802.3 (Ethernet protocol), and other terms are a few of many network communication protocols. When you access a website through a browser, the "http://" at the beginning of the web address indicates you are using HTTP to access the website. Similarly, "ftp://" indicates FTP is being used to download a file.

In the field of network communications, "protocol", "standard", "specification", "technology", and similar words are often interchangeable. For example, IEEE 802.3 protocol, IEEE 802.3 standard, IEEE 802.3 protocol specifications, IEEE 802.3 protocol standard, IEEE 802.3 standard protocol, IEEE 802.3 standard specifications, and IEEE 802.3 technology specifications are all the same thing.

Protocols can be categorized as either proprietary protocols defined by network device manufacturers, or open protocols defined by special standards organizations. These two types of protocols often differ significantly and may not be compatible with each other. To promote universal network interconnection, manufacturers should try to comply with open protocols and reduce the use of proprietary protocols, but due to factors like intellectual property, and competition between manufacturers, this is not always feasible or desirable.

Institutions specifically organized to consolidate, research, develop, and release standard protocols are known as standards organizations. Table 1.4 lists several of the well-known organizations.

1.2.2   OSI Reference Model

To interact with networks and various network applications, network devices must run various protocols to implement a variety of functions. To help you understand, this section will introduce the layered model of network functions from the perspective of the network architecture.

Table 1.4 Well-known network communication standards organizations

Standards organization	Description
International Organization for Standardization (ISO)	ISO is the world's largest non-governmental standardization organization and is extremely important in the field of international standardization. ISO is responsible for promoting global standardization and related activities to facilitate the international exchange of products and services, and the development of mutual international cooperation in information, scientific, technological, and economic events
Internet Engineering Task Force (IETF)	IETF is the most influential Internet technology standardization organization in the world. Its main duties include the study and development of technical specifications related to the Internet. Currently, the vast majority of technical standards for the internet are from IETF. IETF is well known for its request for comments (RFC) standard series
Institute of Electrical and Electronics Engineers (IEEE)	IEEE is one of the world's largest professional technology organizations. The IEEE was founded as an international exchange for scientists, engineers, and manufacturers in the electrical and electronic industries, with the aim to provide professional training and improved professional services. IEEE is well known for its ethernet standard specification
International Telecommunications Union (ITU)	ITU is a United Nations agency that oversees information communications technology. ITU coordinates the shared global use of the radio spectrum, promotes international cooperation in assigning satellite orbits, works to improve telecommunication infrastructure in the developing world, and assists in the development and coordination of worldwide technical standards
Electronic Industries Alliance (EIA)	EIA is a standards developer for the American electronics industry. One of the many standards developed by EIA is the commonly used RS-232 serial port standard
International Electrotechnical Commission (IEC)	IEC is responsible for international standardization in electrical and electronic engineering. It has close ties to ISO, ITU, IEEE, and other organizations

Functions are categorized into layers based on their purposes and roles. Each layer can be clearly distinguished from another.

Running a specific protocol allows network device functions to be realized. The layered model of functions therefore corresponds to the layered model of protocols. Protocols that have identical or similar functional roles are assigned into the same layer. Clear differences exist between layers in terms of protocols' functional roles.

Layering the protocols and functions offers the following benefits:

- Easier standardization: Each layer focuses on specific functions, making the development of corresponding protocols or standards easier.

- Lower dependence: The addition, reduction, update, or change of a layer will not affect other layers; the protocols or functions of each layer can be independently developed.
- Easier to understand: Layering protocols and functions makes it clearer for people to study and research networks, clarifying the working mechanisms of an entire network and the relationships between its many different network protocols.

Open System Interconnection Reference Model (OSI RM) promotes the development of network technology. Launched by ISO in the 1980s, OSI is a seven-layer function/protocol model. Table 1.5 provides a basic description of each layer in this model.

1. The physical layer performs logical conversions between data and optical/electrical signals. It forms the foundation for the communication process. Primarily, the physical layer sends, transmits, and receives single "0"s and "1"s.
2. The data link layer sends and receives strings of "0"s and "1"s. Each string has a certain structure and meaning. Without the data link layer, parties wishing to communicate would see a constantly changing optical/electrical signal and would be unable to organize the "0"s and "1"s into meaningful data.
3. The network layer performs a global data transfer between any two nodes. In contrast, the data link layer performs a local, direct data transfer between adjacent nodes. ("Adjacent node" refers to any node that is connected to the

Table 1.5 Functions of OSI reference model layers

Layer no.	Layer name	Main functions
1	Physical layer	Completes the logical conversion of the "0" and "1" physical signals (optical/electrical signals) carried on the transmission medium, and sends, receives, and transmits physical signals on the medium
2	Data link layer	Establishes a logical data-link through adjacent nodes connected to a physical link, and performs direct point-to-point or point-to-multipoint communications on the data link
3	Network layer	Transmits data from any one node to any other node based on the network layer address information included in the data
4	Transport layer	Establishes, maintains, and cancels one-time end-to-end data transmission processes, controls the transmission speeds, and adjusts data sequencing
5	Session layer	Establishes, manages, and terminates communication sessions between two parties, and determines whether a party can initiate communication
6	Presentation layer	Converts data formats to ensure the application layer of one system can identify and understand the data generated by the application layer of another system
7	Application layer	Provides system application interfaces for user application software

same routing device.) LAN technology is focused within the data link layer and its underlying physical layer.

4. Certain functions of the transport layer improve the reliability of transmission. An analogy is a conversation between two people: if one person speaks too quickly, the other person might say, "Speak slowly". This phrase is used to control the speed of the conversation. And, if a person cannot hear someone speak clearly, the person might say, "Please repeat that", which is used to improve the reliability of the conversation. These phrases are similar to the purpose of certain transport layer functions.

5. The session layer controls and manages the exchange of information. For example, if you went online and requested a specific network service, but mistyped the login credentials, the request will be denied. The service provider verifies login credentials, and terminates the subsequent communication process if the credentials are incorrect. The verification and communication shutoff operation the service provider performs is one of the functions of the session layer.

6. The presentation layer ensures that the application layer of one party can identify and understand data sent from another party's application layer. One of the common functions of the presentation layer operates in a similar manner to applications used to compress and decompress.rar files. To minimize the use of network bandwidth resources, one party will compress a file before sending it to another party. The recipient must decompress the received file to identify and understand its content; otherwise, the content is meaningless.

7. The application layer interacts with software applications that may be controlled by a user. Some TCP/IP protocols (we'll look at TCP/IP in Sect. 1.2.3 "TCP/IP Protocol Suite"), such as HTTP, Simple Mail Transfer Protocol (SMTP), FTP, and Simple Network Management Protocol (SNMP), can be considered as application layer protocols if we make a comparison with the OSI model.

8. An additional layer, known as the "user layer" exists at Layer 8. However, this layer is not within the scope of the OSI model. For example, network browser software, such as Internet Explorer and Firefox, is located in this layer, but such software relies on HTTP in the application layer. Another example is software that sends and receives emails, such as Outlook. This software is also located in Layer 8, but relies on SMTP in the application layer.

Looking at the OSI model, data transmitted from a computer will be transferred from the highest layer (Layer 7) to the lowest layer (Layer 1). The data is encapsulated during the transfer process until it is converted to optical/electrical signals and sent out from the physical layer. Conversely, data received by a computer will be transferred from the lowest layer to the highest layer and be decapsulated. Figure 1.5 shows how data is transferred from one layer to the next in a simple network consisting of only two computers (Computer A and Computer B) connected by a network cable.

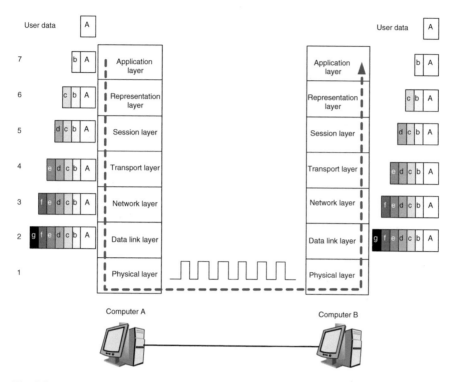

Fig. 1.5 Data encapsulation and decapsulation process on communication terminals in the OSI model

1.2.3   TCP/IP Protocol Suite

Originating from ARPANET and enhanced by the IETF, the TCP/IP model is formed from two important protocols, the Transmission Control Protocol (TCP) and Internet Protocol (IP).

Figure 1.6 shows two different versions of the TCP/IP model and provides a comparison with the OSI model. The standard TCP/IP model has four layers: the network access layer corresponds to Layer 1 and Layer 2 of both the peer TCP/IP model and the OSI model, and the application layer of both the standard and peer TCP/IP models corresponds to Layer 5, Layer 6, and Layer 7 of the OSI model. The five-layer peer TCP/IP model is the most widely used, so unless otherwise specified, this TCP/IP model is the intended reference in this book.

The main difference between the TCP/IP model and the OSI model, and the ways they are divided, is due to the different protocols they use (Fig. 1.7).

Some of the protocols used in the TCP/IP model may be familiar to you, whereas those in the OSI model may not be. The reason why the OSI model protocols may be unfamiliar is that, when designing and applying the Internet and other networks,

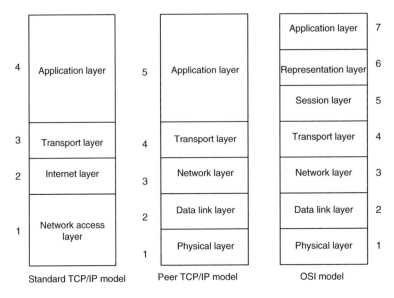

Fig. 1.6 Hierarchical structure of the TCP/IP model

5	Application layer	HTTP, FTP, SMTP, SNMP...
4	Transport layer	TCP, UDP...
3	Network layer	IP, ICMP, IGMP...
2	Data link layer	SLIP, PPP...
1	Physical layer	...

TCP/IP protocol suite

7	Application layer	FTAM, X.400, CMIS...
6	Representation layer	X.226, X.236...
5	Session layer	X.225, X.235...
4	Transport layer	TP0, TP1, TP2...
3	Network layer	CLNP, X.233...
2	Data link layer	ISO/IEC 766...
1	Physical layer	EIA/TIA-232...

OSI protocol suite

Fig. 1.7 Different protocols used by the TCP/IP model and OSI model

most designers opted for the TCP/IP protocol suite instead of the OSI protocol suite.

In the OSI model, we typically refer to the data unit of each layer as a "protocol data unit (PDU)". For example, the data unit in Layer 6 is called an L6 PDU.

In the TCP/IP model, we typically refer to the data unit in the physical layer as a "bit", that in the data link layer as a "frame", and that in the network layer as a "packet". In the transport layer, a data unit encapsulated with TCP is referred to as a "segment" (a "TCP Segment"), and that encapsulated with UDP is referred to as a "datagram" (a "UDP datagram"). And, in the application layer, a data unit encapsulated with HTTP is referred to as an "HTTP datagram", and that encapsulated with FTP is known as an "FTP datagram".

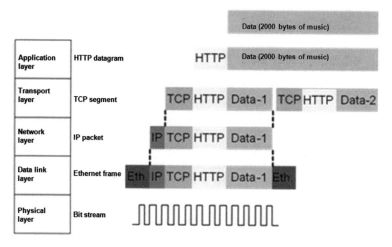

Fig. 1.8 Data encapsulation process in the TCP/IP model

For example, you find a 2000 byte song on the Internet, and to download it, your web browser first sends a request. Before the song is sent, it will be encapsulated through the layers on the web server. The application layer will add an HTTP header to the original song data to form an HTTP datagram. Because the HTTP datagram is too long it will be segmented into two parts in the transport layer, with a TCP header added to the front of each part to form two TCP segments. At the network layer an IP header will be added to each TCP segment to form an IP packet. When the IP packet reaches the data link layer, assuming the layer is using Ethernet technology, it will add an Ethernet frame header and trailer to the IP packet, forming an Ethernet frame. Finally, the physical layer will convert these Ethernet frames into a bit stream (Fig. 1.8).

1.2.4   Review Questions

1. Which of the following are specific network protocols? (Choose all that apply)
   a. HTTP
   b. FTP
   c. OSI
   d. ISO
   e. TCP
   f. IP
   g. TCP/IP

2. In the OSI reference model, what is the order of layers from Layer 1 to Layer 7? (Choose one)

   a. physical layer > transport layer > data link layer > network layer > session layer > presentation layer > application layer
   b. physical layer > transport layer > data link layer > network layer > session layer > application layer > presentation layer
   c. physical layer > data link layer > transport layer > network layer > session layer > application layer > presentation layer
   d. physical layer > data link layer > network layer > transport layer > session layer > presentation layer > application layer
   e. physical layer > data link layer > transport layer > network layer > session layer > presentation layer > application layer

3. In the TCP/IP model, at which layer is the data unit referred to as a "frame"? (Choose one)

   a. Layer 1
   b. Layer 2
   c. Layer 3
   d. Layer 4
   e. Layer 5

4. What are the advantages of layered network protocols? (Choose all that apply)

   a. Conducive to protocol design
   b. Conducive to protocol management
   c. Conducive to learning and understanding protocols
   d. Conducive to improving the efficiency of communications
   e. Conducive to modifying protocols.

1.3 Network Types

LAN, WAN, private network, public network, intranet, extranet, circuit switched network, packet switched network, ring network, star network, optical network— network terminology is very broad, but it all has something to do with the various types of network that exist. There are so many network types because there are many ways in which networks can be divided.

In this section, we will divide networks based on geographical coverage and topological forms. We'll also describe the principles for these two divisions as well as the basic characteristics of all types of networks.

As you progress through this section, please pay attention to the following points:

- Definitions of LAN and WAN and the differences between them
- Common LAN and WAN technologies
- The characteristics of networks with different topologies.

After completing this section, you should be able to:

- Describe the basic concepts of LAN and WAN.
- Understand the basic states of LAN and WAN.
- Understand the characteristics of networks with different topologies.

1.3.1 LAN and WAN

Based on geographical coverage, networks can be divided into Local Area Networks (LANs) and Wide Area Networks (WANs). Table 1.6 compares these two of networks.

Table 1.6 Comparison between LAN and WAN

Network type	Basic features	Technology used
LAN	• Coverage is generally within a few kilometers • Mainly used to connect several computer terminals distributed within close proximity of each other (for example, within a home or office, between several buildings, or across a work campus) • Does not involve telecom operator communication lines	Some examples are: • Token bus • Token ring • Fiber distributed data interface (FDDI) • Ethernet • Wireless LAN (WLAN)
WAN	• Coverage generally ranges from a few kilometers to thousands of kilometers • Mainly used to connect several LANs distributed across great distances (for example, to connect LANs in different cities or countries) • Involves telecom operator communication lines	Some examples are: • T1/E1, T3/E3 • X.25 • High-level data link control (HDLC) • Point-to-point protocol (PPP) • Integrated services digital network (ISDN) • Frame relay (FR) • Asynchronous transfer mode (ATM) • Synchronous digital hierarchy (SDH)

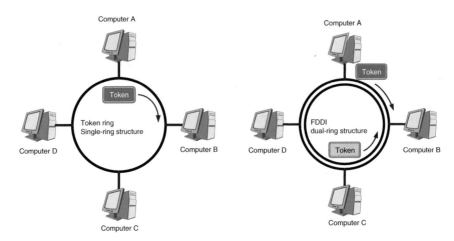

Fig. 1.9 Token bus network and FDDI network topologies

The geographical coverage of LAN and WAN is not firmly established. When we talk about LAN or WAN, we are referring to the technology used by LAN or WAN.

There are many different types of LAN technology, such as Token bus (IEEE 802.4), Token ring (IEEE 802.5), FDDI, Distributed Queue/Dual Bus (DQDB, IEEE 802.6), isoEthernet (IEEE 802.9a), and 100VG-AnyLAN (IEEE 802.12). Two of the most widely used LAN technologies are Ethernet and WLAN, which have achieved active development and widespread application. Most LAN technologies other than Ethernet and WLAN have disappeared or are being phased out due to market changes and developments. As such, a deep understanding of these outdated technologies is not required (unless you're particularly interested in the history of network technology). Figure 1.9 shows the topology of token bus and FDDI networks, which are no longer common but can still be found on some older networks.

WAN's deployment environment and conditions are more complicated than LAN's, and improving and upgrading WAN is also more complicated than for LAN. This is partly why older WAN technologies are still in use. However, the general trend is phasing out antiquated WAN technologies such as T1/E1, T3/E3, ISDN, and FR. Optical network technologies, such as SDH and Optical Transport Network (OTN), are increasingly being used in the field of WAN communication.

1.3.2 Forms of Network Topology

Apart from geographic coverage of the network, network has its topology. Network topology is a graphical representation of a network structure. Table 1.7 illustrates some examples of network topology.

Table 1.7 Various types of network topology

Network type	Topology map	Basic characteristics
Star network		All nodes are connected through a central node • Advantages: New nodes can be easily added to a network. All data to be communicated must pass through the central node, which makes network monitoring easier • Disadvantages: Failure of the central node will disrupt all network communication
Bus network		All nodes are connected along a single bus (such as a coaxial electrical cable) • Advantages: Simpler installation and shorter cable lengths than most other network topologies. Failure of a given node will not usually disrupt all network communication • Disadvantages: Failure of the bus will disrupt all network communication. All nodes connected to the bus can receive information sent out from any given node, lowering security
Ring network		All nodes are connected within a single closed ring • Advantages: Shorter cable lengths than other network topologies • Disadvantages: Adding new nodes will disrupt network communication
Tree network		Nodes are connected in a kind of layered star structure • Advantages: Easy to expand by connecting multiple star networks • Disadvantages: The higher the layer in which a node fails, the greater the disruption caused to network communication
Fully meshed network		All nodes are interconnected • Advantages: High reliability and communication efficiency • Disadvantages: Increased costs because the more nodes connected, the greater the number of physical ports and cables required. Problematic to expand
Partially meshed network		Only strategic nodes are interconnected • Advantages: Costs less than a fully meshed network • Disadvantages: Less reliable than a fully meshed network

Fig. 1.10 Hybrid network
topology

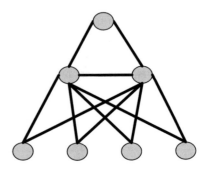

Some of the network topologies shown in Table 1.7 are usually combined to meet various practical requirements such as cost, communication efficiency, and reliability. For example, the network shown in Fig. 1.10 combines the ring, star, and tree topologies.

1.3.3 Review Questions

1. Into which geographical categories can networks be divided? (Choose all that apply)

   a. Local Area Network
   b. Ethernet
   c. Internet
   d. Wide Area Network

2. LAN is typically limited to a range of how many kilometers? (Choose one)

   a. 0.1 km
   b. 1 km
   c. 10 km
   d. 100 km
   e. 1000 km

3. Which of the following networks is most reliable? (Choose one)

   a. Star network
   b. Bus network
   c. Ring network
   d. Tree network
   e. Fully meshed network

4. Which of the following characteristics does not apply to a tree network? (Choose one)

  a. Prone to a single point of failure
  b. Easy to expand
  c. The higher the layer in which a node resides, the lower the requirements for reliability.

1.4 Transmission Media and Methods of Communication

Specific types of transmission media, including optical fibers and copper wires, are used to carry the physical signals in the communication process. "Methods of communication" is a broad term relating to, for example, optical and electronic communication, wireless and wired communication, and unicast and broadcast communication. Specifically, "methods of communication" when used in this section refers to serial and parallel communications as well as simplex, half-duplex, and full-duplex communications.

As you progress through this section, please pay attention to the following points:

- The conceptual difference between a signal's physical speed of dissemination and the rate of information transmission.
- The physical speed of dissemination of optical signals and electrical signals on an optical fiber and copper wire, respectively.
- The main advantages of optical fiber compared to copper wire.
- The major differences between a single-mode optical fiber and a multimode optical fiber (in terms of structure, cost, and performance).
- The maximum information transmission rates that Cat 3, Cat 5, and Cat 5e UTP support in Ethernet scenarios.
- The key factor preventing the use of parallel communication for long-distance communication.

  After completing this section, you should be able to:

- Describe the basic classifications of transmission media commonly used in network communications, and their characteristics.
- Understand the major differences between parallel communication and serial communication.
- Understand the concepts of simplex, half-duplex, and full-duplex communication.

1.4.1 Transmission Media

The main transmission media used to carry physical signals (mainly optical or electrical signals) are space, metal wire, and glass fiber.

Space is primarily used to transmit electromagnetic waves. This transmission medium can be divided into vacuum and air. In a vacuum, electromagnetic waves are transmitted at 299,792,458 meters per second (the speed of light). In air, the speed is approximately 299,705,000 meters per second.

Metal wire is primarily used to transmit current/voltage signals. The metal most widely used for transmission is copper. The speed at which current/voltage signals are transmitted across copper wire is very close to the speed of light. Two types of copper wiring are commonly used in network communication: coaxial cables and twisted pair cables.

Optical fiber is generally made of glass and is used to transmit optical signals (essentially, an optical signal is just a kind of electromagnetic wave in a given spectrum). The speed at which optical signals are transmitted is approximately 200,000,000 meters per second.

The following is a brief introduction to three kinds of transmission media: coaxial cables, twisted pairs, and optical fibers.

Coaxial Cables

Figure 1.11 shows the structure and physical appearance of a coaxial cable. Only the copper wire (the core) is used to transmit current/voltage signals. The shielding layer is used to limit externally-emitted electromagnetic radiation that may interfere with the current/voltage signals. Coaxial cable was used as the bus in

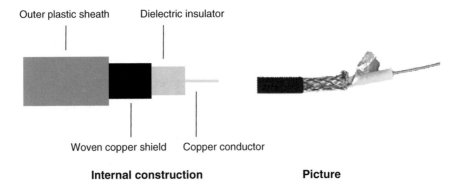

Fig. 1.11 Structure and physical appearance of a coaxial cable

Ethernet-based bus networks; however, as Ethernet evolved and star networks became common, twisted pair and optical fiber cables began to be used instead. Currently, coaxial cables are widely used in cable television network systems.

Twisted Pairs

A twisted pair cable gets its name from the fact that the copper wires are twisted together inside the cable. Twisting pairs of wires together offers better resistance to interference from externally-emitted electromagnetic radiation.

Twisted pair cables can be categorized as shielded twisted pair (STP) or unshielded twisted pair (UTP), depending on whether the cable contains a shielding layer. Figures 1.12 and 1.13 show the structure and physical appearance of STP and UTP cables, respectively. The two figures illustrate how eight copper wires are intertwined to form four pairs of wires, or four coils. By eliminating the shielding layer, UTP is cheaper than STP; however, it is less capable of limiting interference. UTP is suitable for most scenarios, whereas STP is used in scenarios where, for example, strong electromagnetic radiation exists.

Twisted pair cables can be further classified into categories such as Cat 3 and Cat 5. Table 1.8 describes some of the UTP classifications. To ensure that signal attenuation does not exceed a defined threshold in Ethernet networks, the maximum length of a single Cat 3, Cat 5, and Cat 5e cable must not exceed 100 m (this length restriction is overcome by adding specific network devices between cables).

Figure 1.14 shows a common 8-wire Cat cable. In this case both ends of the twisted pair are mounted with an RJ45 connector. Once the eight copper wires in a twisted pair are separated and straightened, they are inserted into the eight

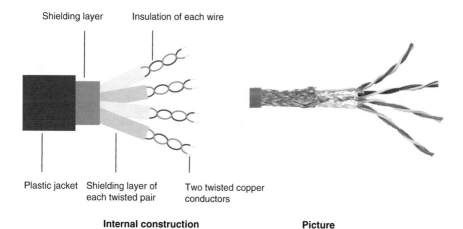

Internal construction   **Picture**

Fig. 1.12 Structure and physical appearance of a shielded twisted pair

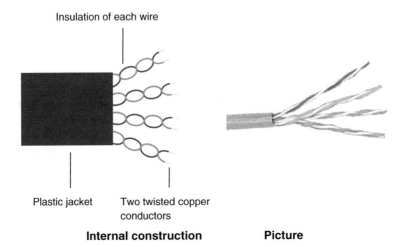

Internal construction   **Picture**

Fig. 1.13 Structure and physical appearance of an unshielded twisted pair

Table 1.8 UTP classification

UTP	Usage	Description
Cat 1	Telephone systems	Defined by Anixter International. Cat 1 is not used in network communications
Cat 2	Token ring networks	Defined by Anixter International. Cat 2 is generally no longer used. Information transmission on Cat 2 has a maximum speed of 4 Mbit/s
Cat 3	Ethernet and telephone systems	Defined by TIA/EIA-568. Cat 3 was used in the first IEEE-standardized star ethernet standard, 10BASE-T. Information transmission on Cat 3 has a maximum speed of 16 Mbit/s
Cat 4	Token ring networks and ethernet	Defined by TIA/EIA-568. Cat 4 is generally no longer used. Information transmission on Cat 4 has a maximum speed of 16 Mbit/s
Cat 5	Ethernet and telephone systems	Defined by TIA/EIA-568. Cat 5 is in widespread use and supports 10BASE-T and 100BASE-TX. Information transmission on Cat 5 has a maximum speed of 100 Mbit/s
Cat 5e	Ethernet	Defined by TIA/EIA-568. Cat 5e ("e" represents "enhanced") is in widespread use and supports 10BASE-T, 100BASE-TX, and 1000BASE-T. An improvement over Cat 5, information transmission on Cat 5e has a maximum speed of 1000 Mbit/s

corresponding slots in the RJ45 connector in a specific order. The sharp pin slots then pierce the insulating layer on the corresponding copper wires and clamp closely to them, fully connecting the RJ45 connector to the twisted pair cable.

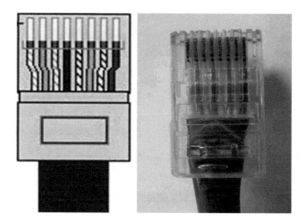

Fig. 1.14 RJ45 connector

Optical Fibers

An optical fiber cable contains one or more fibers and a number of protective layers. Optical fibers are generally made of glass, although some may be made of plastic, and are used to transport infrared wavelengths in an optical network communication system. Figure 1.15 shows the structure and physical appearance of an optical cable and the fibers inside. The protective layers include the housing, reinforcing materials, and buffer layer—optical fiber refers to the fiber core and cladding layers. The refractive index of the cladding layer is less than that of the fiber core.

The two main types of optical fibers are single-mode and multimode optical fibers. Figure 1.16 shows cross-sections of these two types of optical fibers. A single-mode optical fiber has a thinner core and thicker cladding layer compared with a multimode optical fiber. The thickness of an optical fiber refers to the outside diameter of the periphery cladding layer, which is approximately 125 μm. For comparison, the thickness of a human hair is approximately 100 μm.

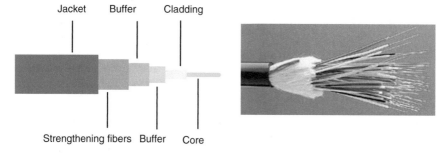

Fig. 1.15 Structure and physical appearance of an optical fiber/optical fiber cable

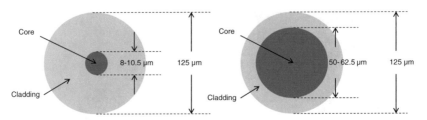

Single-mode optical fiber: thinner core, thicker cladding   Multimode optical fiber: thicker core, thinner cladding

Fig. 1.16 Single-mode optical fiber and multimode optical fiber

In this section, we will only briefly compare the different transmission modes of optical fibers.

- The cost to produce multimode optical fiber is lower compared to single-mode optical fiber, due to the thicker fiber core and simpler production requirements of multimode optical fiber.
- Multimode transmission, used in multimode optical fibers, causes modal dispersion. Modal dispersion greatly reduces the transmission quality of optical signals and causes "pulse broadening" effects, which distort the transmitted optical signals. Single-mode optical fibers do not suffer from modal dispersion.
- The greater the transmission distance, the greater the effects of modal dispersion on optical signal transmission quality (and the greater the optical signal distortion).
- Single-mode optical fiber supports higher information transmission rates than multimode optical fiber at comparable transmission distances, and supports greater transmission distances at comparable information transmission rates.
- Single-mode optical fiber is mostly used in WANs at transmission distances extending thousands of kilometers, whereas multimode optical fiber is mostly used in LANs at transmission distances of no more than a few kilometers. The transmission distance of multimode optical fibers is limited mainly to reduce the effects of modal dispersion on optical signal transmission quality and the degree of signal distortion.

Similar to twisted pair cables, both ends of an optical cable need to be mounted with an optical fiber connector. Figure 1.17 shows some commonly used optical fiber connectors.

Optical fiber has grown in popularity and is increasingly being used to replace copper wire. This is called the "fiber to replace copper" trend. The main advantages of optical fiber over copper wire include:

- Radio waves, electromagnetic noise, electromagnetic induction, and lighting may cause interference to electrical signals on copper wire, whereas optical signals on optical fibers are immune to such interference.
- Optical fiber generally supports far higher information transmission speeds than copper wire.

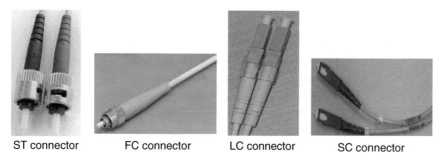

ST connector   FC connector   LC connector   SC connector

Fig. 1.17 Optical fiber connectors

• Signal attenuation is much lower in optical fibers than in copper wires. Therefore, fewer repeaters are required and greater distances can be achieved.
• Optical fibers are lighter and thinner than copper wires and are easier to transport, install, and deploy.

1.4.2   Methods of Communication

Serial Communication and Parallel Communication

Serial communication refers to a method by which data is transmitted sequentially, one bit at a time, on a single data channel. RS-232 line communication is a kind of serial communication.

Parallel communication refers to a method by which sets of data (several bits) are transmitted simultaneously on a set of data channels. In parallel communication, the transmission principle for each data channel is the same as that of serial communication. Typically, parallel communications are transmitted in bytes. Communication between computers and digital projectors is parallel communication.

Switching from serial communication to parallel communication can greatly increase transmission speeds. However, parallel communication requires more data channels and more copper wires or optical fibers, which increases the cost of network construction. Also, in parallel access, the requirements for signal synchronization on data channels are higher. For example, in Fig. 1.18, PC1 sends PC2 two sets of data through parallel communication. Because of interference, the first "1" of datagram 1 arrives at PC2 later than the remaining seven bits that comprise datagram 1. PC2 therefore believes that this bit has been lost. However, this bit arrives almost concurrently with bits two through eight of datagram 2. A bit error occurs because PC2 assumes that the first "1" of datagram 1 is the first bit of datagram 2.

The greater the signal transmission distance, the harder it becomes to realize signal synchronization. Therefore, parallel communication is generally unsuitable for long-distance communication.

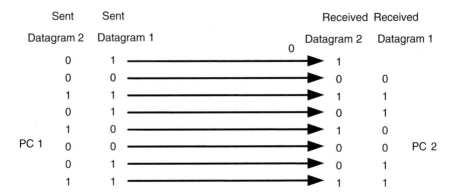

Fig. 1.18 Bit error in parallel communication due to synchronization problems

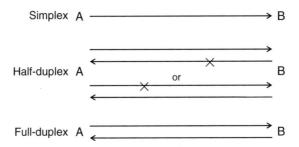

Fig. 1.19 Simplex, half-duplex, and full-duplex methods of communication

Simplex, Half-Duplex, and Full-Duplex Communication

In Fig. 1.19, A and B are communication parties. Communication can be divided into simplex, half-duplex, and full-duplex, based on the direction of communication.

In the simplex method, information flows in only one direction. A can send data to B, but B cannot send data to A. A traditional analog television system is an example of simplex communication.

In the half-duplex method, information can flow from A to B and from B to A, but both parties cannot transmit data simultaneously. If A and B send data simultaneously, neither party will successfully receive the data sent from the other. An intercom system is an example of half-duplex communication.

In the full-duplex method, information can simultaneously flow in either direction. Both A and B can simultaneously send and receive data. Landline and mobile telephone communication systems are examples of full-duplex communication.

1.4.3   Review Questions

1. In an Ethernet network, which of the following media can support an information transfer rate of 100 Mbit/s? (Choose all that apply)

   a. Cat 3 UTP
   b. Cat 5 UTP
   c. Cat 5e UTP

2. In an Ethernet network, what is the maximum transmission distance for Cat 3, Cat 5, and Cat 5e UTP? (Choose one)

   a. 50 m
   b. 100 m
   c. 150 m
   d. 200 m

3. At the same transmission distance, which medium currently supports the fastest information transmission rate? (Choose one)

   a. Coaxial cable
   b. Optical fiber
   c. Twisted pair

4. At comparable transmission rates, the transmission distance of a multimode optical fiber is less than that of a single-mode optical fiber. Why? (Choose one)

   a. Multimode fiber costs less to produce than single-mode fiber.
   b. Modal dispersion in multimode fibers will cause distortion in transmitted optical signals, and the greater the transfer distance, the greater the degree of distortion.
   c. The greater the transmission distance, the greater the effects of attenuation on the optical signals in the multimode fiber.

5. In a global positioning system (GPS), which method does the satellite use to communicate with the GPS receiver on the ground? (Choose one)

   a. Simplex communication
   b. Half-duplex communication
   c. Full-duplex communication.

Chapter 2
VRP Basics

2.1 Introduction to VRP

Versatile Routing Platform (VRP) is a network operating system applied in Huawei network devices like routers and switches. It provides users of these network devices with a consistent and powerful configuration platform by standardizing network, user, and management interfaces. Communication engineers all over the world may have frequqently used these Huawei devices, as Huawei has a large international deployment of network devices. It is required for these engineers to understand the basics of VRP.

Based on the TCP/IP model, VRP's hierarchical system architecture integrates device and network management capabilities, network application technologies, and data communication technologies, such as routing, multiprotocol label switching (MPLS), virtual private network (VPN), and security technologies, with a real-time operating system.

To ensure the configuration platform remains up-to-date and relevant for current technologies, VRP has evolved from VRP1.0, first released in 1998, to VRP8.X, its latest version.

Figure 2.1 illustrates the main features of each version.

Many of the low-end and mid-range network devices currently in use on enterprise networks run VRP5.X. As such, this book focuses on VRP5.12.

2.2 VRP Command Lines

VRP command lines are directly defined to configure and manage Huawei network devices. After completing this section, you should be able to:

- Describe the concepts, functions, and basic structure of a command line.
- Understand the differences between the user, the system, and the interface views.
- Understand command levels and user levels.
- Effectively use command lines.

© Springer Science+Business Media Singapore 2016
Huawei Technologies Co., Ltd., *HCNA Networking Study Guide*,
DOI 10.1007/978-981-10-1554-0_2

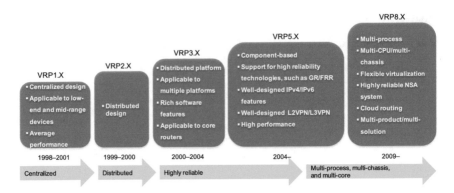

Fig. 2.1 VRP features by version

2.2.1 Basic Concepts

- Command line ·
  VRP command lines are character strings used to configure functions and deploy
  services on Huawei network devices. A command line consists of keywords and
  parameters. Keywords are one or more words that uniquely identify, correspond
  to, and generally describe the instruction that a command line performs, and
  parameters specify the data that is used as input for the keywords. This book
  shows keywords in **bold** and parameters in *italic*. For example, in the command
  line **ping** *ip-address* (which tests a device's connectivity), **ping** is the keyword,
  and *ip-address* represents a user-specified parameter such as 192.168.1.1.
  Huawei's network devices generally are shipped unconfigured by default, so the
  user must enter command lines in the device's command-line interface (CLI) to
  configure the functionality of the device.
- CLI
  A CLI provides a means of interacting with a device. Through the CLI, you can
  enter command lines to configure devices. VRP command lines, of which there are
  thousands, are classified by function and registered in different command views.
- Command view
  The CLI provides several command views, of which the user, the system,
  and the interface views are the most commonly used. To enter and use command lines in the CLI, you must first access the user view (as shown in
  Fig. 2.2). This view allows you to query a device's basic information and status
  and access other views, but does not allow service functions to be configured.
  You can configure service functions and run the basic configuration commands
  in the system view (as shown in Fig. 2.3), which can be accessed from the user
  view by running the **system-view** command.
  The system view also allows you to access other views, such as the interface
  view (as shown in Fig. 2.4). In the interface view, you can configure parameters
  and services for a specified interface.

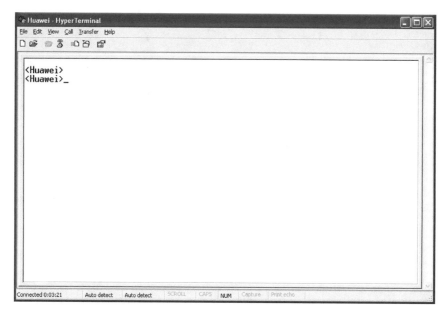

Fig. 2.2 User view interface

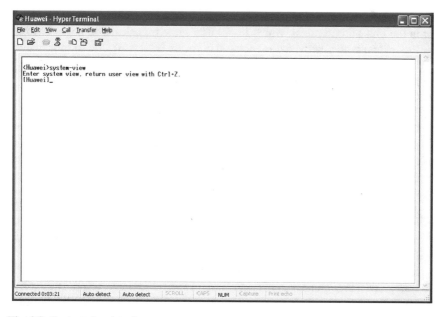

Fig. 2.3 System view interface

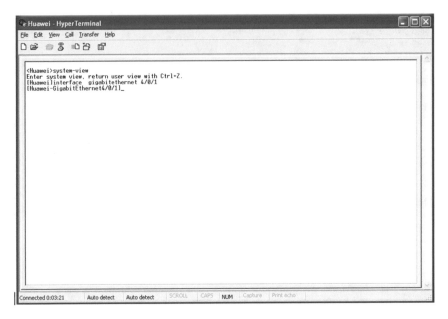

Fig. 2.4 Interface view interface

The command prompt in each view contains the device's host name ("Huawei" in the preceding figures), which in the user view is enclosed in angle brackets (⟨...⟩) and in all other views is enclosed in square brackets ([...]). In some views, the command prompt may contain additional information (such as the interface identifier, GigabitEthernet4/0/1, in the preceding interface view example).

- Command and user levels
  VRP commands are classified based on the function they perform: Level 0 (visit level) commands test network connectivity, Level 1 (monitoring level) commands display network status and basic device information, Level 2 (configuration level) commands configure services for a device, and Level 3 (management level) commands manage certain functions of a device, such as uploading or downloading configuration files.
  To limit which commands a user can run, users are assigned different user levels. In total, 16 user levels are available, from Level 0 to Level 15. Level 0 is the most restrictive, with the permissiveness increasing for each subsequent level. By default, Levels 4 through 15 are the same as Level 3, so users assigned these levels all have the same permissions and can run all VRP commands. However, user levels can be configured if finer granularity of control is required. For example, you can increase to Level 15 the user level of particular commands so that only users assigned this level can run these commands. However, changing the default assignments may complicate operation and maintenance tasks and weaken device security—consulting with Huawei engineers is advisable if you want to change these default assignments. Table 2.1 lists the default mapping between user and command levels.

Table 2.1 Default mapping between user and command levels

User Level	Command Level	Description
0	0	Commands for network diagnostics (such as **ping** and **tracert**) and remote login (such as **telnet**)
1	0, 1	Commands for system maintenance, such as **display**. Specific **display** commands, such as **display current-configuration** and **display saved-configuration**, are management-level commands (requiring a Level 3 user)
2	0, 1, 2	Commands for service configuration, such as routing commands
3–15	0, 1, 2, 3	Commands for controlling basic system operations, such as file systems, FTP download, user management, command level setting, and fault diagnostics

2.2.2 Using Command Lines

This section explains how to use VRP command lines.

- Accessing a command view

  As mentioned in Sect. 2.2.1, the user view is the first view displayed after you enter VRP. If <Huawei> is displayed (and the cursor to the right of > is blinking), you are in the user view. In this view, you can run commands to query the device's basic information and status. To configure an interface, for example, you need to access the system view and then access the interface view. The commands to do this are **system-view** and **interface** *interface-type interface-number*. The following shows how to access the interface view of GigabitEthernet 1/0/0.

```
<Huawei> system-view
[Huawei]            //The system view is displayed.
[Huawei] interface gigabitethernet 1/0/0
[Huawei-GigabitEthernet1/0/0]        //The interface view is displayed.
```

- Exiting from the command view

  The **quit** command allows you to exit from the current view and return to the upper-level view. In the preceding example, the current view is the interface view, and the system view is the upper-level view of the interface view. Running the **quit** command in the interface view will show the following.

```
[Huawei-GigabitEthernet1/0/0] quit
[Huawei]            //Returned to the system view.
```

  To return to the user view, run the **quit** command again.

```
[Huawei] quit
<Huawei>            //Returned to the user view.
```

Sometimes you may want to return to the user view without running the **quit** command multiple times. The **return** command allows you to directly return to the user view.

```
[Huawei-GigabitEthernet1/0/0] return
<Huawei>              //Returned to the user view.
```

You can also use shortcut keys **Ctrl+Z** in any view to return to the user view.

- Editing a command line

  You can enter up to 510 characters per command line. However, if you notice a mistake in a long command line, retyping potentially 510 characters would become laborious. Table 2.2 lists the common function keys, which are case-insensitive, for editing VRP command lines. Note that the cursor cannot move into the prompt (for example, [Huawei-GigabitEthernet1/0/0]), nor can the prompt be edited.

- Entering partial keywords

  Command-line completion automatically fills in partially entered keywords if the system can find a unique match. For example, you can enter combinations such as **d cu**, **di cu**, or **dis cu** and press **Tab**, and the system will automatically display the **display current-configuration** command. **d c** and **dis c**, however, return no match because other commands, such as **display cpu-defend**, **display clock**, and **display current-configuration**, also correspond to these partial keywords.

- Obtaining help

  Memorizing the thousands of VRP command lines can seem like a daunting prospect. The question mark (?) makes things easier. You can enter ? at any time to obtain online help. The help is classified as either full help or partial help.

Table 2.2 Function keys for editing VRP command lines

Key	Function
Backspace	Deletes the character to the left of the cursor
← or **Ctrl+B**	Moves the cursor one character to the left
→ or **Ctrl+F**	Moves the cursor one character to the right (only as far right as the end of the command)
Delete	Deletes the character highlighted by the cursor (characters following the deleted character all move one space to the left)
↑ or **Ctrl+P**	Displays the last historical command that was run. The system stores a list of historically run commands, allowing you to display them one at a time (press repeatedly to view earlier commands)
↓ or **Ctrl+N**	Displays the next most recent historical command in the stored list

Full help, for example, displays a list of commands available in the current view.
Entering ? in the user view will display the following.

```
<Huawei> ?
User view commands:
  arp-ping                 ARP-ping
  autosave                 <Group> autosave command group
  backup                   Backup  information
  cd                       Change current directory
  clear                    Clear
  clock                    Specify the system clock
  cls                      Clear screen
  compare                  Compare configuration file
  copy                     Copy from one file to another
  debugging                <Group> debugging command group
  delete                   Delete a file
  dialer                   Dialer
  dir                      List files on a filesystem
  display                  Display information
  factory-configuration    Factory configuration
  fixdisk                  Try to restore disk
---- More ----
```

From the list, you can determine which command you need. For example, the
display keyword is described as **Display information**. This keyword is contained in more than one command, so enter any letter to quit help, enter **display**
and a space, and then enter ?. The following information is then shown.

```
<Huawei> display ?
  accounting-scheme      Accounting scheme
  acl                    <Group> acl command group
  actual                 Current actual
  ap                     <Group> ap command group
  bfd                    Specify BFD(Bidirectional Forwarding Detection)
  bgp                    BGP information
  binding                Display binding relation of profile
  bridge-link            Bridge link
  bridge-profile         Display Bridge profile
  bridge-whitelist       Bridge Whitelist
  bssid-decode           Display bssid detail information
  calibrate              Global calibrate
  clock                  Clock status and configuration information
  config                 System config
  cpu-defend             Configure CPU defend policy
  cpu-usage              Cpu usage information
  current-configuration  Current configuration
---- More ----
```

From this list, you can determine which keyword to pair with **display**. For example, running the **display current-configuration** command displays the current configurations of a device.

Partial help is ideal for when you already know part of the command line. For example, if you know **dis** for **display** and **c** for **current-configuration** but cannot remember the complete command line, use partial help. Entering **dis** and ? shows the following.

```
<Huawei> dis?
  display  Display information
```

The only keyword that matches **dis** is **display**. To determine the second part of the command line, enter **dis**, a space, **c**, and ?.

```
<Huawei> dis c?
  Cellular                Cellular interface
  calibrate               Global calibrate
  capwap                  CAPWAP
  channel                 Informational channel status and configuration
                          information
  clock                   Clock status and configuration information
  config                  System config
  controller              Specify controller
  cpos                    CPOS controller
  cpu-defend              Configure CPU defend policy
  cpu-usage               Cpu usage information
  current-configuration   Current configuration
  cwmp                    CPE WAN Management Protocol
```

A few keywords start with **c**; however, it is easy to determine that the required command line is **display current-configuration**.

- Using shortcut keys

  Shortcut keys facilitate entering commands. Pre-defined shortcut keys are called system shortcut keys. Some of the commonly used system shortcut keys are listed in Table 2.3.

Table 2.3 Commonly used system shortcut keys

Key	Function
Ctrl+A	Moves the cursor to the beginning of the current line
Ctrl+E	Moves the cursor to the end of the current line
Esc+N	Moves the cursor down one line
Esc+P	Moves the cursor up one line
Ctrl+C	Stops a running function
Ctrl+Z	Returns to the user view
Tab	Provides command-line completion. Pressing **Tab** after entering a partial keyword automatically completes the keyword if the system finds a unique match

System shortcut keys cannot be modified; however, you can define your own (known as user-defined shortcut keys). User-defined shortcut keys can provide added convenience but may conflict with some commands—defining such keys is therefore not recommended.

2.3   Logging into a Device

A number of methods are available for logging into a device to configure it and check its status. After completing this section, you should be able to:

- Log into a device through a console port.
- Log into a device through a MiniUSB port (and install the required driver).

2.3.1   Log into a Device Through a Console Port

One of the login methods uses a network device's console port, which connects to a PC's serial port through a console cable. Figure 2.5 shows the appearance and structure of a console cable.

The following example describes how to log in through the console port.

1. Connect a PC and a network device through a console cable.
   The D-type connector of a console cable connects to the PC's serial port, and the RJ-45 connector connects to the device's console port (Fig. 2.6).
2. Create a connection and specify a communication port.
   📖 **NOTE**
   This example uses a PC running Windows XP.
   Power on the PC and device. Choose **Start** > **Programs** > **Accessories** > **Communications** > **HyperTerminal** to start the HyperTerminal. Create a

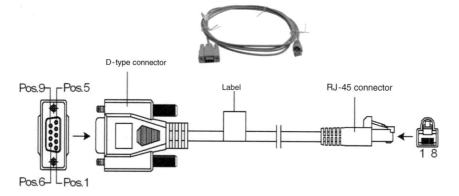

Fig. 2.5 Console cable

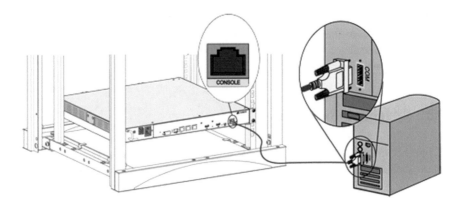

Fig. 2.6 Connecting a PC and network device through a console cable

connection (Fig. 2.7) and specify a communication port (Fig. 2.8). This example names the connection COMM1 and assumes that you connect the console cable to serial port COM1 on your PC.

3. Set communication parameters.
   Communication parameters on both the PC and network device must be the same. All network devices that run VRP have the following default values:

   – Bits per second: 9600
   – Data bits: 8
   – Parity: None
   – Stop bits: 1
   – Flow control: None

Fig. 2.7 Creating a connection

Fig. 2.8 Specifying a
communication port

Fig. 2.9 Setting
communication parameters

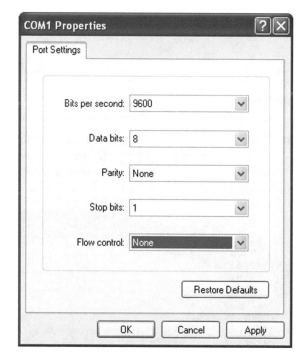

Windows XP also uses these values by default, so to use the default values on your PC, click **Restore Defaults**. Figure 2.9 shows the dialog box used to enter these values in Windows XP.

4. Enter the CLI.

In the dialog box shown in Fig. 2.9, click **OK** or press **Enter** to enter the CLI. If you are logging into the device for the first time, you will be prompted to configure a login password for the console port. After you configure a login password (for example, **huawei123**), the device prompts you whether to stop Auto-Config. If you want to manually configure the device, you must stop Auto-Config by entering **y**.

```
Please configure the login password (maximum length 16):huawei123
<Huawei>
Warning: Auto-Config is working. Before configuring the device, stop
Auto-Config. If you perform configurations when Auto-Config is running, the
DHCP, routing, DNS, and VTY configurations will be lost. Do you want to stop
Auto-Config? [y/n]: y
<Huawei>
```

The device then displays <Huawei>, indicating that you have entered the user view from which you can run VRP command lines.

2.3.2   Log into a Device Through a MiniUSB Port

Another login method uses a network device's MiniUSB port, which connects to a PC's USB port through a MiniUSB cable. Figure 2.10 shows the appearance of a MiniUSB cable.

The following example describes how to log in through the MiniUSB port.

1. Connect a PC and network device through a MiniUSB cable.

The Type-A connector of a MiniUSB cable connects to the PC's USB port, and the Mini-B connector connects to the device's MiniUSB port (Fig. 2.11).

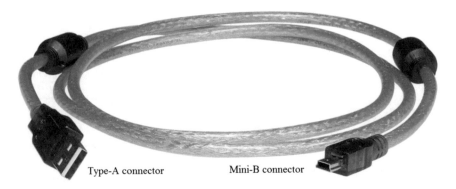

Type-A connector   Mini-B connector

Fig. 2.10 Appearance of a MiniUSB cable

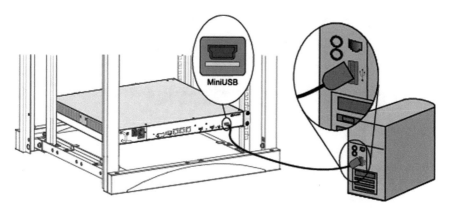

Fig. 2.11 Connecting a PC and network device through a MiniUSB cable

2. Install the MiniUSB driver.

📖 NOTE

This example uses a PC running Windows XP.

The MiniUSB driver enables communication between the PC and device. To install the driver on your PC, perform the following steps:

Step 1   Download the MiniUSB driver AR_MiniUSB_driver from http://support. huawei.com/enterprise. The driver is compatible with Windows XP, Windows Vista, and Windows 7. After the download is complete, double-click the driver installation file, and then click **Next** in the displayed **InstallShield Wizard** dialog box (Fig. 2.12).

Step 2   Select the **I accept the terms in the license agreement** check box after reading and confirming you agree to the terms and click **Next** (Fig. 2.13).

Step 3   In the **Destination Folder** dialog box, click **Change** to change the driver directory (if required), and then click **Next** (Fig. 2.14).

Step 4   Click **Install** to decompress the driver (Fig. 2.15). After the system finishes decompressing the driver, click **Finish** (Fig. 2.16).

Step 5   Navigate to the file decompression path and open the folder DISK1 (Fig. 2.17).

Step 6   Double-click **setup.exe**, and in the displayed **InstallShield Wizard** dialog box, click **Next** (Fig. 2.18).

Step 7   Select the **I accept the terms in the license agreement** check box after reading and confirming you agree to the terms and click **Next** to install the driver (Fig. 2.19).

Step 8   After the installation is complete, click **Finish** (Fig. 2.20).

Step 9   To confirm that the driver is successfully installed, right-click **My Computer** and choose **Computer Management > Device Manager > Ports (COM & LPT)**. If **TUSB3410 Device** is shown, the driver is installed successfully (Fig. 2.21).

Fig. 2.12 InstallShield Wizard dialog box

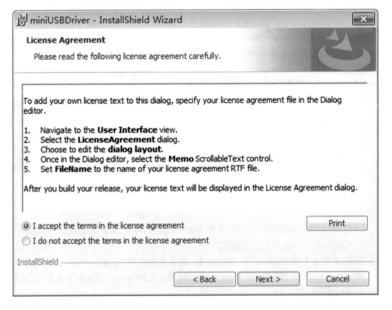

Fig. 2.13 License Agreement dialog box

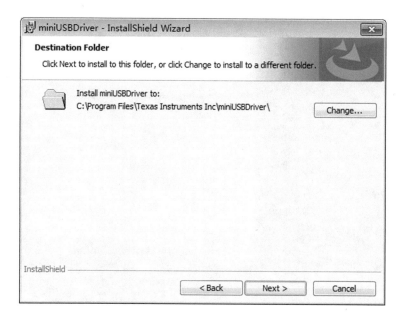

Fig. 2.14 Selecting the installation path

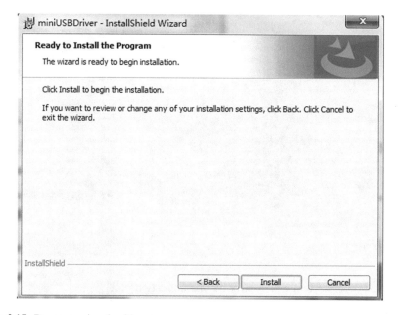

Fig. 2.15 Decompressing the driver

Fig. 2.16 Finishing driver decompression

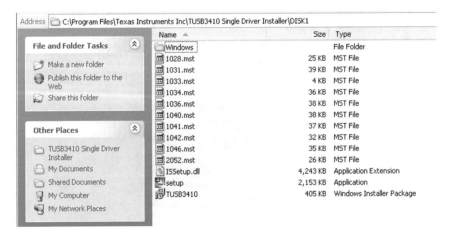

Fig. 2.17 DISK1 folder

1. Create a connection and specify a communication port.
   Choose
   Start > **Programs** > **Accessories** > **Communications** > **HyperTerminal** to
   start the HyperTerminal. Create a connection (Fig. 2.22) and specify a

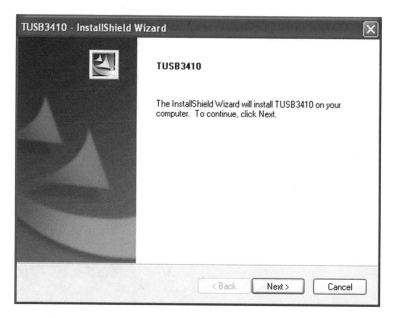

Fig. 2.18 InstallShield dialog box

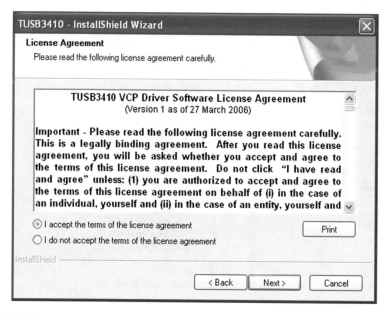

Fig. 2.19 License Agreement

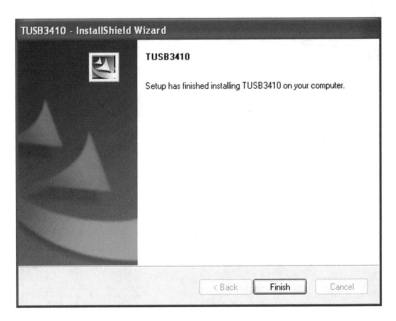

Fig. 2.20 Completing the installation

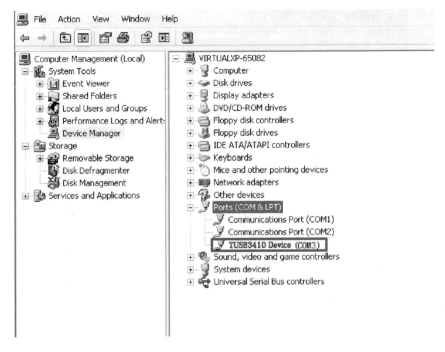

Fig. 2.21 Confirming the driver installation

communication port (Fig. 2.23). This example names the connection MiniUSB and specifies COM3 as the communication port.

2. Set communication parameters.

Communication parameters on both the PC and network device must be the same. All network devices that run VRP have the following default values:

Fig. 2.22 Creating a connection

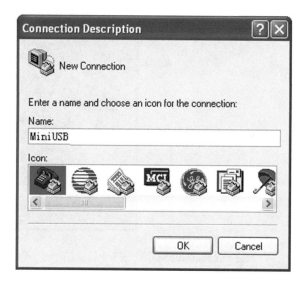

Fig. 2.23 Specifying a connection port

Fig. 2.24 Setting
communication parameters

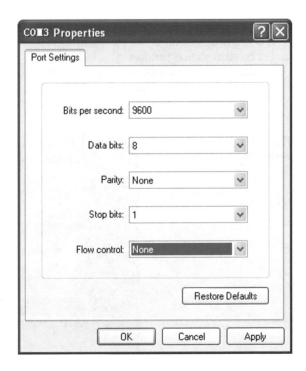

- Bits per second: 9600
- Data bits: 8
- Parity: None
- Stop bits: 1
- Flow control: None

Windows XP also uses these values by default, so to use the default values on your PC, click **Restore Defaults**. Figure 2.24 shows the dialog box used to enter these values in Windows XP.

3. Enter the CLI.

In the dialog box shown in Fig. 2.24, click **OK** or press **Enter** to enter the CLI.

2.4   Basic Configurations

Huawei's network devices generally are shipped unconfigured by default, so to use a device you must first configure some of its basic functions. After completing this section, you should be able to:

- Set the host name.
- Set the system time.
- Configure IP addresses.
- Configure the user interface.

2.4.1 Setting the Host Name

In the CLI, the host name (the name of the device) is enclosed in angle brackets
(⟨...⟩) or square brackets ([...]). The default host name is **Huawei**, but this name
should be changed so that multiple devices can be better differentiated. To change
the host name, use the **sysname** *host-name* command.

The following example shows how to change the host name to **Huawei-AR-01**.

```
<Huawei> system-view
Enter system view, return user view with Ctrl+Z.
[Huawei] sysname Huawei-AR-01
[Huawei-AR-01]
```

2.4.2 Setting the System Time

By default, Huawei devices use Coordinated Universal Time (UTC). To specify a
different time zone for a device, run the **clock timezone** *time-zone-name* {**add** |
minus} *offset* command. You can name the time zone in the *time-zone-name*
parameter, and specify whether the time zone's offset to UTC is positive (**add**
offset) or negative (**minus** *offset*). Note that {...} indicates that one of the enclosed
parameters must be selected. For example, if you want to set the time zone of the
device as Beijing time, run the following command:

```
[Huawei-AR-01] clock timezone BJ add 08:00
```

After setting the time zone, run the **clock datetime** *HH:MM:SS YYYY-MM-DD*
command to set the time and date. The *HH:MM:SS* parameter specifies the time, in
24-hour format, and *YYYY-MM-DD* specifies the date. (Huawei devices support
only the 24-hour format.) For example, to set a time and date of 18:30 on March 10,
2015, run the following command:

```
[Huawei-AR-01] clock datetime 18:30:00 2015-03-10
```

2.4.3 Configuring an IP Address for the Device

In addition to the login methods described in Sect. 2.3, you can also use Telnet to
log into a device. However, Telnet requires that an IP address be set on the device's
interface. To set an IP address, run the **ip address** *ip-address* {*mask* | *mask-length*}
command in the interface view. The *ip-address* and *mask* parameters specify the IP
address and subnet mask, respectively, in dotted decimal notation, and *mask-length*
specifies the number of consecutive "1"s in the binary notation of the subnet mask.

The following example shows how to set an IP address of 10.1.1.100 and subnet
mask of 255.255.255.0 for the management interface **Ethernet 1/0/0**:

```
<Huawei-AR-01> system-view
[Huawei-AR-01] interface ethernet 1/0/0        //Enter the interface view.
[Huawei-AR-01-Ethernet1/0/0] ip address 10.1.1.100 255.255.255.0
```

📖 **NOTE**

The length of the subnet mask's binary notation is 24 (255.255.255.0 is equivalent to the binary value 11111111.11111111.11111111.00000000), so in this example you can replace 255.255.255.0 with 24.

2.4.4 User Interface Configurations

Basic concepts

If you log into a device through the console port, a console user interface is displayed. If you log in through Telnet, a virtual type terminal (VTY) user interface is displayed. To implement user control on the console port, for example, to set the user level to 2, you can run the following commands:

```
<Huawei> system-view
[Huawei] user-interface console 0      //Enter the console user interface.
[Huawei-ui-console0] user privilege level 2
```

Other users may also log into the device while you are logged into it. Each user has a separate user interface (the number of VTY interfaces supported varies depending on the device), so to differentiate multiple user interfaces, the device implements user interface numbering.

User interface numbering

When a user logs into a device, the device allocates to the user the lowest numbered idle user interface according to the login method used. User interfaces are numbered either relatively or absolutely.

- Relative numbering
  The numbering format is user interface type + number. Generally, a device has one console port (some devices may have more) and 15 VTY user interfaces (5 VTY user interfaces enabled by default). When relative numbering is used, the ports are displayed as follows:

  − Console user interface: CON 0
  − VTY user interfaces: The first VTY user interface is VTY 0, the second VTY 1, and so on.

- Absolute numbering

  An absolute number uniquely identifies a user interface. Absolute and relative numbers are in one-to-one mapping. The console user interface has a relative number of CON 0 and an absolute number of 0. A VTY user interface has a relative number ranging from VTY 0 to VTY 14 and an absolute number ranging from 129 to 143.

To check the user interfaces that a device supports, run the **display user-interface** command. For example:

```
<Huawei> display user-interface
  Idx      Type      Tx/Rx     Modem  Privi  ActualPrivi  Auth Int
    0      CON 0     9600        -     15       -            -
+ 129      VTY 0                 -     15       15           P   -
  130      VTY 1                 -     15       -            A   -
  131      VTY 2                 -     15       -            A   -
  132      VTY 3                 -     15       -            A   -
  133      VTY 4                 -     15       -            P   -
  134      VTY 5                 -     15       -            P   -
  135      VTY 6                 -     15       -            P   -
  136      VTY 7                 -     15       -            P   -
  137      VTY 8                 -     15       -            P   -
  138      VTY 9                 -     15       -            P   -
  139      VTY 10                -     15       -            P   -
  140      VTY 11                -     15       -            P   -
  141      VTY 12                -     15       -            P   -
  142      VTY 13                -     15       -            P   -
  143      VTY 14                -     15       -            P   -
UI(s) not in async mode -or- with no hardware support:
1-128
    +    : Current UI is active.
    F    : Current UI is active and work in async mode.
    Idx  : Absolute index of UIs.
    Type : Type and relative index of UIs.
    Privi: The privilege of UIs.
    ActualPrivi: The actual privilege of user-interface.
    Auth : The authentication mode of UIs.
        A: Authenticate use AAA.
        N: Current UI need not authentication.
        P: Authenticate use current UI's password.
    Int  : The physical location of UIs.
```

In the command output, the **Idx** column shows the absolute numbers, and the **Type** column shows the relative numbers.

User authentication

To ensure that only authorized users are allowed to access a device, the device supports password authentication and AAA authentication. None authentication is also supported.

- Password authentication
  This mode is used by default and requires users to enter the correct login password. If no password is configured, login is denied.
- AAA authentication
  This mode requires a correct user name and password combination. Using a user name and password combination improves security compared to password authentication. In addition, users are differentiated and do not affect each other during authentication. AAA authentication is generally used for Telnet logins because of its enhanced security.
- None authentication
  This mode performs no authentication on users and is not recommended. None authentication allows users to log in directly without any login credentials.

The user authentication mechanism verifies user login. By default, after a user logs into a device using Telnet, the user is granted Level 0.

Example: configuring VTY user interfaces

During device commissioning, many users may log into the device to configure services. To limit the number of users who can log in through Telnet to 15, configure 15 VTY user interfaces. Then, to enable the users to configure services, set the user level to 2.

1. Set the maximum number of VTY user interfaces to 15.
   Run the **user-interface maximum-vty** *number* command. Specify *number* as 15.
   ```
   <Huawei> system-view
   [Huawei] user-interface maximum-vty 15
   ```
2. Enter the VTY user interface view.
   Run the **user-interface vty** *first-ui-number* [*last-ui-number*] command. Specify *first-ui-number* as 0 and *last-ui-number* as 14 (relative numbers of VTY user interfaces). Note that [...] indicates that the enclosed parameter is optional; however, in this example, the parameter is required to limit the number of allowed users.
   ```
   [Huawei] user-interface vty 0 14
   [Huawei-ui-vty0-14]            //Enter the VTY user interface view.
   ```
3. Set the user level to 2 for the VTY user interface.
   Run the **user privilege level** *level* command. Specify *level* as 2.
   ```
   [Huawei-ui-vty0-14] user privilege level 2
   ```

4. Set the user authentication mode to AAA for the VTY user interface.
   Run the **authentication-mode** {**aaa** | **none** | **password**} command.
   ```
   [Huawei-ui-vty0-14] authentication-mode aaa
   ```
5. Configure a user name and password used in AAA authentication.
   Exit from the VTY user interface view and run the **aaa** command to enter the
   AAA view. Run the **local-user** *user-name* **password cipher** *password* command
   to configure a user name and password (**cipher** indicates that the specified
   password is saved in ciphertext in the configuration file). Then, run the **local-user**
   user-name **service-type telnet** command to set the service type to Telnet.
   ```
   [Huawei--ui-vty0-14] quit
   [Huawei] aaa
   [Huawei-aaa] local-user admin password cipher admin@123
   [Huawei-aaa] local-user admin service-type telnet
   [Huawei-aaa] quit
   ```
   After the configuration is complete, the user name (admin) and password (ad-
   min@123) must be entered before the command interface is displayed.

Example: configuring the console user interface

Password authentication is used for console port logins. Generally, only adminis-
trators are allowed to log into a device through the console port, and therefore the
highest user level is required.

1. Enter the console user interface.
   Run the **user-interface console** *interface-number* command, where *interface-
   number* specifies the relative number of the console user interface. In this
   example, interface 0 is used.
   ```
   [Huawei] user-interface console 0
   ```
2. Set the authentication mode and save the password in ciphertext.
   Run the **authentication-mode** {**aaa** | **none** | **password**} command to configure
   an authentication mode, and run the **set authentication password cipher**
   password command to configure a ciphertext password.
   ```
   [Huawei-ui-console0] authentication-mode password
   [Huawei-ui-console0] set authentication password cipher admin@123
   ```

After the configuration is complete, save the configurations to the memory. To check
the configurations, run the **display current-configuration** command. If the configurations are not saved, they will be lost after the device is powered off or restarted.

2.5   Configuration File Management

After completing this section, you should be able to:

- Understand the three basic concepts involved in file management.
- Save the current device configurations.
- Set the next startup configuration file.

2.5.1 Basic Concepts

To configure file management, you need to understand three concepts: current configurations, configuration file, and next startup configuration file.

1. Current configurations
   The configurations in the device memory are the configurations that the device is currently running. When a device is powered off or restarted, the configurations in the memory are lost.
2. Configuration file
   The configuration file contains the device configurations. Current configurations can be saved to this file, which is stored in an external storage device in either **.cfg** or **.zip** format. The configurations are loaded to device memory each time the device restarts. The configuration file can be queried, backed up, and even migrated to other devices. By default, the device saves the current configurations to **vrpcfg.zip**, which is stored in the root directory of the device's external storage device.
3. Next startup configuration file
   The next startup configuration file is the file from which the device imports configurations upon restart. By default, the next startup configuration file is named **vrpcfg.zip.**

2.5.2 Saving the Current Configurations

The current configurations can be saved either manually or automatically.

1. Saving configurations manually
   You can run the **save** [*configuration-file*] command at any time to save the current configurations to the configuration file specified by *configuration-file*. The specified configuration file must be in the **.cfg** or **.zip** format. If *configuration-file* is not specified, the configurations will be saved to the configuration file **vrpcfg.zip** by default.
   To save the current configurations to the configuration file **vrpcfg.zip**, perform the following operations:

   ```
   [Huawei] save
   The current configuration will be written to the device.
   Are you sure to continue?[Y/N]:y        //Enter y to confirm the saving.
   It will take several minutes to save configuration file, please wait...
   Configuration file had been saved successfully
   Note: The configuration file will take effect after being activated
   ```

   To back up the configuration file **vrpcfg.zip** to **backup.zip**, perform the following operations:

```
[Huawei] save backup.zip
Are you sure to save the configuration to flash:/backup.zip?[Y/N]:y
Now saving the current configuration to the slot 17.
Save the configuration successfully
```

2. Saving configurations automatically

Autosaving configurations helps avoid configuration loss if they are forgotten to be manually saved. Autosaving can be performed either periodically or at a scheduled time.

Periodical autosaving enables the device to automatically save the configurations when a specified period elapses, regardless of whether the configurations have been changed. In contrast, scheduled autosaving enables the device to automatically save the configurations at a specified time every day. By default, autosaving is disabled.

To enable periodical autosaving, run the **autosave interval on** command, and then run the **autosave interval** *time* command to set an interval at which configurations are automatically saved. *time* specifies a time period, in minutes. The default value is 1440 min (24 h).

To enable scheduled autosaving, run the **autosave time on** command, and then run the **autosave time** *time-value* command to set a time at which configurations are automatically saved. *time-value* specifies a time, in the format of hh:mm:ss. The default value is 00:00:00.

The device saves the configurations to **vrpcfg.zip** or to the next startup configuration file if you have specified one for the next startup.

📖 **NOTE**

The two autosaving modes, periodical and scheduled, cannot be used together. To use one autosaving mode, the other mode must be disabled. However, you can manually save the configurations at any time by running the **save** command, regardless of the autosaving mode in use.

2.5.3   Setting the Next Startup Configuration File

The **startup saved-configuration** *configuration-file* command allows you to specify the configuration file that a device uses upon restart. This next startup configuration file must be in either **.cfg** or **.zip** format and stored in the root directory (**flash:**/for example) of a device's external storage. *configuration-file* specifies a configuration file. If the specified configuration file does not exist in the root directory, an error will occur.

To specify the file **backup.zip** as the next startup configuration file, perform the following operations:

```
[Huawei] startup saved-configuration backup.zip
This operation will take several minutes, please wait...
Info: Succeeded in setting the file for booting system
```

The configurations in the specified file take effect only after the device restarts. By default, saving the current configurations will overwrite the configurations stored in the specified next startup configuration file.

Generally, devices are maintained by more than one engineer. As such, the current configurations may not be consistent with those in the specified next startup configuration file. To compare the current configurations against the next startup configuration file, you can run the **compare configuration** command. If the configuration commands differ, the device displays 120 characters (by default) starting from the line with differences.

For example, to compare the current configurations against the next startup configuration file **backup.zip**, perform the following operation:

```
[Huawei] compare configuration
The current configuration is not the same as the next startup configuration file.
 ====== Current configuration line 14 ======
 undo http server enable
#
 drop illegal-mac alarm
#
 vlan batch 10 to 11
#
 dot1x enable
 mac-authen
#
set transceiver-monitoring disable
 ====== Configuration file line 14 ======
 http server enable
#
 drop illegal-mac alarm
#
 vlan batch 10 to 11
#
 dot1x enable
 mac-authen
#
set transceiver-monitoring disable
```

The command output shows that line 14 differs between the current configurations and the next startup configuration file (the **undo http server enable** command is included in the current configurations, but is replaced with the **http server enable** command in the next startup configuration file). Then, you can determine whether to save the current configurations.

2.6   Remote Login Through Telnet

After completing this section, you should be able to:

- Understand the basic concepts of Telnet.
- Use Telnet to log into a device.

2.6.1 Introduction to Telnet

Telnet is an application-layer protocol in the TCP/IP model. This protocol enables a device (Telnet client) to log into a remote host (Telnet server) using TCP as the transport-layer protocol. Generally, the Telnet server listens for Telnet connections on TCP port 23.

A device that runs VRP can function as both a Telnet client and a Telnet server. For example, you can log into a device and use it as a Telnet client to telnet to another device. Figure 2.25 shows such a scenario, in which R1 functions as the Telnet server and the Telnet client for the PC and R2, respectively.

2.6.2 Logging into a Device Through Telnet

To log into a device from a PC running a Windows operating system, choose **Start** > **Run** and run the **telnet** *ip-address* command. For example, to log into a device whose IP address is 10.137.217.177, run the **telnet** *10.137.217.177* command and click **OK** (Fig. 2.26).

In the displayed login dialog box, enter the user name and password. If the authentication is successful, the command line prompt <Huawei> will be displayed.

2.7 File Management

VRP uses a file system to manage all files and directories on a device. After completing this section, you should be able to:

- Understand the basic concepts of the file system.
- Back up a device's configuration file.
- Use TFTP and FTP to transfer files.

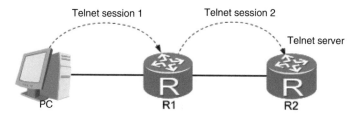

Fig. 2.25 Level-2 Telnet connection

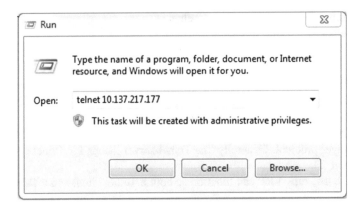

Fig. 2.26 CLI on the PC

- Delete files in a device.
- Configure the startup file of a device.

2.7.1 Basic Concepts

The VRP file system is used to create, delete, modify, copy, and display files and directories that are stored in a device's external storage, which for Huawei routers is flash memory and SD cards and for Huawei switches is flash memory and CF cards. Some devices also use external USB disks as supplementary storage devices.

An external storage device can store various types of files, including the configuration file, system software file, license file, and patch file. The system software file is the VRP operating system file and must be stored in **.cc** format in the root directory of the external storage device. The contents of this file are loaded to device memory and run when a device is powered on.

2.7.2 Backing up a Configuration File

In some scenarios such as a system upgrade, you may need to back up a device's configuration file to a specific folder in an external storage device. The following example describes the backup process, assuming that you have already logged into R1 through the PC (Fig. 2.27).

1. Locate the file to be backed up.
   The **dir** [/**all**] [*filename* | *directory*] command displays files in a specified path. **all** indicates that all files and directories in the current path are displayed, including any files in the recycle bin. *filename* specifies a file. *directory* specifies a directory.

Fig. 2.27 Backing up a configuration file

To check files and directories in the root directory of R1's flash memory, run the following command:

```
[Huawei] dir
Directory of flash:/

  Idx  Attr    Size(Byte)  Date          Time(LMT)    FileName
    0  -rw-    94,777,088  Jan 19 2013   16:20:29     software.cc
    1  -rw-             0  Jan 28 2013   09:16:34     brdxpon_snmp_cfg.efs
    2  -rw-           396  Jan 28 2013   09:18:27     rsa_host_key.efs
    3  -rw-         1,317  Mar 20 2013   10:22:32     private-data.txt
    4  -rw-        44,192  Mar 20 2013   10:26:25     mon_file.txt
    5  -rw-           540  Jan 28 2013   09:18:26     rsa_server_key.efs
    6  drw-             -  Jun 21 2012   10:25:25     cdr
    7  -rw-         1,351  Mar 08 2013   13:55:28     vrpcfg.zip
    8  -rw-     7,301,397  Jan 28 2013   09:18:26     abcd.zip
    9  drw-             -  Aug 21 2012   11:21:58     dhcp

217,168 KB total (94,104 KB free)
<Huawei>
```

In this example, the configuration file **vrpcfg.zip** of 1351 bytes in size will be backed up.

2. Create a directory.
   Run the **mkdir** *directory* command to create a directory. *directory* specifies the name of a directory (including its path) to be created. To create a directory **backup** in the root directory of a device's flash memory, run the following command:
   ```
   [Huawei] mkdir flash:/backup
   Info: Create directory flash:/backup......Done
   ```
3. Copy and rename the configuration file.
   Run the **copy** *source-filename destination-filename* command to copy a file. *source-filename* specifies the path and name of a source file. *destination-filename* specifies the path and name of a destination file.
   To copy the configuration file **vrpcfg.zip** to the directory **backup** and rename the file to **vrpcfgbak.zip**, run the following command:
   ```
   [Huawei] copy vrpcfg.zip flash:/backup/vrpcfgbak.zip
   Copy flash:/vrpcfg.zip to flash:/backup/vrpcfgbak.zip? (y/n)[n]:y
   ```

```
100% complete
Info: Copied file flash:/vrpcfg.zip to flash:/backup/vrpcfgbak.zip...Done
```

4. Check that the file has been backed up.

Run the **cd** *directory* command to change the current working directory. To check whether the configuration file has been successfully backed up, run the following commands:

```
[Huawei] cd flash:/backup
[Huawei] dir
Directory of flash:/backup/

  Idx  Attr     Size(Byte)  Date          Time(LMT)  FileName
   0   -rw-          1,351   Mar 20 2013   14:36:15   vrpcfgbak.zip

217,168 KB total (94,072 KB free)
<Huawei>
```

The command output shows that the directory **backup** contains the file **vrpcfgbak.zip**, meaning that the configuration file **vrpcfg.zip** has been backed up.

2.7.3 Transferring Files

1. TFTP

The Trivial File Transfer Protocol (TFTP) is a simple application-layer protocol in the TCP/IP model used to transfer files. It uses UDP as the transport-layer protocol with port 69.

TFTP works in the client/server model. Huawei routers and switches function only as TFTP clients. In Fig. 2.28, a PC functions as the TFTP server, and a router functions as the TFTP client. TFTP is used to transfer the VRP system software file on the PC to the router.

The **tftp** *tftp-server* {**get** | **put**} *source-filename* [*destination-filename*] command configures TFTP for file transfer. *tftp-server* specifies the IP address of a TFTP server. **get** indicates that a file is to be downloaded from a TFTP server to a TFTP client. **put** indicates that a file is to be uploaded from a TFTP client to a TFTP server. *source-filename* specifies a source file name. *destination-filename*

Fig. 2.28 Using TFTP to transfer a file

Fig. 2.29 Using FTP to transfer a file

specifies a destination file name. To download the VRP system software file **devicesoft.cc** from the PC to the router, run the following command:

```
[Huawei] tftp 10.1.1.1 get devicesoft.cc
Info: Transfer file in binary mode.
Downloading the file from the remote TFTP server. Please wait...\
TFTP: Downloading the file successfully.
93832832 bytes received in 722 seconds.
```

TFTP is easy to implement and use, but offers no security (for example, it does not verify user credentials or encrypt data). Anyone can upload or download files to or from TFTP servers, making TFTP suitable for file transfers only within secure network environments. For improved security, use FTP or SFTP.

2. FTP

Similar to TFTP, the File Transfer Protocol (FTP) is an application-layer protocol in the TCP/IP model. It uses TCP as the transport-layer protocol with port 21. Huawei routers and switches that run VRP can function as FTP servers as well as FTP clients. Compared to TFTP, FTP is more secure as it requires user credentials to establish an FTP connection. In addition, FTP allows you to delete files, and create and delete file directories on the FTP server.

In Fig. 2.29, a PC functions as the FTP server, and a router functions as the FTP client. FTP is used to transfer the VRP system software file on the PC to the router. Run the **ftp** *host-ip* [*port-number*] command to create an FTP connection. *host-ip* specifies the IP address of an FTP server. *port-number* specifies the port number of an FTP server. By default, TCP port 21 is used.

```
[Huawei] ftp 10.1.1.1
Trying 10.1.1.1 ...
Press CTRL+K to abort
Connected to 10.1.1.1.
220 FTP service ready.
User(10.1.1.1:(none)):admin      //Specify the user name of the server.
331 Password required for admin.
Enter password:                  //Specify the password of the server.
230 User logged in.

[Huawei-ftp]
```

Run the **dir** command to check a list of files on the FTP server.

```
[Huawei-ftp] dir
200 Port command successful.
150 Opening data connection for directory list.
drw-rw-rw-  1 ftp       ftp              0    Apr 17 10:53 back
drw-rw-rw-  1 ftp       ftp              0    Apr 17 10:53 backup
-rwxrwxrwx  1 noone     nogroup          0    Mar 23 15:49 aaa.cfg
-rwxrwxrwx  1 noone     nogroup       1351    Apr 02 20:37 vrpcfgbak.zip
-rwxrwxrwx  1 noone     nogroup     286620    Apr 07 08:56 sacrule.dat
-rw-rw-rw-  1 ftp       ftp       93832832    Mar 30 18:29 vrpsoft.cc
8 File sent ok
FTP: 734 byte(s) received in 0.129 second(s) 5.68Kbyte(s)/sec.

[Huawei-ftp]
```

Similar to TFTP, FTP uses **get** and **put** keywords: **get** in the **get** *source-filename* [*destination-filename*] command indicates that a file is to be downloaded from an FTP server to an FTP client, and **put** in the **put** *source-filename* [*destination-filename*] command indicates that a file is to be uploaded from an FTP client to an FTP server.

In this example, the **get** *vrpsoft.cc devicesoft.cc* command is run to download the VRP system software file **vrpsoft.cc** from the FTP server (the PC) to the FTP client (the router) and rename the file **devicesoft.cc**.

```
[Huawei-ftp] get vrpsoft.cc devicesoft.cc
200 Port command okay.
150 Opening ASCII mode data connection for vrpsoft.cc.
226 Transfer complete.
FTP: 93832832 byte(s) received in 722 second(s) 560.70byte(s)/sec.
```

FTP transfers data in plaintext. For improved security, use the Secure File Transfer Protocol (SFTP) to transfer files. SFTP encrypts data and protects the integrity of the data being transferred.

2.7.4 Deleting a File

You may need to delete files occasionally to free up storage space. To do so, run the **delete [/unreserved] [/force]** *filename* command. **/unreserved** indicates that the file to be deleted cannot be restored. **/force** indicates that no confirmation is required to delete the specified file. *filename* specifies the name of a file to be deleted.

If **/unreserved** is not configured, the file to be deleted is moved to the recycle bin and can be restored using the **undelete** command. The file will still occupy storage space inside the recycle bin. The **reset recycle-bin** command deletes all files in the recycle bin. Once files are deleted from the recycle bin, they cannot be restored.

To permanently delete a file, for example, **abcd.zip**, perform the following operations:

```
[Huawei] delete /unreserved abcd.zip
Warning: The contents of file flash:/backup/abcd.zip cannot be recycled.
Continue? (y/n)[n]:y
Info: Deleting file flash:/backup/abcd.zip...
Deleting file permanently from flash will take a long time if
needed.............succeed.
```

2.7.5 Setting a System Startup File

Startup files include the system software file and other files loaded from an external storage device to the memory for the device startup. Before setting the next startup file, run the **display startup** command to check the startup files used for the next startup.

```
[Huawei] display startup
MainBoard:
    Startup system software:                    flash:/software.cc
    Next startup system software:               flash:/software.cc
    Backup system software for next startup:    null
    Startup saved-configuration file:           flash:/vrpcfg.zip
    Next startup saved-configuration file:      flash:/vrpcfg.zip
    Startup license file:                       null
    Next startup license file:                  null
    Startup patch package:                      null
    Next startup patch package:                 null
    Startup voice-files:                        null
    Next startup voice-files:                   null
```

The command output shows that the system software file **software.cc** will be used for the next startup of the device. The **startup system-software** *system-file* command sets the system software file for the next startup. *system-file* specifies the file. To use the file **devicesoft.cc** for the next startup, run the following command:

```
[Huawei] startup system-software devicesoft.cc
This operation will take several minutes, please wait...
Info: Succeeded in setting the file for booting system
```

To verify whether the setting has taken effect, run the **display startup** command.

```
[Huawei] display startup
MainBoard:
  Startup system software:                   flash:/software.cc
  Next startup system software:              flash:/devicesoft.cc
  Backup system software for next startup:   null
  Startup saved-configuration file:          flash:/vrpcfg.zip
  Next startup saved-configuration file:      flash:/vrpcfg.zip
  Startup license file:                 null
  Next startup license file:            null
  Startup patch package:                null
  Next startup patch package:            null
  Startup voice-files:                  null
  Next startup voice-files:             null
```

The command output shows that the system software file for the next startup has been set to **devicesoft.cc**.

2.8   Basic Configuration Commands

Some commands are used more frequently than others and so are worth remembering. Table 2.4 lists some of the basic configuration commands that are most frequently used.

Table 2.4 VRP basic configuration commands

Command	Description
authentication-mode {**aaa** | **password** | **none**}	Sets an authentication mode for login to a user interface
autosave interval {*value* | *time* | **configuration** *time*}	Sets periodical autosaving
autosave time {*value* | *time-value*}	Sets scheduled autosaving
cd *directory*	Changes the working directory
clock datetime *HH:MM:SS YYYY-MM-DD*	Sets the current date and time
clock timezone *time-zone-name* {**add** | **minus**} *offset*	Sets a local time zone
compare configuration [*configuration-file*] [*current-line-number save-line-number*]	Compares the current configurations against the next startup configuration file
copy *source-filename destination-filename*	Copies a file
delete [**/unreserved**] [**/force**] {*filename* | *devicename*}	Deletes a file
dir [**/all**] [*filename* | *directory*]	Displays all files and directories or a specified file or directory

(continued)

Table 2.4 (continued)

Command	Description
display current-configuration	Displays the current configurations
display startup	Displays the system startup file
display this	Displays the running configurations in the current view
display user-interface [*ui-type ui-number1* | *ui-number*] [**summary**]	Displays the user interface
ftp *host-ip* [*port-number*]	Configures a device to establish a connection with an FTP server
get *source-filename* [*destination-filename*]	Downloads a file from a server to a client
local-user *user-name* **password cipher** *password*	Creates a local user and sets a password
local-user *user-name* **service-type telnet**	Configures the access type for a local user
mkdir *directory*	Creates a directory
move *source-filename destination-filename*	Moves a source file to a destination directory
put *source-filename* [*destination-filename*]	Uploads a file from a client to a server
quit	Returns to the upper-level view, or quits the system if the current view is the user view
reboot	Reboots a device
reset recycle-bin	Deletes files in the recycle bin permanently
save	Saves the current configurations
schedule reboot {**at** *time* | **delay** *interval*}	Configures scheduled restart of a device
startup saved-configuration *configuration-file*	Sets a next startup configuration file
sysname *host-name*	Sets a host name for a device
system-view	Displays the system view from the user view
telnet *host-name* [*port-number*]	Enables a device to use Telnet to log into another device
tftp *tftp-server* {**get** | **put**} *source-filename* [*destination-filename*]	Uploads a file to or downloads a file from a TFTP server
user-interface [*ui-type*] *first-ui-number* [*last-ui-number*]	Displays one or more user interfaces
user-interface maximum-vty *number*	Sets the maximum number of login users
user privilege level *level*	Sets a user level

2.9   Review Questions

1. What is VRP? (Choose all that apply)

   A. A network operating system
   B. System software
   C. A network device
   D. A software platform applicable to multiple network devices

2. Which prompt indicates the interface view? (Choose one)

   A. <Huawei>
   B. [Huawei]
   C. [Huawei-GigabitEthernet0/0/1]
   D. [Huawei-Vlan1]

3. Which of the following VRP command levels can Level-2 users run? (Choose one)

   A. Levels 0 and 1
   B. Levels 0, 1, and 2
   C. Level 2
   D. Levels 0, 1, 2, and 3

4. What is the default FTP port number? (Choose one)

   A. 23
   B. 69
   C. 21
   D. 24

5. What configurations must be performed after you log into a device for the first time? (Choose all that apply)

   A. Set a host name.
   B. Set the system time.
   C. Set a device IP address.
   D. Set a user interface.

Chapter 3
Ethernet

3.1 Ethernet Cards

A network interface card (NIC), often called a network card, is a key component
used by computers, switches, routers, and other network devices to connect directly
to external networks around the world. According to the technology used, NICs can
be divided into many types, such as token ring, FDDI, SDH, and Ethernet NICs. In
this chapter, our focus is Ethernet, so all network cards will refer to Ethernet
interface cards.

After completing this section, you should be able to:

- Understand the basic composition and operating principles of a network card.
- Understand the differences between a computer network card and a switch
  network card.

3.1.1 Computer Network Cards

A computer network card provides a port that can accommodate a network cable to
connect the computer to another device or to a network. Logically, a network card
provides seven functional modules: control unit (CU), output buffer (OB), input
buffer (IB), line coder (LC), line decoder (LD), transmitter (TX), and receiver (RX).
Figure 3.1 shows the logical architecture of a computer network card.

The following describes how a computer uses a network card to send information (see Fig. 3.1).

1. Application software installed on the computer generates the data to be sent. The
   data then passes through the application, transport, and network layers of the
   TCP/IP model. The network layer encapsulates the data into packets, and then
   transmits them to the network card's CU.

© Springer Science+Business Media Singapore 2016
Huawei Technologies Co., Ltd., *HCNA Networking Study Guide*,
DOI 10.1007/978-981-10-1554-0_3

Fig. 3.1 Architecture of a
computer network card

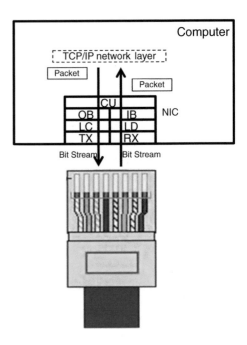

2. Upon receipt, the CU encapsulates each packet into an Ethernet frame. Then, the CU transmits these frames to the OB.
3. The OB arranges the frames according to the order in which they are received, and then transmits them in a "first in, first out" manner to the LC.
4. Upon receipt, the LC performs line encoding for the frames. Logically, a frame is a series of 0 s and 1 s with a finite length. The representation of 0 s and 1 s in the OB is not suitable for transmission across the transmission medium (such as a twisted pair). Therefore, the role of the LC is to convert this representation of 0 s and 1 s into physical signals, such as current/voltage, suitable for the transmission medium.
5. The TX receives the physical signals from the LC and adjusts their power and other characteristics before transmitting them across the transmission medium.

Now let's see how the computer uses the network card to receive information (see Fig. 3.1):

1. The network card's RX receives the physical signals (for example, current/voltage) from the transmission medium, and then adjusts their power and other characteristics before sending them to the LD.
2. The LD performs line decoding on the received physical signals. Line decoding logically identifies the 0 s and 1 s in the physical signal and converts them into a representation suitable for the buffer. These 0 s and 1 s will then be transmitted as frames to the IB.

3. The IB arranges the frames according to the order in which they are received, and then transmits them in a "first in, first out" manner to the CU.
4. Upon receipt, the CU processes the frames. The CU either discards the frames due to specific conditions or removes their headers and trailers to extract the encapsulated packets. Then, the CU transmits the packets to the TCP/IP model's network layer.
5. The packets are processed at the network layer, then at the transport layer, and then at the application layer. Ultimately, the processed data is sent to be used by the application software. However, data may be preemptively discarded by one of the layers due to specific conditions.

3.1.2 Switch Network Cards

A switch network card is similar to a computer network card. In a switch, each port that forwards data has a corresponding network card. Different ports correspond to different network cards. Switch network cards provide the same functional modules as computer network cards, specifically, the CU, OB, IB, LC, LD, TX, and RX modules.

Figure 3.2 shows the logical architecture of a switch network card.

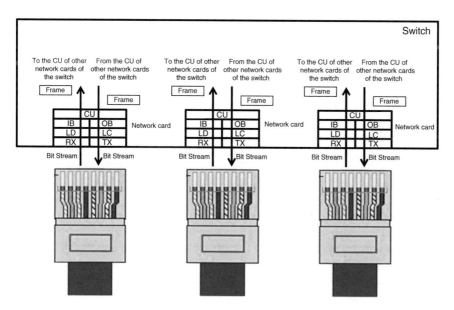

Fig. 3.2 Architecture of a switch network card

Forwarded data can be classified as incoming data and outgoing data. The following describes how a switch uses a network card to receive incoming data (see Fig. 3.2):

1. The network card's RX receives the physical signals (for example, current/voltage) from the transmission medium (such as a twisted pair), and then adjusts their power and other characteristics before sending them to the LD. This process is the same as that used by the computer network card's RX module.
2. The LD performs the same process as the computer network card's LD module. For details, see Sect. 3.1.1.
3. The IB performs the same process as the computer network card's IB module. For details, see Sect. 3.1.1.
4. The CU processes the frames received from the IB. The CU may discard the frames due to specific conditions, transmit them to a specific CU on the switch, or replicate them and send a copy of each frame to N CUs on the switch.

Now let's see how a switch uses a network card to transfer data out (see Fig. 3.2):

1. Unlike the computer network card's CU, switch network card CUs receive frames directly from the switch's other network card CUs. The CUs transmit these frames to the OB.
2. The OB performs the same process as the computer network card's OB. For details, see Sect. 3.1.1.
3. The LC performs the same process as the computer network card's LC. For details, see Sect. 3.1.1.
4. The TX performs the same process as the computer network card's TX. For details, see Sect. 3.1.1.

We can summarize computer and switch network cards as follows:

1. Network cards operate at the data link and physical layers of the TCP/IP model and posses functions of both layers.
2. A computer network card is used to receive and send data, whereas a switch network card is used to forward data.
3. The composition of the computer network card and the switch network card are the same, consisting of the CU, OB, IB, LC, LD, TX, and RX functional modules.
4. Except for that of the CU, the process performed by each module is the same for both the computer network card and the switch network card.
5. A computer network card's CU must encapsulate and decapsulate frames, convert them into packets, and deliver the packets to the network layer of the TCP/IP model. In contrast, a switch network card's CU neither encapsulates nor decapsulates frames; instead, it directly sends them to other network card CUs in the switch.

Each port has its own network card, regardless of whether the card is a computer or switch network card. The purpose of a network card is to send or forward, and receive, data. When we say that a port is sending, receiving, or forwarding data, what is actually meant is that the port's network card is sending, receiving, or forwarding the data.

In general, if a computer has multiple ports for connecting to a network, the network cards of these ports appear as stand-alone devices, with each network card installed at the location of its port. On a switch, however, a network card often appears as integrated chips. For example, a switch with eight ports may include two integrated chips, with four network cards concentrated on each chip. The location of the integrated chips within the switch is immaterial.

3.1.3 Review Questions

1. Which of the following descriptions are correct? (Choose all that apply)

   A. A network card operates at and possesses functions of only the data link layer.
   B. A network card operates at and possesses functions of both the data link layer and the physical layer.
   C. The LC and LD of a network card posses only data link layer functions.
   D. The LC and LD of a network card posses only physical layer functions.

2. Which of the following descriptions are incorrect? (Choose all that apply)

   A. The TX and RX of a network card posses only data link layer functions.
   B. The TX and RX of a network card posses only physical layer functions.
   C. A network card cannot exchange data with the network layer of the TCP/IP model.
   D. A network card can exchange data with the network layer of the TCP/IP model.

3. Which of the following descriptions are correct? (Choose all that apply)

   A. Referring to a port as an Ethernet port is actually referring to the port's network card as an Ethernet card.
   B. A computer network card must encapsulate and decapsulate frames.
   C. A computer cannot contain more than one network port, because a computer is not a data forwarding device.
   D. A switch will always contain many network ports, because a switch is a data forwarding device.

4. Which of the following descriptions are incorrect? (Choose all that apply)

   A. A single network card can control only a single network port in sending or forwarding, and receiving data.

B. A single network card can simultaneously control multiple network ports in sending or forwarding, and receiving data.

C. Multiple network cards can simultaneously control a single network port in sending or forwarding, and receiving data.

3.2   Ethernet Frames

The frame used by Ethernet technology is an Ethernet frame; the frame used by a token ring is a token ring frame; the frame used by FR technology is an FR frame, and so on and so forth. When we mention frames herein, unless specifically stated otherwise, it will always be in reference to Ethernet frames.

After completing this section, you should be able to:

- Describe MAC address structures and classifications.
- Describe the Ethernet II frame structure.
- Distinguish the differences and relationships between unicast, multicast, and broadcast MAC addresses and frames.

3.2.1   MAC Addresses

In February 1980, the IEEE convened a meeting to launch a major standardization project called IEEE Project 802. The 80 in 802 stands for 1980, while the 2 stands for February.

The project's aim was to formulate a series of LAN standards. The Ethernet (IEEE 802.3), token bus (IEEE 802.4), token ring (IEEE 802.5), and other such LAN standards are the result of IEEE 802. As such, the standards developed under IEEE Project 802 are collectively referred to as IEEE 802 standards.

The IEEE 802 standard defines and standardizes the Medium Access Control (MAC) address for all network interface cards (such as Ethernet and token ring network cards) that must have a MAC address. Not every network interface card must have a MAC address. For example, SDH network interface cards do not have MAC addresses, and so do not comply with the IEEE 802 standard. Hereinafter, all references to network cards will refer to Ethernet cards.

Every network card has its own globally unique MAC address, which is 48 bits (6 bytes) in length and identifies the card. A network card manufacturer must register with the IEEE to obtain an Organizationally-Unique Identifier (OUI), which is 24 bits (3 bytes) in length and identifies the manufacturer. During card production, the manufacturer burns to the Read Only Memory (ROM) of each card the MAC address (referred to as a Burned-In Address, BIA). The first three bytes of the BIA is the manufacturer's OUI, with the last three bytes being determined by the manufacturer.

Fig. 3.3 BIA format

For different network cards produced by the same manufacturer, the last three bytes of the BIA must be different. The BIA of a network card cannot be altered and can only be read. Figure 3.3 shows the format of a BIA.

A BIA is a kind of unicast MAC address. MAC addresses can be divided into three types: unicast, multicast, and broadcast MAC addresses.

1. A unicast MAC address is identified by its least significant bit of the first byte being 0.
2. A multicast MAC address is identified by its least significant bit of the first byte being 1.
3. A broadcast MAC address is identified by all its bits being 1.
4. A unicast MAC address (such as a BIA address) identifies a network card; a multicast MAC address identifies a group of network cards; a broadcast MAC address is a special kind of multicast MAC address which identifies all network cards.

In Fig. 3.4, we can see that only the unicast MAC address contains an OUI, whereas the multicast and broadcast MAC addresses do not, because only unicast MAC addresses identify individual network cards and multicast and broadcast MAC addresses are logical MAC addresses that identify multiple network cards.

A MAC address is often expressed in one of two common formats. In one of the formats, the MAC address is expressed as six groups of hexadecimal digits, with each group (1 byte) connected by a dash. In the other format, the MAC address is expressed as three groups of hexadecimal digits, with each group (2 bytes) connected by a dash. Figure 3.5 shows the two formats.

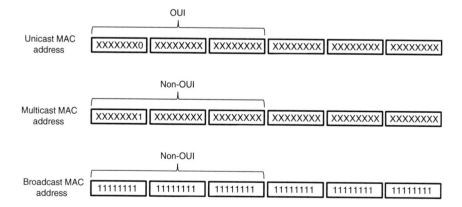

Fig. 3.4 MAC address types and formats

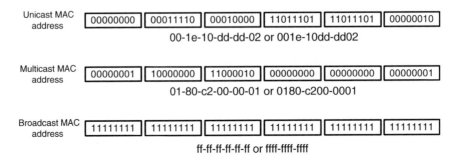

Unicast MAC address
| 00000000 | 00011110 | 00010000 | 11011101 | 11011101 | 00000010 |
00-1e-10-dd-dd-02 or 001e-10dd-dd02

Multicast MAC address
| 00000001 | 10000000 | 11000010 | 00000000 | 00000000 | 00000001 |
01-80-c2-00-00-01 or 0180-c200-0001

Broadcast MAC address
| 11111111 | 11111111 | 11111111 | 11111111 | 11111111 | 11111111 |
ff-ff-ff-ff-ff-ff or ffff-ffff-ffff

Fig. 3.5 MAC address formats

3.2.2 Ethernet Frame Formats

There are two standard types of Ethernet frame formats: the IEEE 802.3 format, which is defined by IEEE 802.3, and the Ethernet II format (also called the DIX format), which is jointly defined by Digital Equipment Corporation (DEC), Intel, and Xerox. Figure 3.6 shows the two types of format.

Despite the differences between the two formats, current network devices support both. The Ethernet II format is most widely used, whereas the IEEE 802.3 format is generally used only in certain scenarios where the frames are required to carry specific protocol information.

The following describes the different fields in an Ethernet II frame:

1. Destination MAC address (6 bytes): contains the MAC address of the entity to which the frame is sent. A destination MAC address can be a unicast, multicast, or broadcast MAC address (frames containing such are called unicast, multicast, or broadcast frames, respectively).
2. Source MAC address (6 bytes): contains the MAC address of the entity from which the frame is sent. A source MAC address can only be a unicast MAC address.
3. Type (2 bytes): contains the payload data type. For example, a value of 0x0800 indicates that the payload data is an IPv4 packet, a value of 0x86dd indicates an IPv6 packet, a value of 0x0806 indicates an ARP packet, and a value of 0x8848 indicates an MPLS packet.
4. Payload Data (46–1500 bytes, variable): contains the payload of the frame.
5. CRC Field (4 bytes): contains a checksum (an integrity check) of the frame. CRC stands for Cyclic Redundancy Check. The working mechanism of CRC is beyond the scope of this book.

The destination MAC address, source MAC address, type, payload data, and CRC fields are the same in both an Ethernet II and an IEEE 802.3 frame. The remaining fields in an IEEE 802.3 frame are beyond the scope of this book.

IEEE 802.3 format

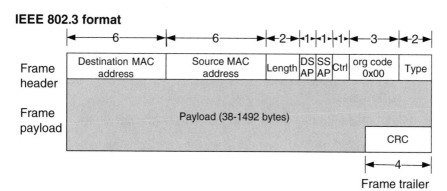

Ethernet II format

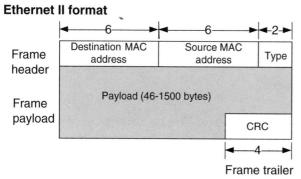

Fig. 3.6 Two standard Ethernet frame formats

3.2.3 Review Questions

1. How many network cards can a network card manufacturer produce with a single OUI? (Choose one)

   A. 1
   B. 16,777,216
   C. 256
   D. 65,536

2. Which of the following identifies a MAC address of 05-1e-10-0d-d0-03? (Choose one)

   A. Unicast MAC address
   B. Multicast MAC address
   C. Broadcast MAC address

3. Which of the following descriptions are correct? (Choose all that apply)

   A. The two types of Ethernet frame format are the IEEE 802.3 format and the IEEE 802.4 format.

B. The two types of Ethernet frame format are the IEEE 802.3 format and the Ethernet II format.
C. The two types of Ethernet frame format are the Ethernet I format and the Ethernet II format.
D. The two types of Ethernet frame format are the IEEE 802.3 format and the DIX format.

4. Which of the following descriptions are correct? (Choose all that apply)

A. The destination MAC address of an Ethernet frame can only be a unicast MAC address.
B. The source MAC address of an Ethernet frame can only be a unicast MAC address.
C. The source MAC address of a multicast frame can only be a unicast MAC address.

3.3   Ethernet Switches

Currently, the majority of LAN switches are Ethernet switches. Consequently, the terms Ethernet switch and LAN switch have become practically synonymous. Unless stated otherwise, hereinafter we are referring exclusively to Ethernet switches.

After completing this section, you should be able to:

- Understand the three types of forwarding operations.
- Describe the forwarding principle and process for unicast and broadcast frames.
- Understand how switches learn the mapping between MAC addresses and ports.
- Describe the process by which computer ports process unicast and broadcast frames.
- Describe the aging mechanism of the MAC address table.

3.3.1   Three Types of Forwarding Operations

A switch can perform three types of operations on frames received from transmission medium. The three operations are:

1. Flooding: The switch forwards a frame received on one port out from all ports other than the port on which the frame is received. A flooding operation is a kind of point-to-multipoint forwarding.
2. Forwarding: The switch forwards a frame received on one port out from another port. A forwarding operation is a kind of point-to-point forwarding.
3. Discarding: The switch discards a frame received on a port.

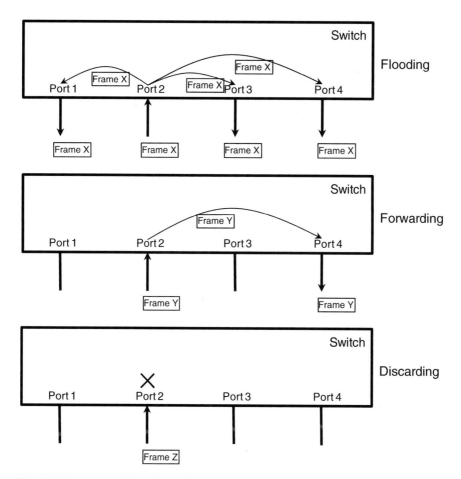

Fig. 3.7 Three types of frame forwarding operations

The arrows in Fig. 3.7 indicate the directions in which a frame is forwarded. For details, see Sect. 3.1.2.

Flooding, forwarding, and discarding operations are often collectively generalized as forwarding operations. Therefore, when we encounter the word "forwarding", we must determine whether it refers to this generalization or the specific operation based on the context in which it is used.

3.3.2 Switch Operating Principle

The switch operating principle primarily refers to the process in which a switch forwards a frame received on one of its ports from a transmission medium. Some concepts, such as a "MAC address table", may currently be unfamiliar to you. As we progress through the following topics, you will gain a better understanding of these concepts.

A MAC address table is where a switch stores the mapping relationship between MAC addresses and switch ports. Such a table exists within every switch's working memory. The MAC address table is empty after a switch is started and is populated when the switch learns the mapping between MAC addresses and switch ports during the process of data forwarding. The mappings are lost if the switch is reset or powered off.

The following describes the switch operating principle in general terms:

1. Upon receipt of a unicast frame, the switch queries the MAC address table for the frame's destination MAC address.

   a. If no mapping exists for the destination MAC address, the switch floods this frame out of all ports except the port on which the frame is received.
   b. If a mapping exists for the destination MAC address, the switch checks if the port number mapped to the destination MAC address is the port number of the port on which the frame is received.

      1. If the port numbers are not the same, the switch forwards the frame to the port mapped to the frame's destination MAC address in the MAC address table, and sends the frame out from that port.
      2. If the port numbers are the same, the switch discards the frame.

2. Upon receipt of a broadcast frame, the switch floods the frame out of all ports other than the port on which the frame is received, without querying the MAC address table.
3. Upon receipt of a multicast frame, the switch performs complex processing that goes beyond the scope of this book.

To learn new mapping, the switch reads the source MAC address of received frames (regardless of whether the frames are unicast, multicast, or broadcast). The switch then stores the mapping between the source MAC address and port number if the mapping does not exist in the MAC address table.

3.3.3 Examples of Data Forwarding on a Single Switch

In Fig. 3.8, four PCs each connect to a single switch by a twisted pair cable. The four ports on the switch are numbered 1 through 4. For information about how the cables connect between PC and switch, see Sect. 3.1. Assume that the MAC addresses of PCs 1 through 4's computer network card are MAC1 through MAC4, respectively, and that the MAC address table is currently empty.

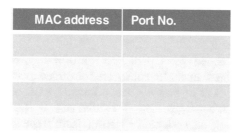

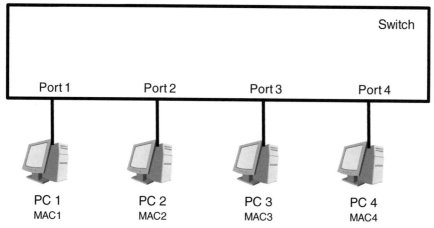

Fig. 3.8 Single switch networking

If PC 1 knows the MAC address of PC 3's network card and sends a unicast frame, frame X, to PC 3, PC 1 is deemed the source host and PC 3 the destination host. The process to transfer frame X from PC 1 to PC 3 is as follows:

1. The application software running on PC 1 generates data, which passes through the application, transport, and network layers of the TCP/IP model for processing. The network layer generates a packet from the data, and then transmits it to the CU of PC 1's network card, which in turn encapsulates it into a frame—frame X. The CU specifies its MAC address (MAC1) as the source MAC address of frame X, and MAC3 as the destination MAC address. For now, we can ignore the content of the other fields in frame X.
2. Frame X is forwarded as follows: CU of PC 1's network card → OB of PC 1's network card → LC of PC 1's network card → TX of PC 1's network card → twisted pair → RX of Port 1's network card → LD of Port 1's network card → IB of Port 1's network card → CU of Port 1's network card. This process is explained in Sect. 3.1.
3. Upon frame X's arrival at the CU of Port 1's network card, the switch queries the MAC address table for the frame's destination MAC address, MAC3. However, the MAC address table is currently empty. The switch, therefore, floods frame X out of all ports except the port on which frame X is received.

Because frame X arrived at the switch on Port 1 and frame X's source MAC address is MAC1, the switch maps MAC1 to Port 1 and stores this mapping in the MAC address table.

4. After frame X is flooded, the CU of Port n's (n = 2, 3, or 4) network card receives a copy of the frame. The copies are forwarded as follows: CU of Port n's network card $\rightarrow$ OB of Port n's network card $\rightarrow$ LC of Port n's network card $\rightarrow$ TX of Port n's network card $\rightarrow$ twisted pair $\rightarrow$ RX of PC n's network card $\rightarrow$ LD of PC n's network card $\rightarrow$ IB of PC n's network card $\rightarrow$ CU of PC n's network card. This process is explained in Sect. 3.1.

5. The CUs of PC 2, 3, and 4's network cards compare whether their MAC address is the same as the destination MAC address of the received frame X. Both PC 2 and 4 discard frame X because the MAC addresses are not the same.

6. Because the MAC address of PC 3's network card is the same as the destination MAC address of frame X, the CU of PC 3's network card extracts the packet from frame X. Based on the value of frame X's Type field, the CU sends the packet to the relevant processing module on the network layer of the TCP/IP model. After the network, transport, and application layers process the data, it arrives at the intended application software running on PC 3.

The current status of the example network is shown in Fig. 3.9. Frame X has been successfully sent from source host PC 1 to destination host PC 3. The traffic generated by frame X on PC 2 and 4's twisted pairs was of no practical use and was immediately discarded. Such traffic, generated by a switch's flooding operation, is known as junk traffic.

Based on the network status shown in Fig. 3.9, assume that PC 4 knows the MAC address of PC 1's network card and sends frame Y, a unicast frame, to PC 1. In this scenario, PC 4 is the source host, and PC 1 is the destination host. The process to transfer frame Y from PC 4 to PC 1 is as follows:

1. The application software running on PC 4 generates data, which passes through the application, transport, and network layers of the TCP/IP model for processing. The network layer generates a packet from the data, and then transmits it to the CU of PC 4's network card, which in turn encapsulates it into a frame— frame Y. The CU specifies its MAC address (MAC4) as the source MAC address of frame Y, and MAC1 as the destination MAC address. For now, we can ignore the content of the other fields in frame Y.

2. Frame Y is forwarded as follows: CU of PC 4's network card $\rightarrow$ OB of PC 4's network card $\rightarrow$ LC of PC 4's network card $\rightarrow$ TX of PC 4's network card $\rightarrow$ twisted pair $\rightarrow$ RX of Port 4's network card $\rightarrow$ LD of Port 4's network card $\rightarrow$ IB of Port 4's network card $\rightarrow$ CU of Port 4's network card.

3. Upon frame Y's arrival at the CU of Port 4's network card, the switch queries the MAC address table for the frame's destination MAC address, MAC1. The result of the query indicates that MAC1 maps to Port 1. Port 1 is not the port on which frame Y arrived, so the switch performs a point-to-point forwarding operation for frame Y and sends it to the CU of Port 1's network card.

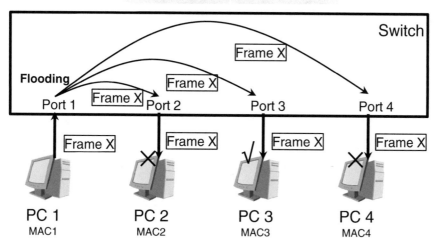

Frame X: The destination MAC address is MAC3, and the source MAC address is MAC1.

Fig. 3.9 Unicast frame sent from PC 1 to PC 3

Because frame Y arrived at the switch on Port 4 and frame Y's source MAC address is MAC4, the switch maps MAC4 to Port 4 and stores this mapping in the MAC address Table

4. The CU of Port 1's network card forwards the received frame Y as follows: CU of Port 1's network card → OB of Port 1's network card → LC of Port 1's network card → TX of Port 1's network card → twisted pair → RX of PC 1's network card → LD of PC 1's network card → IB of PC 1's network card → CU of PC 1's network card.

5. The CU of PC 1's network card compares whether its MAC address is the same as the destination MAC address of the received frame Y. Because the MAC addresses are the same, the CU extracts the packet from frame Y. Based on the

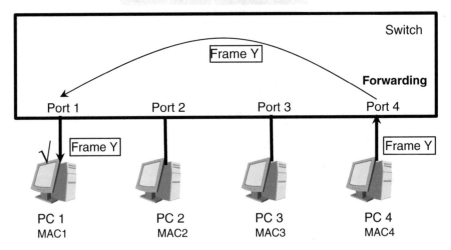

MAC address	Port No.
MAC1	1
MAC4	4

Frame Y: The destination MAC address is MAC1,
and the source MAC address is MAC4.

Fig. 3.10 Unicast frame sent from PC 4 to PC 1

value of frame Y's Type field, the CU sends the packet to the relevant processing module on the network layer of the TCP/IP model. After the network, transport, and application layers process the data, it arrives at the intended application software running on PC 1.

The current status of the example network is shown in Fig. 3.10. Frame Y has been successfully sent from source host PC 4 to destination host PC 1, and because the switch performed a point-to-point forwarding operation for frame Y, no junk traffic was generated.

Based on the network status shown in Fig. 3.10, assume that PC 1 sends a unicast frame, frame Z. However—due to a bug, for example—the CU of PC 1's network card specifies MAC1 as frame Z's destination MAC address and MAC5 as the source MAC address during frame creation. The process to transfer frame Z is as follows:

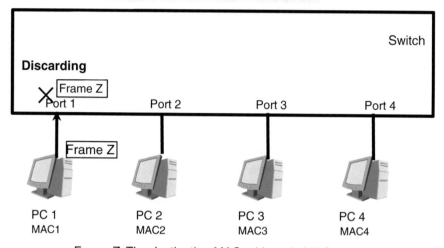

MAC address	Port No.
MAC1	1
MAC4	4
MAC5	1

Frame Z: The destination MAC address is MAC1, and the source MAC address is MAC5.

Fig. 3.11 PC 1 sending a unicast frame

1. CU of PC 1's network card → OB of PC 1's network card → LC of PC 1's network card → TX of PC 1's network card → twisted pair → RX of Port 1's network card → LD of Port 1's network card → IB of Port 1's network card → CU of Port 1's network card.
2. Upon frame Z's arrival at the CU of Port 1's network card, the switch queries the MAC address table for the frame's destination MAC address, MAC1. The result of the query indicates that MAC1 maps to Port 1. However, because Port 1 is the port on which frame Z arrived, the switch discards the frame. The switch also maps MAC5 to Port 1 and stores this mapping in the MAC address table.

The current status of the example network is shown in Fig. 3.11.

The preceding examples have shown and described how a switch floods, forwards, and discards a unicast frame sent from a PC. Now, let's look at an example of a broadcast frame sent from a PC. Based on the network status shown in Fig. 3.11, assume that PC 3 sends a broadcast frame, frame W. The process to transfer frame W is as follows:

1. The application software running on PC 3 needs to simultaneously send data to all other computers. It generates the data, which passes through the application, transport, and network layers of the TCP/IP model for processing. The network layer generates a packet from the data, and then transmits it to the CU of PC 3's network card, which in turn encapsulate it into a broadcast frame—frame W. The CU specifies its MAC address (MAC3) as the source MAC address of frame W, and the broadcast MAC address as the destination MAC address. For now, we can ignore the content of the other fields in frame W.

2. Frame W is forwarded as follows: CU of PC 3's network card → OB of PC 3's network card → LC of PC 3's network card → TX of PC 3's network card → twisted pair → RX of Port 3's network card → LD of Port 3's network card → IB of Port 3's network card → CU of Port 3's network card.

3. Upon frame W's arrival at the CU of Port 3's network card, the switch floods the frame to all ports other than the port on which the frame is received, without querying the MAC address table. Because frame W arrived at the switch on Port 3 and frame W's source MAC address is MAC3, the switch maps MAC3 to Port 3 and stores this mapping in the MAC address table.

4. After frame W is flooded to all ports, the CU of Port n's (n = 1, 2, 4) network card receives a copy of the frame. The copies are forwarded as follows: CU of Port n's network card → OB of Port n's network card → LC of Port n's network card → TX of Port n's network card → twisted pair → RX of PC n's network card → LD of PC n's network card → IB of PC n's network card → CU of PC n's network card.

5. Because frame W is a broadcast frame, the CU of PC n's network card extracts the packet from frame W. Based on the value of frame W's Type field, the CU sends the packet to the relevant processing module on the network layer of the TCP/IP model. After the network, transport, and application layers process the data, it arrives at the intended application software running on PC n.

The current status of the example network is shown in Fig. 3.12. The application software running on PCs 1, 2, and 4 have successfully received the same data broadcast from PC 3's application software.

As multicast frames go beyond the scope of this book, no examples are provided of forwarding multicast frames.

In concluding this section, we must emphasize the following points:

1. Upon receipt of a unicast frame, a computer network card compares its own MAC address with the destination MAC address of the frame. If the MAC addresses are the same, the network card sends the payload data to the relevant processing module on the network layer, depending on the value of the unicast frame's Type field. Otherwise, the network card discards the unicast frame.

2. Upon receipt of a broadcast frame, a computer network card directly sends the payload data to the relevant processing module on the network layer, depending on the value of the broadcast frame's Type field.

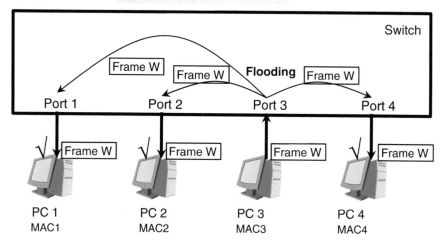

MAC address	Port No.
MAC1	1
MAC4	4
MAC5	1
MAC3	3

Frame W: The destination MAC address is ff-ff-ff-ff-ff-ff, and the source MAC address is MAC3.

Fig. 3.12 PC 3 sending a broadcast frame

3. Upon receipt of a unicast frame, a switch network card directly queries the MAC address table and then implements one of the three forwarding operations on the unicast frame.
4. Upon receipt of a broadcast frame, a switch network card floods the frame out of all ports other than the port on which the frame was received.

3.3.4 Examples of Data Forwarding Between Multiple Switches

In Fig. 3.13, four PCs connect through twisted pairs to three switches, forming a moderately complex network. Assume that the switch MAC address tables are currently empty. In this section, we'll provide some examples to help you understand the frame forwarding process in this multi-switch network. These examples

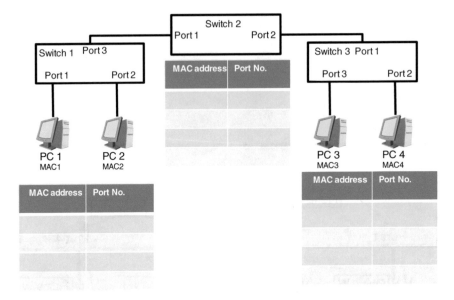

Fig. 3.13 Multi-switch networking

will be brief because we have described the forwarding process in Sect. 3.3.2. You can refer back to that section if needed.

Assume that PC 1 knows the MAC address of PC 3 is MAC3 and sends a unicast frame, frame X, to PC 3. The process to transfer frame X from PC 1 to PC 3 is as follows:

1. The CU of PC 1's network card encapsulates frame X, and specifies the destination MAC address as MAC3 and the source MAC address as MAC1.
2. Frame X is forwarded as follows: CU of PC 1's network card → CU of Port 1's network card on Switch 1.
3. Switch 1 floods frame X out of Port 3 (to Port 1 of Switch 2) and Port 2 (to PC 2). Switch 1 stores the mapping between MAC1 and Port 1 in its MAC address table.
4. Switch 2 floods frame X (which arrived on the CU of Port 1's network card) out of Port 2 (to Port 1 of Switch 3). Switch 2 stores the mapping between MAC1 and Port 1 in its MAC address Table
5. Switch 3 floods frame X (which arrived on the CU of Port 1's network card) out of Port 2 (to PC 4) and Port 3 (to PC3). Switch 3 stores the mapping between MAC1 and Port 1 in its MAC address Table
6. PC 2 and PC 4's network cards discard frame X. PC 3 sends the payload data of frame X to the network layer.

The current status of the example network is shown in Fig. 3.14. Frame X has been successfully sent from source host PC 1 to destination host PC 3. PC 2 and PC 4 also received frame X (causing junk traffic), but discard it.

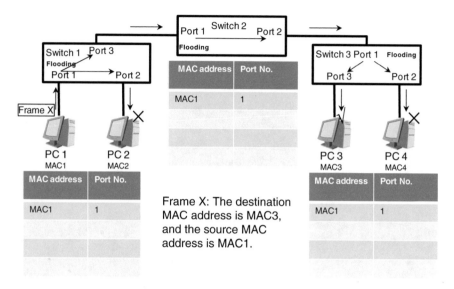

Fig. 3.14 PC1 sending a unicast frame to PC 3

Based on the network status shown in Fig. 3.14, assume that PC 4 knows the MAC address of PC1's network card, which is MAC1, and sends a unicast frame, frame Y, to PC 1. The process to transfer frame Y from PC 4 to PC 1 is as follows:

1. The CU of PC 4's network card encapsulates frame Y, and specifies the destination MAC address as MAC1 and the source MAC address as MAC4.
2. Frame Y is forwarded as follows: the CU of PC 4's network card → the CU of Port 2's network card on Switch 3.
3. Switch 3 performs a point-to-point forwarding operation for frame Y, which is on Port 2's network card CU. Frame Y arrives at Switch 2's Port 2 through Switch 3's Port 1. Switch 3 stores the mapping between MAC4 and Port 2 in its MAC address Table
4. Switch 2 performs a point-to-point forwarding operation for frame Y, which is on Port 2's network card CU. Frame Y arrives at Switch 1's Port 3 through Switch 2's Port 1. Switch 2 stores the mapping between MAC4 and Port 2 in its MAC address table.
5. Switch 1 performs a point-to-point forwarding operation for frame Y, which is on Port 3's network card CU. Frame Y arrives at PC 1 through Switch 1's Port 1. Switch 1 stores the mapping between MAC4 and Port 3 in its MAC address table.
6. PC 1 receives frame Y and sends the frame's payload data to the network layer.

The current status of the example network is shown in Fig. 3.15. Frame Y has been successfully sent from source host PC 4 to destination host PC 1, without generating any junk traffic.

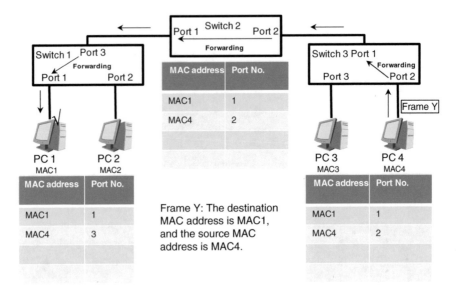

Fig. 3.15 PC4 sending a unicast frame to PC 1

Based on the network status shown in Fig. 3.16, assume that PC 2 knows the MAC address of PC 1's network card, which is MAC1, and sends a unicast frame, frame Z, to PC 1. Currently, no entry exists for MAC1 in Switch 1's MAC address table; however, such an entry does exist in Switch 2's MAC address table.

The process to transfer frame Z from PC 2 to PC 1 is as follows:

1. The CU of PC 2's network card encapsulates frame Z, and specifies the destination MAC address as MAC1 and the source MAC address as MAC2.
2. Frame Z is forwarded as follows: CU of PC 2's network card → CU of Port 2's network card on Switch 1.
3. Switch 1 floods frame Z out of Port 1 (to PC 1) and Port 3 (to Port 1 of Switch 2) because no mapping currently exists for MAC1 in the MAC address table. Then, Switch 1 stores the mapping between MAC2 and Port 2 in its MAC address table.
4. Switch 2 discards frame Z because the port on which the frame is received is Port 1, which maps to MAC1 in its MAC address table. Then, Switch 2 stores the mapping between MAC2 and Port 1 in its MAC address table.
5. PC 1 receives frame Z and sends the frame's payload data to the network layer.

The current status of the example network is shown in Fig. 3.17. Frame Z has been successfully sent from source host PC 2 to destination host PC 1.

Based on the network status shown in Fig. 3.17, assume that PC 3 sends a broadcast frame, frame W. The process to transfer frame W is as follows:

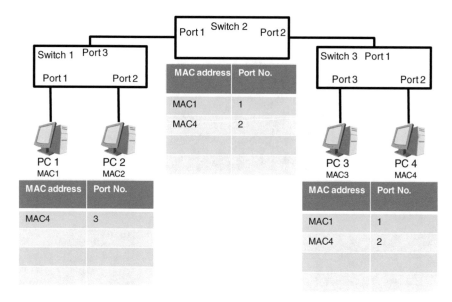

Fig. 3.16 PC 2 sending a unicast frame to PC 1

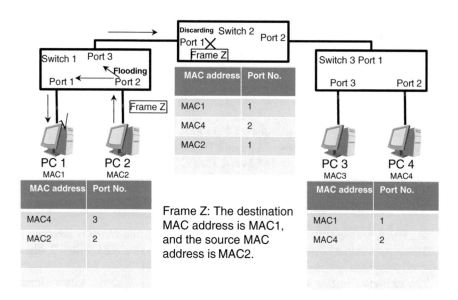

Fig. 3.17 PC2 sending a unicast frame to PC 1

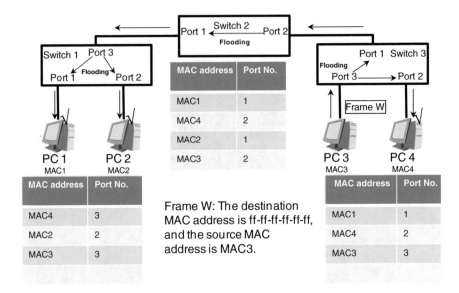

Fig. 3.18 PC 3 sending a broadcast frame

1. The CU of PC 3's network card encapsulates frame W, and specifies the destination MAC address as ff-ff-ff-ff-ff-ff and the source MAC address as MAC3.
2. Frame W is forwarded as follows: CU of PC 3's network card → CU of Port 3's network card on Switch 3.
3. Switch 3 floods frame W out of Port 1 (to Port 2 of Switch 2) and Port 2 (to PC 4). Then, Switch 3 stores the mapping between MAC3 and Port 3 in its MAC address table.
4. Switch 2 floods frame W out of Port 1 (to Port 3 of Switch 1). Then, Switch 2 stores the mapping between MAC3 and Port 2 in its MAC address table.
5. Switch 1 floods frame W out of Port 1 (to PC 1) and Port 2 (to PC 2). Then, Switch 1 stores the mapping between MAC3 and Port 3 in its MAC address table.
6. After the network cards of PC 1, 2, and 4 receive frame W, they send the frame's payload data to the network layer.

The current status of the example network is shown in Fig. 3.18. PC 1, 2, and 4 have all successfully received broadcast frame W from PC 3.

The examples in this section have described how frames move within simple networks, such as the one shown in Fig. 3.13. However, you can apply the same understanding to other more complex networks, such as the one shown in Fig. 3.19.

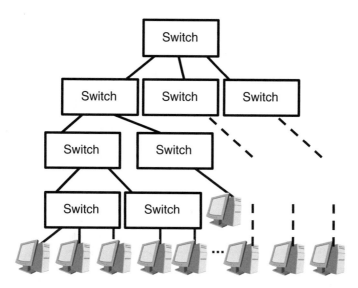

Fig. 3.19 Complex network

3.3.5 MAC Address Table

A switch MAC address table is also known as a MAC address mapping table, the entries in which are known as address table entries. An address table entry describes the mapping relationship between a MAC address and a port. In the preceding two sections, you learned how a switch ascertains the mapping relationship between MAC addresses and ports, as well as how it stores this mapping in the MAC address table.

But, what if the location of a switch or computer in a network changes? If you changed the switch's port to which your computer is connected, from port 1 to port 2, some entries in the switch's MAC address table will be inaccurate. In addition, the more entries stored in the MAC address table, the longer it takes for the switch to query the table (remember that, for unicast frames, the switch must check the destination MAC address in the MAC address table to determine which forwarding operation to execute). To mitigate such problems, entries in a MAC address table have a finite lifetime, defined by an aging mechanism.

Assume that X indicates any frame with the source MAC address, MACx. (Note that X can be a unicast, multicast, or broadcast frame.) Also assume that N indicates the switch has N ports (Port 1, Port 2, …, Port N). The following describes the MAC address table's aging mechanism based on these assumptions:

1. Upon X's arrival at the switch on Port k ($1 \leq k \leq N$), if no entry for MACx exists in the MAC address table, a new entry will be created with the content "MACx ← → Port k". At the same time, the value of the entry's countdown

MAC address	Port No.	Countdown Timer (Second)	
00-1e-10-00-00-02	3	240	⬅60 seconds has elapsed since the establishment or last update of the entry.
00-1e-10-00-0d-07	5	300	⬅The entry is just established or updated.
			⬅The entry has been deleted (aged out).
00-1e-10-00-00-a8	2	95	⬅205 seconds has elapsed since the establishment or last update of the entry.
00-1e-10-00-00-05	1	10	⬅290 seconds has elapsed since the establishment or last update of the entry.
...	...	...	
...	...	...	

Fig. 3.20 Example of MAC address table content

timer (a timer that determines the entry's lifetime) is set to the initial default value of 300 s. If MACx exists in the MAC address table, the content of the entry will be updated to "MACx ← → Port k", and the countdown timer for this entry will be reset to the default value of 300 s.

2. When the value of the countdown timer of any entry in the MAC address table reaches 0, the entry will be immediately deleted (called "aged out").

Each entry in the MAC address table has its own countdown timer. The content of an entry in the MAC address table is dynamic, and new entries are constantly added while old entries are constantly updated or deleted. Figure 3.20 shows the content of a MAC address table at a given time.

The smaller the initial countdown timer value, the more dynamic the MAC address table. The standard default initial value is 300 s, but this value can often be changed through configuration commands. Consider what impact changing the default value to 1 s or 3 days might have on the MAC address table.

For most modern switches in general, a MAC address table can store several thousand entries on a low-end switch, tens of thousands of entries on a mid-range switch, and hundreds of thousands of entries on a high-end switch.

3.3.6 Review Questions

1. Assume that a single switch has eight ports, one of which receives a unicast frame. However, no entry in the MAC address table matches this frame's destination MAC address. Which of the following forwarding operation will the switch perform for this frame? (Choose one)

   A. Discarding
   B. Flooding
   C. Point-to-point forwarding

2. Assume that a single switch has eight ports, one of which receives a unicast frame. An entry in the MAC address table matches this frame's destination

MAC address. Which of the following forwarding operation will the switch perform for this frame? (Choose one)

A. Definitely point-to-point forwarding
B. Definitely discarding
C. Maybe point-to-point forwarding, maybe discarding
D. Flooding

3. Which of the following descriptions are correct? (Choose all that apply)

A. Upon receipt of a broadcast frame, the computer port definitely sends the frame's payload data to the upper layer protocol for processing.
B. Upon receipt of a broadcast frame, the computer port performs a flooding operation.
C. Upon receipt of a broadcast frame, the switch port definitely sends the frame's payload data to the upper layer protocol for processing.
D. Upon receipt of a broadcast frame, the switch port performs a flooding operation.

4. Which of the following descriptions are correct? (Choose all that apply)

A. Computer MAC address tables have an aging mechanism.
B. In terms of probability, the fewer the entries in a switch MAC address table, the greater the possibility that the switch will execute a flooding operation.
C. In terms of probability, the fewer the entries in a switch MAC address table, the greater the possibility of junk traffic on the network.

5. What is the standard default initial value of the countdown timer for entries in a MAC address table? (Choose one)

A. 100 s
B. 5 min
C. 30 min

3.4   ARP

Address Resolution Protocol (ARP) is a commonly used protocol that resolves known IP addresses to MAC addresses. It is an important network layer protocol that involves data link layer information.

After completing this section, you should be able to:

- Understand the operating principle of ARP.
- Describe the roles of an ARP packet's various fields.
- Understand the role of the ARP cache table.

3.4.1   Basic Principles of ARP

In Sect. 3.3, we assumed that the source PC already knew the destination PC's MAC address. However, when a source device first starts working, it does not know the MAC address of the destination device. The source device must first obtain the IP address (we'll describe IP addresses in subsequent chapters) of the destination device through mechanisms such as the Domain Name System (DNS) and then use ARP to resolve the IP address into the destination device's MAC address. (Devices always know their own MAC address and IP address.)

To resolve an IP address, a source device sends a broadcast frame, the payload data of which is an ARP request packet. Upon receiving the ARP request packet, the destination device sends a unicast frame to the source device, the payload data of which is an ARP reply packet that includes the destination device's MAC address.

The following example will help you understand ARP's basic operating principle. In Fig. 3.21, PC 1 (source host) knows PC 2's (destination host) IP address is 10.0.0.2. Assume that PC 1 needs to obtain PC 2's MAC address. The process by which PC 1 obtains PC 2's MAC address is as follows:

1. PC 1 sends a broadcast frame, in which the source MAC address is MAC1 and the Type field value is 0x0806 (indicating that the payload data is an ARP packet). The ARP request packet specifies that PC 1's IP address is 10.0.0.1 and MAC address is MAC1, and requests the MAC address that corresponds to IP address 10.0.0.2.
2. Because the frame is a broadcast frame, both PC 2 and PC 3 receive the frame. Based on the Type field value (0x0806), the ARP request packet is sent to the ARP module on the network layer for processing.
3. PC 3's ARP module determines that 10.0.0.2 is not its IP address, so it does not send a reply. However, PC 3 stores the mapping between 10.0.0.1 and MAC1 in its ARP cache table. PC 3 then discards the ARP request packet.
4. PC 2's ARP module determines that 10.0.0.2 is its IP address, so it sends to PC 1 a reply: a unicast frame in which the destination MAC address is MAC1, the

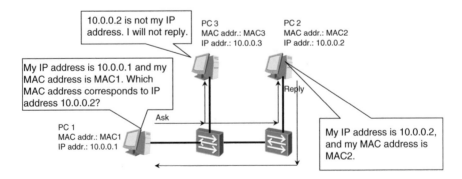

Fig. 3.21 ARP operating principle

source MAC address is MAC2, and the Type field value is 0x0806. The frame's payload data is an ARP reply packet that contains PC 2's IP address (10.0.0.2) and MAC address (MAC2). In addition, PC 2 stores the mapping between 10.0.0.1 and MAC1 in its ARP cache table.

5. Upon receipt of the unicast frame sent by PC 2, PC 1 sends the ARP reply packet to the Layer-3 ARP module. PC 1's ARP module obtains PC 2's MAC address, MAC 2, from the reply packet. In addition, PC 1 stores the mapping between 10.0.0.2 and MAC2 in its ARP cache table.

An ARP cache table temporarily stores the mapping between IP addresses and MAC addresses. When a device sends a unicast frame to a destination device, it first checks the ARP cache table for a MAC address matching the destination IP address. If a match is found, the device sends the frame to the destination MAC address. Otherwise, it broadcasts an ARP request to obtain the MAC address.

The ARP cache table is dynamic. A single entry (specifically, the mapping between an IP address and a MAC address) expires 180 s (configurable) after it is established or matched. Each time the entry is matched, its aging time is reset to 180 s. Upon reaching this aging time, the entry will be deleted.

3.4.2   ARP Packet Format

ARP packets can be divided into ARP request and ARP reply packets, both of which have the same structure but different values of their fields. The shaded area in Fig. 3.22 shows the structure of an ARP packet, and Table 3.1 describes the ARP packet's fields.

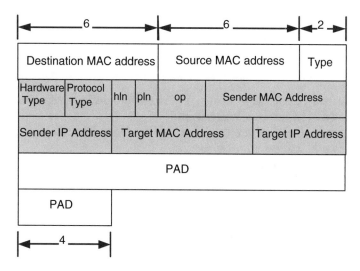

Fig. 3.22 ARP packet structure

Table 3.1 ARP packet's fields

Field	ARP Request	ARP Reply
Destination MAC Address	ff-ff-ff-ff-ff-ff	Requester MAC address
Source MAC Address	Requester MAC address	Requested MAC address
Type	2 bytes. The value is 0x0806	
Hardware type	2 bytes. Specifies the network type. For Ethernet, the value is 1	
Protocol type	2 bytes. Specifies the protocol address type. For IP address-based mapping, the value is 0x0800	
Hardware address length (hln)	1 byte. Specifies the length of the hardware address. For Ethernet, the value is 6 (indicating that the MAC address length is 6 bytes)	
Protocol address length (pln)	1 byte. Specifies the length of the protocol address. For IP, the value is 4 (indicating that the length of the IP address is 4 bytes)	
op	2 bytes. Specifies the type of ARP packet. The value is 1	2 bytes. Specifies the type of ARP packet. The value is 2
Sender MAC address	Requester MAC address	Requested MAC address
Sender IP address	Requester IP address	Requested IP address
Target MAC address	This field is ignored because the requester does not know this MAC address	Requester MAC address
Target IP address	IP address that the requester wants to map (also the requested IP address)	Requester IP address
PAD	18 bytes. The PAD field is used for padding, to ensure that Ethernet frames attain their minimum payload length of 46 bytes	

3.4.3   Review Questions

1. Which of the following descriptions are correct? (Choose all that apply)

   A. The role of ARP is to obtain IP address information that corresponds to known MAC address information.
   B. The role of ARP is to obtain MAC address information that corresponds to known IP address information.
   C. ARP is a data link layer protocol.
   D. ARP is a network layer protocol.

2. What type of frame should carry an ARP reply packet? (Choose one)

   A. Broadcast frame
   B. Multicast frame
   C. Unicast frame

3. What type of frame should carry an ARP request packet? (Choose one)

   A. Broadcast frame
   B. Multicast frame
   C. Unicast frame

4. Which of the following Type field value indicates that a frame is carrying an ARP packet? (Choose one)

   A. 0x0800
   B. 0x0806
   C. 0x8006

5. What is stored in the ARP cache table? (Choose one)

   A. The mapping between IP addresses and ports
   B. The mapping between MAC addresses and IP addresses
   C. The mapping between MAC addresses and ports

Chapter 4
STP

Spanning tree protocol (STP) is a data link layer protocol used to prevent loops on switched networks. The acronym STP is also used for other terms, such as shielded twisted pair and signal transfer point, so be careful not to confuse them.

After completing this chapter, you should be able to:

- Describe STP's background.
- Understand the STP port roles and states.
- Describe the process in which an STP tree is generated.
- Describe the roles of BPDU fields.

4.1 Loops

A loop is a complete cycle where packets continue traveling in it and never reach the destination. The switched networks that we have studied thus far have been star or tree topologies, neither of which is prone to loops.

In the network shown in Fig. 4.1, switches S1, S2, and S3 form a ring topology. This network is simple; however, it is susceptible to loops that may result in MAC address flapping, broadcast storms, and multiple frame copies.

MAC Address Flapping

Based on Fig. 4.1, assume that PC 1 sends a broadcast frame, frame X. Upon receipt of frame X, S1 floods out a copy of it in both counterclockwise and clockwise directions. The paths that each copy traverses are as follows:

- Counterclockwise
  S1 Port 1 → S2 Port 1 → S2 Port 2 → S3 Port 1 → S3 Port 2 → S1 Port 2 → S1 Port 1 → S2 Port 1 → S2 Port 2 → S3 Port 1 → S3 Port 2 → S1 Port 2 → S1 Port 1 …

Fig. 4.1 A simple network
susceptible to loops

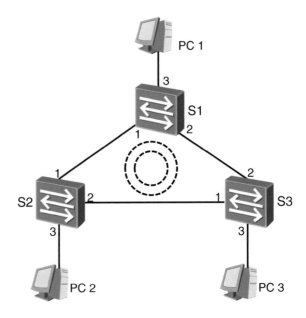

- Clockwise
  S1 Port 2 → S3 Port 2 → S3 Port 1 → S2 Port 2 → S2 Port 1 → S1 Port
  1 → S1 Port 2 → S3 Port 2 → S3 Port 1 → S2 Port 2 → S2 Port 1 → S1
  Port 1 → S1 Port 2 …

Copies of frame X will continue to traverse the three switches, in both directions,
indefinitely. Upon arrival of each copy at S1's Port 1, S1 updates the entry in its
MAC address table for PC 1's MAC address to "PC 1's MAC address ← → Port
1". However, upon arrival of each copy at S1's Port 2, S1 updates the entry to "PC
1's MAC address ← → Port 2". The continual updating of S1's MAC address
table (alternating the mapping of PC 1's MAC address between Port 1 and Port 2) is
known as MAC address flapping. The same phenomenon occurs to S2 and S3's
MAC address tables. MAC address flapping wastes a large amount of switch
processing resources, resulting in switch overload and potential failure.

Broadcast Storm

Based on Fig. 4.1, upon receipt of frame X, switch Sn (n = 1, 2, 3) performs a
flooding operation and PC n receives a copy of the frame. Sn constantly performing
flooding operations and PC n constantly receiving copies of frame X is known as a
broadcast storm. A broadcast storm wastes network bandwidth resources and
computer processing resources. Because a computer must send the payload data of
each received broadcast frame to the network layer for processing, a sufficient
volume of frames may overload the computer and cause failure.

Multiple Frame Copies

Receiving multiple copies of the same frame generally wastes computer resources. Based on Fig. 4.1, assume that PC 1 sends a unicast frame, frame Y, to PC 2, S1's MAC address table does not contain an entry for PC 2's MAC address, S2's MAC address table contains the entry "PC 2's MAC address ← → Port 3", and S3's MAC address table contains the entry "PC 2's MAC address ← → Port 1". Therefore, for frame Y, S1 will perform a flooding operation, whereas S2 and S3 will perform point-to-point forwarding operations. As a result, PC 2 will receive two copies of frame Y, which is known as multiple frame copies.

Despite the preceding drawbacks, such a network topology can offer advantages. For example, a ring network can improve the reliability of network connections. In Fig. 4.1, the ring ensures network connectivity even if a link between any two switches fails.

To realize these advantages and mitigate the drawbacks, IEEE 802.1D defined STP. Some common terms involved in STP include bridge, bridge MAC address, bridge ID, and port ID. These terms are described as follows.

Bridge

Because of performance limitations and other such factors, early switches typically could only have two forwarding ports (if there were more ports, the slow forwarding would be unbearable), so at that time, switches were often referred to as "network bridges", or simply "bridges". In IEEE terminology, the term "bridge" is still used to this date, but rather than only referring to those switches with just two ports, it is also used to refer to any multi-port switch.

Bridge MAC Address

Each port of a bridge has its own MAC address. Generally, the MAC address of the lowest-numbered port serves as the MAC address of the entire bridge.

Bridge Identifier (BID)

A BID specifies the bridge's priority and MAC address. Figure 4.2 shows the BID structure, in which the first two bytes specify the bridge's priority, and the latter six bytes specify its MAC address. The default value of the bridge priority is 0x8000 (decimal equivalent of 32,768), but this value can be manually specified.

Port Identifier (PID)

Figure 4.3 shows two of the many ways in which a port can be identified. Both of the PIDs shown in the figure contain two bytes that specify a port's priority and number. However, the number of bits used for the port's priority and number differ between the two PIDs. In the first PID, the first 8 bits (1 byte) specify the port's priority, and the latter 8 bits specify the port number. In the second PID, the first 4 bits specify the port's priority, and the latter 12 bits specify the port number. The value of the port priority can be manually specified. Different vendors may use different methods for defining PID.

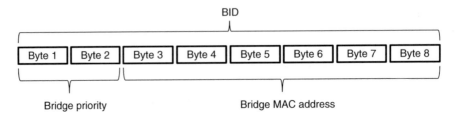

Fig. 4.2 BID structure

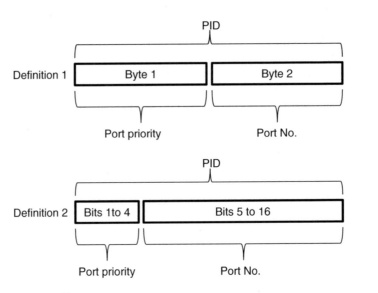

Fig. 4.3 PID composition

4.2 STP Tree Generation

In switched networks with a physical loop, switches run STP to automatically generate a loop-free topology. Such a topology is known as an STP tree. The STP tree can contain only one root bridge; each of the other bridges connects to this root bridge through only one active path (which is the optimal path). In the STP tree generation process, a root bridge is first elected, then a root port (RP) and a designated port (DP) are elected, and then the alternate port (AP) is blocked. If the network topology changes, STP automatically updates the tree accordingly.

4.2.1 Root Bridge Election

Before an STP tree can be generated, a root bridge must be elected. A root bridge is the logical (not necessarily the physical) center of an entire switched network. Changes to the network topology may change the root bridge.

Switches running STP (we'll refer to such switches as STP switches) exchange STP frames, the payload data of which is known as bridge protocol data units (BPDUs). A BPDU contains STP-specific information, including the BID. However, despite STP frames carrying this data unit, a BPDU is not a network layer unit of data (We'll describe BPDUs in Sect. 4.3). The BPDU producer, receiver, and processor are all STP switches rather than computers.

After bootup, all STP switches assume that they are the root bridge. They announce this assumption in the BPUDs that they send to other switches. Upon receiving such a BPDU, the switch compares its own BID with that of the root bridge specified in the BPDU. The switches continue to exchange and compare BPDUs until the switch with the smallest BID is elected as the root bridge.

In Fig. 4.4, switches S1, S2, and S3 all use the default bridge priority of 32,768. However, because S1's BID is the smallest, it will be elected as the root bridge.

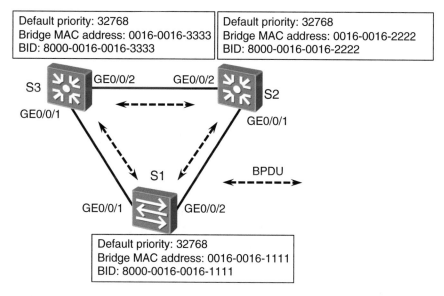

Fig. 4.4 Root bridge election

4.2.2   Root Port Election

Bridges other than the root bridge are known as non-root bridges. Each non-root bridge may have multiple ports connected to the network, so to ensure that each non-root bridge has only one active path (the optimal path) to the root bridge, one "root port" must be elected per non-root bridge. The non-root bridge uses the root port to exchange packets with the root bridge.

STP elects the root port based on root path cost (RPC), which is the total cost of all the links along the path from a port to the root bridge. Path cost is related to the port rate, and the faster the port forwarding, the lower the path cost. Table 4.1 lists this relationship.

📖 NOTE

The values and their relationship specified in this table are defined in IEEE 802.1t. However, the values used in real-world scenarios may differ from vendor to vendor.

Based on Fig. 4.5, assume that S1 is the root bridge and that the path cost adheres to IEEE 802.1t. S3 must elect either GE0/0/1 or GE0/0/2 as the root port. Because the RPC of GE0/0/1 is 20000 and that of GE0/0/2 is 200,000 + 20,000 = 220,000, S1 elects GE0/0/1 as its root port.

However, different ports on a non-root bridge device may have the same RPC. In such a scenario, the process shown in Fig. 4.6 is used to elect the root port.

In Fig. 4.7, S1 is the root bridge. Assume that the RPC of S4's GE0/0/1 and GE0/0/2 are the same. S4 compares the BID of S2 and S3. If S2's BID is smaller

Table 4.1 Port rate to path cost relationship

Port rate	Path cost (IEEE 802.1t standard)
10 Mbps	2,000,000
100 Mbps	200,000
1 Gbps	20,000
10 Gbps	2000

Fig. 4.5 Root port election (different RPCs)

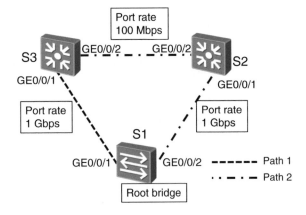

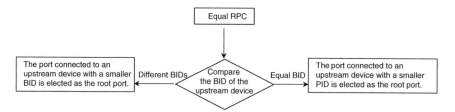

Fig. 4.6 Root port election process (same RPC)

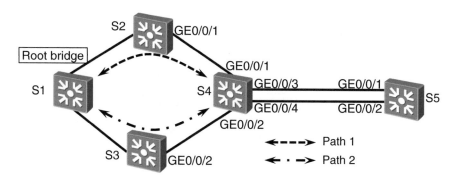

Fig. 4.7 Root port election (same RPC)

than S3's BID, S4 elects GE0/0/1 as its root port; or, if S3's BID is smaller than S2's BID, S4 elects GE0/0/2 as its root port. For S5, assume that the RPC of its GE0/0/1 and GE0/0/2 are the same. Because these two ports are connected to the same device (S4), S5 compares the PID of S4's GE0/0/3 and GE0/0/4. If the PID of GE0/0/3 is smaller than that of GE0/0/4, S5 elects GE0/0/1 as its root port; or, if the PID of S4's GE0/0/4 is smaller than that of S4's GE0/0/3, S5 elects GE0/0/2 as its root port.

4.2.3 Designated Port Election

A root port ensures that a switch has only one active path (the optimal path) to the root bridge. To prevent loops, each network segment must have only one active path (the optimal path) to the root bridge. If a network segment has two or more such paths (for example, the network segment is connected to different switches or different ports on the same switch), the corresponding switch or switches must have only one designated port.

The designated port is elected by comparing RPC. The port with the smallest RPC is elected as such. If the RPC is the same, the BID and PID must be compared. For details, see Fig. 4.8.

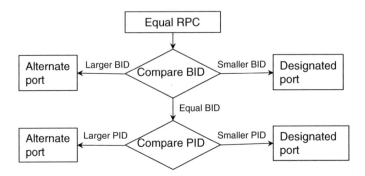

Fig. 4.8 Designated port election (same RPC)

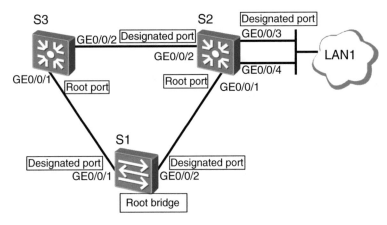

Fig. 4.9 Designated port election (same RPC)

Based on Fig. 4.9, assume that S1 is the root bridge and that the costs of all links are the same. S3's GE0/0/1 has a smaller RPC than that of GE0/0/2, so S3 elects GE0/0/1as its root port. Similarly, S2's GE0/0/1 has a smaller RPC than that of GE0/0/2, so S2 elects GE0/0/1 as its root port.

For the network segment between S3's GE0/0/2 and S2's GE0/0/2, S3's GE0/0/2 and S2's GE0/0/2 have the same RPC, so S3's BID and S2's BID must be compared. If S2's BID is smaller than S3's BID, S2's GE0/0/2 will be elected as the designated port for the network segment between S3's GE0/0/2 and S2's GE0/0/2.

Network segment LAN1 is connected only to S2. As such, only the PIDs of S2's GE0/0/3 and GE0/0/4 need to be compared. If GE0/0/3 has a smaller PID than GE0/0/4, S2's GE0/0/3 will be elected as the designated port for the network segment LAN1.

Finally, it must be noted that there are no root ports on the root bridge and only designated ports. Consider for a moment why this might be.

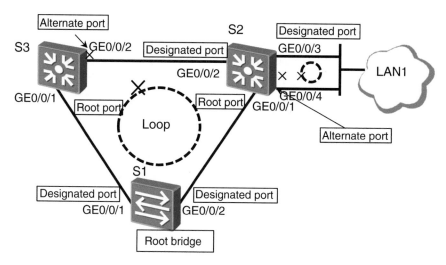

Fig. 4.10 Alternate port blocking

4.2.4 Alternate Port Blocking

All ports other than the root port and designated port on a switch are collectively known as alternate ports. STP logically blocks these alternate ports, which prevents them from forwarding user frames (frames generated and sent from computers). However, these ports can receive and process STP frames. The root and designated ports can forward user data frames in addition to sending and receiving STP frames.

Logically blocking the alternate ports completes the STP tree (loop-free topology) generation process. Figure 4.10 shows the blocked ports.

4.3 STP Packet Format

An STP switch generates, sends, receives, and processes STP frames, which are a type of multicast frame that contains the multicast address 01-80-c2-00-00-00. The switch establishes and maintains an STP tree through STP frames and reestablishes a new STP tree if the network's physical topology changes.

STP frames use the IEEE 802.3 encapsulation format, with a payload data known as a BPDU. The two types of BPDU are configuration BPDUs and Topology Change Notification (TCN) BPDUs.

4.3.1   Configuration BPDUs

During the initial STP tree generation process, STP switches periodically (every 2 s by default) generate and send configuration BPDUs. During periods in which an established STP tree is stable, only the root bridge periodically (every 2 s by default) generates and sends configuration BPDUs. Likewise, non-root switches periodically receive configuration BPDUs from their root ports and immediately generate their own configuration BPDUs, which the switches send from their designated port. This process is equivalent to the root bridge's configuration BPDUs traversing other switches one-by-one.

Table 4.2 describes the format of BPDUs.

Configuration BPDU parameters can be divided into three types:

- The BPDU's own identifiers, including the protocol identifier, version number, BPDU type, and flags.

Table 4.2   BPDU format

Field	Length (Bytes)	Description
Protocol identifier	2	Always 0x0000
Protocol version identifier	1	Always 0x00
BPDU type	1	0x00, indicates a configuration BPDU 0x80, indicates a TCN BPDU
Flags	1	Network topology change flag: Uses the least significant and most significant bits Least significant bit is the topology change (TC) flag Most significant bit is the TC acknowledgment (TCA) flag
Root identifier	8	Current root bridge BID
Root path cost	4	RPC of the port that sends the BPDU
Bridge identifier	8	BID of the switch that sends the BPDU
Port identifier	2	PID of the port that sends the BPDU
Message Age	2	Age of BPDU message This refers to the total time required to send a certain configuration BPDU from the root bridge up until it arrives at the current switch, including transmission delays. If a configuration BPDU is sent from a root bridge, the Message Age is 0. Otherwise, the Message Age is equal to the period from when the BPDU was sent by the root bridge to when the BPDU is received by the current bridge, including transmission delays. In live networks, the Message Age increases by one for each bridge the configuration BPDU traverses

(continued)

Table 4.2 (continued)

Field	Length (Bytes)	Description
Max Age	2	BPDU's maximum lifecycle for configuration BPDUs The value of the Max Age is designated by the root bridge and set to 20 s by default. Once the STP switch receives a configuration BPDU, it will compare the Message Age and Max Age. If the Message Age is less than or equal to the Max Age, the configuration BPDU will trigger the switch to generate and send a new configuration BPDU. Otherwise, the configuration BPDU will be discarded (ignored) and will not trigger the switch to generate and send a new configuration BPDU
Hello Time	2	The interval at which the root bridge and other switches send configuration BPDUs. The default value of Hello time is 2 s Once the network topology and STP tree are stable, the entire network will use the Hello Time of the root bridge. To change this parameter, you must change it on the root bridge
Forward Delay	2	The time for which a port remains in the listening and learning state This parameter is used to defer the transition to the forwarding state of a port. It requires a certain amount of time to generate an STP tree. During this process, the switch's port state will change, but may not simultaneously. If a new root port and designated port are elected and immediately begin to forward user data frames, it may lead to a temporary loop. For this, STP has introduced the Forward Delay mechanism: only after two times the Forward Delay can the newly selected root port and designated port enter the forwarding state to forward user data frames. This guarantees that the topology is loop-free at this time

- The parameters used in STP computing, including the BID of the switch that sends the BPDU and the current root bridge, and the RPC and PID of the port that sends the BPDU.
- Time parameters, which are Hello Time, Forward Delay, Message Age, and Max Age.

4.3.2   TCN BPDUs

In terms of their structure and content, TCN BPDUs are simple. They contain only the protocol identifier, version number, and type fields (the first three fields listed in Table 4.2).

If the failure of a network link causes the topology to change, the switch located at the point of failure detects this change through the port state. Other switches,

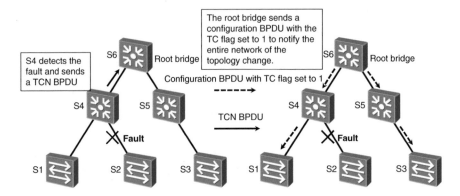

Fig. 4.11 Network topology change notification process

however, cannot directly detect this change. The switch located at the point of failure constantly sends TCN BPDUs to its upstream switch through its root port, at the interval of Hello Time, until it receives a configuration BPDU (with TCA flag set to 1) sent from the upstream switch. After receiving the TCN BPDU, the upstream switch replies with configuration BPDUs (with TCA flag set to 1) through its designated port and constantly sends TCN BPDUs at the interval of Hello Time to its own upstream switch through its root port. This process is repeated until the root bridge receives the TCN BPDU. Upon receipt of the TCN BPDU, the root bridge sends a configuration BPDU (with TC flag set to 1) to notify all other switches about the network topology change. Figure 4.11 illustrates this process.

After receiving the configuration BPDU whose TC flag is set to 1, the switch learns of the network topology change. This change may mean the content of the switch's MAC address table is incorrect. As a result, the switch reduces its aging time (300 s by default) to the length of the Forward Delay (15 s by default), which accelerates the aging of the original entries in the MAC address table.

4.4   STP Port States

In addition to the three different port roles, STP defines fives port states based on whether the port can send and receive STP frames and whether the port can forward user data frames. Table 4.3 describes the five port states.

Upon enabling an STP switch port, the port transitions from the disabled state to the blocking state. If the port is elected as the root or designated port, it will enter the listening state. This state will last for the interval defined by Forward Delay, set to 15 s by default. Then, in the absence of any exceptions that cause the port to revert to the blocking state, the port enters the learning state and remains in this state for the interval defined by Forward Delay. Ports in the learning state may build a MAC address mapping table to better prepare for forwarding user data frames;

Table 4.3 STP port states

Port state	Description
Disabled	The port is administratively down and cannot send or receive any frames
Blocking	The port can only receive STP frames; it cannot send STP frames or forward user data frames
Listening	The port can send and receive STP frames but cannot learn MAC addresses or forward user data frames
Learning	The port can send and receive STP frames and can learn MAC addresses but cannot forward user data frames
Forwarding	The port can send and receive STP frames, learn MAC addresses, and forward user data frames

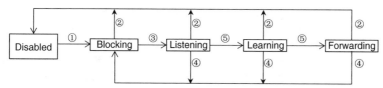

①The port is initialized or enabled.   ②The port is disabled or the link is faulty.
③The port is elected as the root or designated port.   ④The port is no longer the root or designated port.
⑤Forward Delay Timer expires.

Fig. 4.12 Port status transitioning

however, such ports cannot forward user data frames, because the network may not be synchronized (due to the STP tree computing process), and as such, may create a temporary loop. From the learning state, ports transition to the forwarding state and begin to forward user data frames. If a port is shut down or a link fails, the port will enter the disabled state. During the transitioning process of port states, if a port's role is defined as non-root or non-designated, its state immediately reverts to the blocking state. Figure 4.12 illustrates this process.

📖 **NOTE**

The STP implemented on Huawei switches uses the port states defined in MSTP: discarding, learning, and forwarding.

The following example describes how a port transitions from one state to another, based on the network shown in Fig. 4.13.

1. Assume that switches S1, S2, and S3 are simultaneously powered on. Each port of each switch will immediately enter the blocking state from the disabled state. Because a port in blocking state can only receive and not send BPDUs, no ports will receive BPDUs. After the Max Age time (20 s by default) elapses, each switch will assume that it is a root bridge, all port roles will become designated ports, and the ports will transition to the listening state.

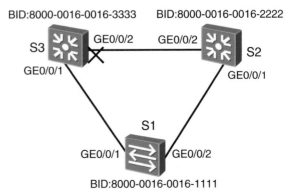

Fig. 4.13 Port state transition

2. After a switch port transitions to the listening state, it begins to send its own configuration BPDUs and receive the configuration BPDUs sent by other switches.

   Assume that S2 sends the first configuration BPDU. After receiving the configuration BPDU sent from S2 through GE0/0/2, S3 learns that S2 should be the root bridge (because S2's BID is smaller than S3's BID). As a result, S3 changes its GE0/0/2 from a designated port to a root port, regenerates a configuration BPDU with the root bridge set to S2, and sends this BPDU from its GE0/0/1. Upon receiving the configuration BPDU sent from S3, S1 learns that its own BID is the smallest and that it should become the root bridge. As a result, it immediately sends its own configuration BPDU to S3. If S1 receives the configuration BPDU sent from S2 through its GE0/0/2, it will also send its own configuration BPDU to S2.

   When S2 and S3 receive the configuration BPDU sent by S1, they confirm that S1 is the root bridge. S2's GE0/0/1 and S3's GE0/0/1 will therefore become root ports, and S2 and S3 will send the new configuration BPDUs from their GE0/0/2. Then, S3's GE0/0/2 will become an alternate port and enter the blocking state, and S2's GE0/0/2 will remain as a designated port.

   Because the length of time required for each switch to send a BPDU may differ slightly, the aforementioned process may not be the only process that occurs. However, regardless of which switch port is first to enter which state and regardless of how different the interim process may be, the ultimate result is the same: the switch with the smallest BID will become the root bridge, and port roles will change to reflect the roles of each port.

   After a port is in the listening state for the interval defined by Forward Delay (15 s by default), it transitions to the learning state. Note that S3's GE0/0/2 has already become an alternate port, so its state will become the blocking state.

3. After each port (except for S3's GE0/0/2) enters the learning state, it remains in this state for the interval defined by Forward Delay (15 s by default). During this period, the switch can learn the mapping relationships between MAC addresses

and ports. Full convergence of the STP tree may also be possible during this period.

4. After the Forward Delay elapses, ports (except for S3's GE0/0/2 port) enter the forwarding state and begin to forward user data frames.

4.5   STP Improvements

In an STP network, an STP tree's full convergence depends on a timer. A port state transition from blocking to forwarding requires at least twice the interval defined by Forward Delay, and therefore the total convergence time lasts for at least 30 s. To speed up convergence, IEEE 802.1w defined the Rapid Spanning Tree Protocol (RSTP). RSTP improves STP to greatly reduce convergence times to less than 10 s. Generally, STP has been superseded by RSTP and is no longer used.

Some of the improvements made by RSTP include:

Three Types of Port States

In RSTP, there are only three port states: discarding, learning, and forwarding. Table 4.4 compares these states with STP's port states.

P/A Mechanism

In STP, a designated port can transition to the forwarding state only after an interval equal to twice that defined by Forward Delay has elapsed. In RSTP, however, such a port first enters the discarding state, and then uses the Proposal/Agreement (P/A) mechanism to actively negotiate with peer ports. Through these negotiations, the port can immediately enter the forwarding state.

Table 4.4 Comparison of RSTP and STP port states

RSTP port state	Equivalent STP port state	Description
Forwarding	Forwarding	Can forward user data frames and learn MAC addresses
Learning	Learning	Cannot forward user data frames but can learn MAC addresses
Discarding	Listening	Cannot forward user data frames and cannot learn MAC addresses
Discarding	Blocking	
Discarding	Disabled	

4.6   Examples of STP Configurations

Figure 4.14 shows a basic STP configuration.

Configuration Process

1. Configure the STP mode.
2. Designate the root bridge.
3. Designate the secondary root bridge (optional).

Procedure

By default, a switch's STP function is enabled. If STP is disabled, use the **stp enable** command in the system view to enable STP.

#On S1, set the spanning tree operating mode to STP. Use the **stp mode {mstp| rstp|stp}** command, from which you can set the mode to MSTP, RSTP, or STP. The mode is set to MSTP by default.

```
<Quidway> system-view
[Quidway] sysname S1
[S1] stp mode stp
```

#On S2, set the spanning tree operating mode to STP.

```
<Quidway> system-view
[Quidway] sysname S2
[S2] stp mode stp
```

Fig. 4.14 Basic STP configuration

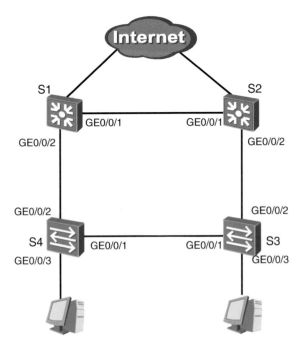

#On S3, set the spanning tree operating mode to STP.
```
<Quidway> system-view
[Quidway] sysname S3
[S3] stp mode stp
```

#On S4, set the spanning tree operating mode to STP.
```
<Quidway> system-view
[Quidway] sysname S4
[S4] stp mode stp
```

Even though STP will automatically elect the root bridge, we first designate a switch closer to the center of the network. The network structure shown in Fig. 4.14 is simple: S1 and S2 are connected through the Internet, and the core switches, S3 and S4, are access switches. We can change S1's bridge priority to ensure that S1 is elected as the root bridge. The command **stp priority** *priority* is used to set a device's bridge priority; the *priority* value ranges from 0 to 61440, in increments of 4096. The default value is 32,768. The smaller the *priority*, the greater the likelihood that the device will be elected as the root bridge. You can also use the command **stp root primary** to designate S1 as the root bridge. Once the command is run on the device, the device's bridge priority value is automatically set to 0. The device's bridge priority cannot be changed thereafter using the command **stp priority** *priority*.

```
[S1] stp root primary
```

Next, we will designate S2 as the secondary root bridge so that S2 replaces S1 as a new root bridge in case of failure. Once the command **stp root secondary** is run on the device, the device's bridge priority value is automatically set to 4096 and cannot be changed thereafter using the command **stp priority** *priority*.

```
[S2] stp root secondary
```

This concludes the network's basic STP configuration. To check the SPT tree state and statistics, you can run the command **display stp [interface** *interface-type interface-number*] [**brief**].

On S1, use the command **display stp brief** to display basic STP information

```
[S1] display stp brief
MSTID   Port                    Role    STP State    Protection
    0   GigabitEthernet0/0/1    DESI    FORWARDING   NONE
    0   GigabitEthernet0/0/2    DESI    FORWARDING   NONE
```

In the example output, because S1 is the root bridge, S1's GE0/0/2 and GE0/0/1 are both designated ports in the normal forwarding state.

The following output is S4's basic STP information.

```
[S4] display stp brief
MSTID   Port                   Role    STP State    Protection
   0    GigabitEthernet0/0/1   ALTE    DISCARDING   NONE
   0    GigabitEthernet0/0/2   ROOT    FORWARDING   NONE
```

S4's GE0/0/2 is a root port in the normal forwarding state. However, its GE0/0/1 is an alternate port in the blocking state.

4.7   Review Questions

1. Which of the following descriptions about STP is correct? (Choose one)

   A. STP is a data link layer protocol.
   B. STP is a network layer protocol.
   C. STP is a transport layer protocol.

2. Which of the following descriptions about STP is correct? (Choose one)

   A. The STP tree convergence process usually takes tens of minutes to complete.
   B. The STP tree convergence process usually takes tens of seconds to complete.
   C. The STP tree convergence process usually takes several seconds to complete.

3. Which of the following descriptions about STP are correct? (Choose all that apply)

   A. No designated port exists on a root bridge.
   B. No root port exists on a root bridge.
   C. One root port and multiple designated ports may exist on a single non-root bridge.
   D. Multiple root ports and a single designated port may exist on a non-root bridge.

4. Which of the following descriptions about STP are correct? (Choose all that apply)

   A. A port state may transition directly from the listening state to the forwarding state.
   B. A port state may transition directly from the learning state to the listening state.
   C. A port in the blocking state cannot send or receive STP frames.
   D. A port in the blocking state cannot forward user data frames.

5. Which of the following descriptions about STP are correct? (Choose all that apply)

    A. A root bridge cannot send TCN BPDUs.
    B. A non-root bridge cannot send a configuration BPDU whose TC flag is set to 1.
    C. STP frames are unicast frames.
    D. STP frames are multicast frames.

6. Which of the following descriptions about STP are correct? (Choose all that apply)

    A. The smaller the bridge priority value, the higher the bridge priority.
    B. The smaller a switch's BID value, the higher the possibility that the switch is elected as a root bridge.
    C. The PID value is not considered during root bridge election.

7. Which of the following descriptions about STP are correct? (Choose all that apply)

    A. The default Hello Time interval is 2 s.
    B. The default Max Age interval is 15 s.
    C. The default Forward Delay interval is 20 s.

Chapter 5
VLAN

This chapter will discuss Virtual Local Area Networks (VLANs) and how they offer multiple benefits to users wanting to securely manage large network configurations.
After completing this section, you should be able to:

- Understand the concept of Layer 2 broadcast domains.
- Learn about why do we need to control the size of Layer 2 broadcast domains.
- Understand the differences between Layer 2 and Layer 3 communication.
- Understand why the VLAN is needed and how the VLAN works.
- Be familiar with the IEEE 802.1Q frame structure.
- Differentiate between common VLAN configurations.
- Understand how the Access and Trunk ports work.
- Understand the purposes of GVRP.

5.1 VLAN Purposes

Figure 5.1 shows a typical switching network involving only PCs and switches without VLAN technology applied to it. When PC 0 sends a broadcast frame, the switch broadcasts this frame to all other computers within the switching network. This makes the broadcast range of the frame a Layer 2 broadcast domain.

Figure 5.2 shows how PC 0 can send a unicast frame Y to PC 10 over the same broadcast domain explained in Fig. 5.1. For the example in Fig. 5.2 you may assume that:

- S1, S3, and S7 have PC 10's MAC address entry in their MAC address tables.
- S2 and S5 do not have PC 10's MAC address entry.

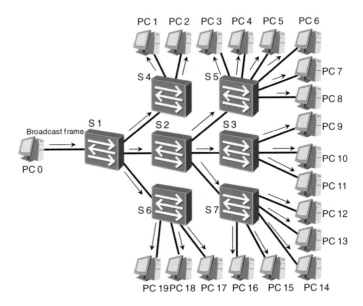

Fig. 5.1 Broadcast domain

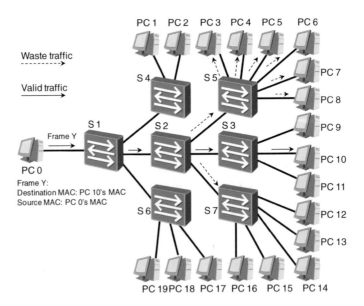

Fig. 5.2 Security and waste traffic issues within a broadcast domain

S1 and S3 will forward frame Y to the next hop. S7 will discard frame Y, and S2 as well as S5 will flood frame Y within the domain. This means that not only PC 10, but also PC 3, PC 4, PC 5, PC 6, PC 7, and PC 8 receive frame Y. This network set up reveals two key issues:

- **Network security**
  If a computer is able to receive frames it does not require on a network, the transmissions across the network are not secure. In this example, if PC 8 belongs to a malicious user, PC 8 can receive information from PC 0 that was intended for PC 10.
- **Waste traffic**
  Waste traffic refers to traffic transmitted from the source received by computers that are not the intended destination. This excess traffic wastes network bandwidth and processing resources.

On a large-sized broadcast domain these issues become more severe. VLAN technology assigned onto switches logically divides a large broadcast domain into multiple smaller domains, improving network security and resources while reducing waste traffic.

In VLAN, LAN refers to a broadcast domain, but not only a local area network covering a small physical range. The large-sized broadcast domain before division is a LAN, and the small-sized broadcast domain after division is a VLAN. For example, when we divide a large-sized broadcast domain into four small-sized broadcast domains, we actually divide a LAN into four VLANs.

Any two computers within the same broadcast domain can communicate with each other at Layer 2 and directly exchange frames. Each Layer 2 frame can contain the destination and source MAC addresses, type field, payload, and CRC. (Note: These frames will not be exchanged through routers, or switches supporting Layer 3 forwarding.)

Attempting to use Layer 3 communications however would involve frames passing through a router, which would modify the frame during the transmission. At least, the source and destination MAC addresses will be modified.

A VLAN is a broadcast domain, so the computers within a VLAN perform Layer 2 communication. If the source and destination are located on different VLANs, they can only perform Layer 3 communication.

5.2   VLAN Scenario

Illustrated in Fig. 5.3, six computers are connected to one switch and have divided the broadcast domain into VLAN 2 and VLAN 3. On the switch, Ports 1, 2, and 6 have been added to VLAN 2 and Ports 3, 4, and 5 have been added to VLAN 3. VLAN configurations are not performed on computers, and computers are unaware of VLAN configurations on the switch.

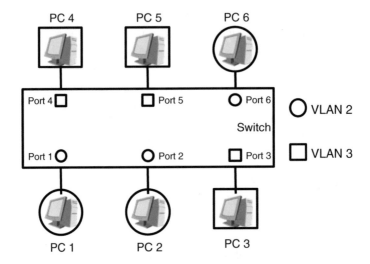

Fig. 5.3 VLAN network with one switch

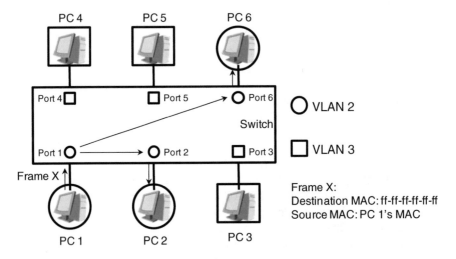

Fig. 5.4 VLAN scenario 1

Using this network set up a few typical VLAN scenarios can be discussed:

1. PC 1 sends a broadcast frame X.

Frame X in Fig. 5.4 enters the switch through Port 1, which belongs to VLAN 2. The switch recognizes that frame X belongs to VLAN 2 and floods the frame to Port 2 and Port 6, resulting in PC 2 and PC 6 receiving the frame, whereas PCs on the VLAN 3 domain do not.

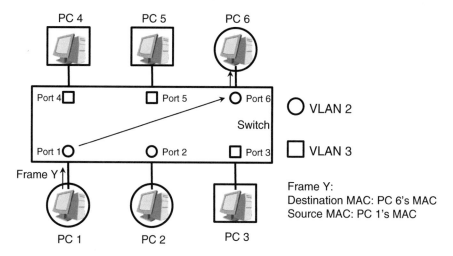

Fig. 5.5 VLAN scenario 2

2. PC 1 sends unicast frame Y to PC 6.

(For the following scenario in Fig. 5.5, assume that the MAC address table corresponding to VLAN 2 on the switch contains PC 6's MAC address entry.)

Frame Y enters the switch through Port 1, which belongs to VLAN 2. The switch recognizes that the frame belongs to VLAN 2. After querying the MAC address table corresponding to VLAN 2, the switch forwards the frame to Port 6, which also belongs to VLAN 2. Then PC 6 receives the frame. If the MAC address table corresponding to VLAN 2 does not contain PC 6's MAC address entry, the switch floods frame Y to Port 2 and Port 6. In this situation, PC 2 discards the frame, whereas PC 6 accept the frame.

3. PC 1 sends unicast frame Z to PC 3.

Figure 5.6 shows frame Z enters the switch through Port 1, which belongs to VLAN 2. The switch recognizes that the frame belongs to VLAN 2. By default, the MAC address table corresponding to VLAN 2 on the switch does not contain PC 3's MAC address entry. The switch then floods the frame to Port 2 and Port 6. PC 2 and PC 6 discards frame Z, and PC 3, due to residing in another VLAN, does not receive frame Z at all.

Figure 5.7 details a more complicated network scenario: a network comprised of three switches and six computers that are then divided into VLAN 2 and VLAN 3. VLAN configurations on the three switches are as follows:

	Switch 1	Switch 2	Switch 3
VLAN 2	Port 1 and Port 2	Port 1	–
VLAN 3	Port 3	Port 2 and Port 3	–
VLAN 2 and VLAN 3	Port 4	Port 4	Port 1 and Port 2

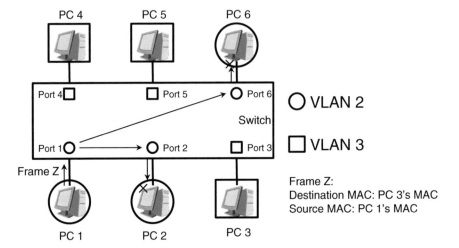

Fig. 5.6 VLAN scenario 3

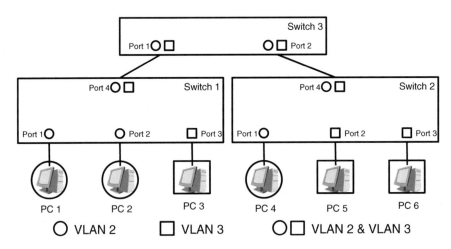

Fig. 5.7 VLAN network with three switches

4. **PC 1 sends a broadcast frame X.**

In Fig. 5.8, Frame X enters Switch 1 through Port 1, which belongs to VLAN 2. Switch 1 recognizes frame X belongs to VLAN 2 and floods the frame to Port 2 and Port 4. Switch 3 receives frame X from Port 1 and, when finding it is from VLAN 2, floods the frame to Port 2. Switch 2 receives frame X and, recognizing that the frame belongs to VLAN 2, floods the frame to Port 1. In this network both PC 2 and PC 4 receive frame X.

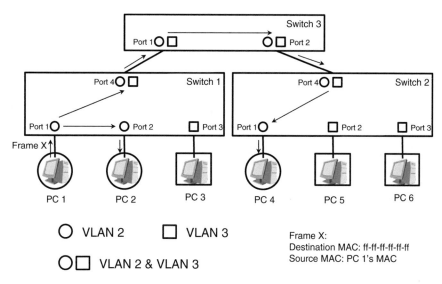

Fig. 5.8 VLAN scenario 4

5. **PC 1 sends unicast frame Y to PC 4.**

For Fig. 5.9 assume that the MAC address table corresponding to VLAN 2 on each switch contains PC 4's MAC address entry.

Frame Y enters Switch 1 through Port 1, which belongs to VLAN 2. Switch 1 recognizes that the frame belongs to VLAN 2. After querying the MAC address table corresponding to VLAN 2, Switch 1 forwards the frame to Port 4. When receiving frame Y through Port 1, Switch 3 finds that the forwarded frame belongs to VLAN 2, queries the MAC address table corresponding to VLAN 2, and forwards the frame to Port 2. When receiving frame Y through Port 4, Switch 2 finds that the frame belongs to VLAN 2. Switch 2 also queries the MAC address table corresponding to VLAN 2, and forwards the frame to Port 1, allowing PC 4 to receive frame Y. (By the way, think about what will happen if some switches have PC 4's MAC address entries and some switches do not have.)

6. **PC 1 sends unicast frame Z to PC 6.**

In Fig. 5.10, by default, the MAC address table corresponding to VLAN 2 on each switch does not contain PC 6's MAC address entry.

Frame Z enters Switch 1 through Port 1, which belongs to VLAN 2. Switch 1 recognizes that the frame belongs to VLAN 2. Because Switch 1 cannot find PC 6's MAC address entry in the MAC address table corresponding to VLAN 2, Switch 1 floods frame Z to Port 2 and Port 4. When Switch 3 receives frame Z through Port 1, it finds that the frame belongs to VLAN 2. Switch 3 also cannot find PC 6's MAC address entry in the MAC address table corresponding to VLAN 2, and

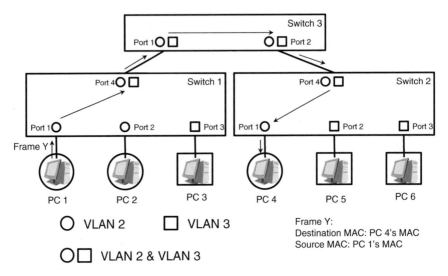

Fig. 5.9 VLAN scenario 5

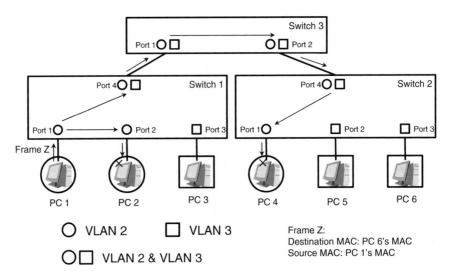

Fig. 5.10 VLAN scenario 6

floods frame Z to Port 2. When Switch 2 receives the forwarded frame, it finds that the frame belongs to VLAN 2. Switch 2 cannot find PC 6's MAC address entry in the MAC address table corresponding to VLAN 2, and floods frame Z to Port 1. PC 2 and PC 4 discard frame Z and PC 6, due to residing on another VLAN, cannot receive frame Z.

5.3   802.1Q Frame Structure

IEEE 802.1Q is the networking standard that supports VLANs on an Ethernet network. IEEE 802.1Q is backward compatible with IEEE 802.1D and incorporates many of its standards. Unless otherwise specified, all switches mentioned in this chapter support VLAN and comply with 802.1Q.

Switches determine the VLAN to which a frame belongs depending on the port that receives the frame. After identifying the VLAN of a frame, the switch will insert a tag into a specified bit of the frame to identify the VLAN the frame belongs to. When another switch receives the frame, that switch can also identify the frame's VLAN based on the tag in the frame. Figure 5.11 illustrates the IEEE 802.1Q structure of tagged frames, called IEEE 802.1Q frames or VLAN frames.

Table 5.1 describes the fields in an 802.1Q (or VLAN) tag.

VLAN configurations are not performed on computers, so computers do not generate or send tagged frames. When a computer receives a tagged frame, it cannot recognize the value 0x8100, thereby discarding the frame.

5.4   VLAN Types

When a VLAN-capable switch receives an untagged frame from a computer, the switch must allocate the frame to a VLAN based on a certain rule. VLANs are classified into three different types as follows:

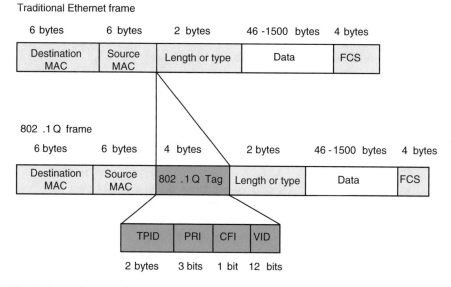

Fig. 5.11 IEEE 802.1Q frame structure

Table 5.1 Fields in an 802.1Q tag

Field	Length	Name	Explanation
TPID	2 bytes	Tag protocol ID	Indicates whether the frame carries a tag. The value 0x8100 indicates a tagged frame; other values indicate an untagged frame. This field is compatible with the **Type/Length** field in an untagged Ethernet frame
PRI	3 bits	Priority	Specifies the priority of a frame, with value ranges from 0 to 7. A larger value indicates a higher priority. When a switch is congested with traffic, it preferentially sends the frames with high priority
CFI	1 bit	Canonical format indicator	This field is not discussed further in this chapter
VID	12 bits	VLAN identifier	Specifies the VLAN that the frame belongs to with value ranges from 1 to 4094 (values 0 and 4095 are reserved for other purposes respectively)

Port-based VLAN

VLAN IDs are mapped to physical ports on a switch. The switch allocates the untagged frames received through a port to the VLAN of the port, making port-based VLAN a secure and easy to implement method.

If however a computer connects to another port on a switch, the VLAN ID of the frames sent by this computer may change. Port-based VLAN is also known as Layer 1 VLAN.

MAC-based VLAN

A switch creates and maintains a MAC address and VLAN ID mapping table. When receiving an untagged frame from a computer, the switch checks the source MAC address in the frame and searches for the VLAN ID matching this MAC address, and then allocates the frame to the VLAN.

This method improves VLAN allocation flexibility. For example, if a computer connects to another port on the switch, the VLAN ID of the frames sent by this computer is unchanged because the computer's MAC address is unchanged. However, this method is not secure because malicious users may create and use fake MAC addresses. MAC-based VLAN is also known as Layer 2 VLAN.

Protocol-based VLAN

A switch determines the VLAN an untagged frame belongs based on the Type field in the frame. For example, the switch allocates a frame with the Type field value of 0x0800 to one VLAN, and a frame with the Type field value of 0x86dd to another VLAN (meaning the switch allocates frames with IPv4 and IPv6 packets into different VLANs). Protocol-based VLAN is also known Layer 3 VLAN.

While this chapter has discussed three types of VLAN, theoretically there are many other VLAN types. VLAN allocation is flexible and can be based on a combination of multiple rules. You should choose an appropriate method according to your network requirements and cost. Currently, port-based VLAN is the most widely used VLAN application.

Unless otherwise specified, the VLANs mentioned in this chapter refer to port-based VLANs.

5.5   Link Types and Port Types

When a frame is allocated to VLAN *i*, *i* refers to the value of the VLAN ID field in the frame's tag (see Table 5.1). This means other switches can identify the VLAN a frame belongs to based on the VID value in the tag. When a switch receives an untagged frame (for example, from a computer), the switch determines the VLAN of the frame based on a certain rule, such as the port receiving the frame.

On a VLAN switching network, such as the one illustrated in Fig. 5.12, a computer connects to a switch through an Access link with the switch-side port on the link becoming an Access port. Two switches connect through a Trunk link with the port on each end becoming the Trunk port. Untagged frames that transmit over an Access link belong to only one VLAN. Tagged frames that transmit over a Trunk link may belong to different VLANs. An Access port can belong to only one VLAN, and allows only the frames from this VLAN to pass through. A Trunk port can belong to multiple VLANs, and allows frames from different VLANs to pass through.

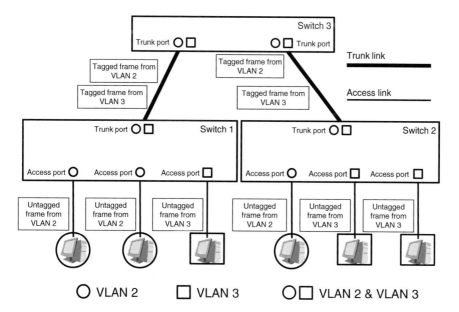

Fig. 5.12 Link and port types

Each port on a switch, whether they are Access or Trunk ports, should have a Port VLAN ID (PVID). All untagged frames received by a port are allocated to the VLAN corresponding to the PVID. For example, if the PVID of a port is 5, the switch allocates all untagged frames received by this port to VLAN 5. By default, the value of PVID is 1.

Frames transmitted between different ports on a switch must be tagged.

Now, let's examine the handling and forwarding rules used by Access and Trunk ports.

Access port

- After an Access port receives an untagged frame, the switch adds a tag carrying the PVID to the frame and forwards the tagged frame.
- After an Access port receives a tagged frame, the switch checks whether the VID in the tag is the same as the PVID. If they are the same, the switch forwards the frame; otherwise, the switch discards the frame.
- When a tagged frame is received by an Access port from another port on the same switch, the switch checks whether the VID in the tag is the same as the PVID. If they are the same, the switch removes the tag from the frame, and forwards the untagged frame. If the VID and the PVID are different, the switch discards the tagged frame.

Trunk port

You must configure an allowed VLAN ID list in addition to the PVID for a Trunk port.

- When a Trunk port receives an untagged frame, the switch inserts a tag carrying the PVID into the frame and checks whether the PVID is in the allowed VLAN ID list. If it is the switch forwards the tagged frame, otherwise the switch discards the frame.
- When a Trunk port receives a tagged frame, the switch checks whether the VID in the tag is in the allowed VLAN ID list. If it is the switch forwards the tagged frame, otherwise the switch discards the frame.
- When a tagged frame is received by a Trunk port from another port on the same switch, if the VID in the tag is not in the allowed VLAN ID list, the switch discards the tagged frame.
- When a tagged frame is received by a Trunk port from another port on the same switch, if the VID in the tag is in the allowed VLAN ID list and is the same as the PVID, the switch removes the tag from the frame and forwards the untagged frame.
- When a tagged frame is received by a Trunk port from another port on the same switch, if the VID in the tag is in the allowed VLAN ID list but is different from the PVID, the switch does not remove the tag from the frame and forwards the tagged frame.

5.6   VLAN Forwarding Examples

For all following examples you may assume this information:

PVID	Switch 1	Switch 2
2	Port 1 and 2	Port 1
3	Port 3	Port 2 and 3

Example 1 For Fig. 5.13 you may assume that:

- The PVIDs of all Trunk ports are 1.
- All Trunk ports allow the frames from VLAN 2 and VLAN 3 to pass through.

PC 1 sends an untagged broadcast frame X:

1. When Port 1 receives frame X, Switch 1 inserts VID 2 into the frame as a tag and floods the frame to Port 2 and Port 4.
2. When Port 2 receives frame X, it removes the tag and forwards the untagged frame to PC 2. When Port 4 receives frame X, it forwards the tagged frame to Port 1 of Switch 3.

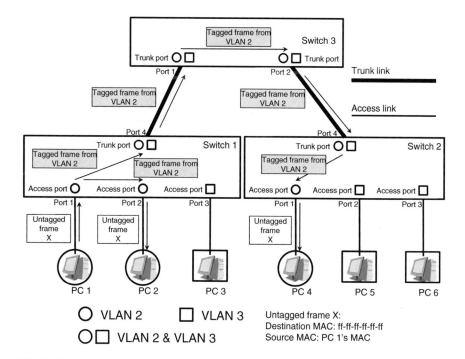

Fig. 5.13 VLAN forwarding example 1

3. Switch 3 floods the tagged frame to Port 2, which then forwards the tagged frame to Port 4 of Switch 2.
4. Switch 2 floods the tagged frame to Port 1. When Port 1 of Switch 2 receives frame X, it removes the tag from the frame and forwards the untagged frame to PC 4.

PC 2 and PC 4 have now received the untagged frame X.

Example 2 For Fig. 5.14 you may assume that:

- The PVIDs of all Trunk ports are 1 and all Trunk ports allow the packets from VLAN 2 and VLAN 3 to pass through.
- The MAC address table corresponding to VLAN 2 on each switch contains PC 4's MAC address entry.

PC 1 sends an untagged unicast frame Y to PC 4.

1. When Port 1 receives frame Y of Switch 1, Switch 1 inserts VID 2 into the frame as a tag.
2. After querying the MAC address table corresponding to VLAN 2, Switch 1 forwards the frame to Port 4.
3. When Port 4 receives frame Y, it forwards the tagged frame to Port 1 of Switch 3.

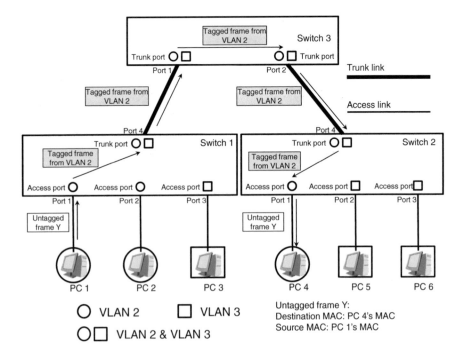

Fig. 5.14 VLAN forwarding example 2

4. Switch 3 queries the MAC address table corresponding to VLAN 2 and forwards the frame to Port 2, which then forwards the tagged frame to Port 4 of Switch 2.
5. Switch 2 queries the MAC address table corresponding to VLAN 2 and forwards the frame to Port 1. When Port 1 of Switch 2 receives the tagged frame Y, it removes the tag from the frame and forwards the untagged frame to PC 4.

PC 4 has now received untagged frame Y.

Example 3 For Fig. 5.15, you may assume that:

- The PVIDs of all Trunk ports are 1.
- All Trunk ports allow the frames from VLAN 2 and VLAN 3 to pass through.

(By default, the MAC address table corresponding to VLAN 2 on each switch does not contain PC 6's MAC address entry.)

PC 1 attempts to send an untagged unicast frame Z to PC 6.

1. Port 1 of Switch 1 receives frame Z. Switch 1 inserts VID 2 into the frame as a tag.
2. Switch 1 cannot find PC 6's MAC address entry in the MAC address table corresponding to VLAN 2, so Switch 1 floods tagged frame Z to Port 2 and Port 4.

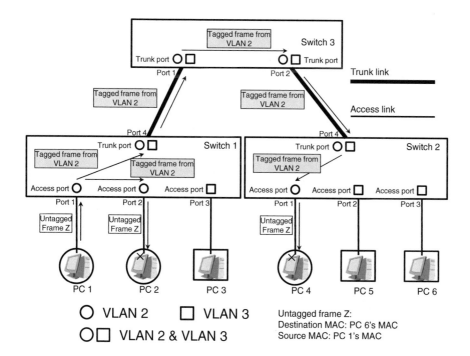

Fig. 5.15 VLAN forwarding example 3

3. When Port 2 receives frame Z, it removes the tag from the frame and forwards the untagged frame to PC 2. When Port 4 receives frame Z, it forwards the tagged frame to Port 1 of Switch 3.
4. Switch 3 cannot find PC 6's MAC address entry in the MAC address table corresponding to VLAN 2, so Switch 3 floods frame Z to Port 2, which then forwards the tagged frame to Port 4 of Switch 2.
5. Switch 2 cannot find PC 6's MAC address entry in the MAC address table corresponding to VLAN 2, so floods frame Z to Port 1. When Port 1 receives frame Z, it removes the tag from the frame and forwards the untagged frame to PC 4.

PC 6 cannot receive the frame as the switches have blocked Layer 2 communication between PC 1 and PC 6.

5.7 VLAN Configuration Example

A company has three independent departments configured with VLAN technology. Figure 5.16 shows PC 1 and PC 2 belong to the same department (VLAN 10), PC 3, PC 4, and PC 5 belong to another department (VLAN 20), and PC 6 belongs to another separate department (VLAN 30).

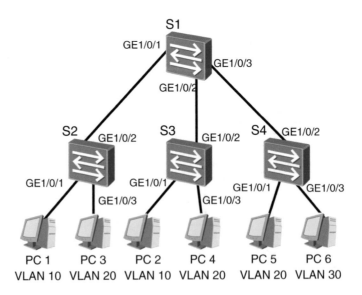

Fig. 5.16 VLAN configuration example

Configuration Roadmap

1. Create VLANs on switches.
2. Set the link types of the ports connected to PCs to Access and add the ports to VLANs.
3. Set the link types of the ports connected to switches to Trunk and add the ports to VLANs.

Procedure

The following procedure uses VLAN 10 as the configuration example.

Enter the system view on a switch, and then run the **vlan** *vlan-id* command to create a VLAN. For example:

\# Configure S2.

```
<S2> system-view
[S2] vlan 10
[S2-vlan10] quit
```

\# Configure S3.

```
<S3> system-view
[S3] vlan 10
[S3-vlan10] quit
```

\# Configure S1.

```
<S1> system-view
[S1] vlan 10
[S1-vlan10] quit
```

You must now add ports to VLAN 10 as newly created ports contain no VLANs.

The default link type of a port on a switch is Hybrid. Run the **port link-type** {**access**| **trunk**} command to change the link types of the ports to be added to VLANs to Access or Trunk. To set a PVID for an Access port, run the **port default vlan** *vlan-id* command. To configure allowed VLANs for a Trunk port, run the **port trunk allow-pass vlan** *vlan-id1* [**to** *vlan-id2*] command.

\# Configure S2.

```
[S2] interface gigabitethernet 1/0/1
[S2-GigabitEthernet1/0/1] port link-type access
[S2-GigabitEthernet1/0/1] port default vlan 10
[S2-GigabitEthernet1/0/1] quit
[S2] interface gigabitethernet 1/0/2
[S2-GigabitEthernet1/0/2] port link-type trunk
[S2-GigabitEthernet1/0/2] port trunk allow-pass vlan 10
[S2-GigabitEthernet1/0/2] quit
```

Configure S3.

```
[S3] interface gigabitethernet 1/0/1
[S3-GigabitEthernet1/0/1] port link-type access
[S3-GigabitEthernet1/0/1] port default vlan 10
[S3-GigabitEthernet1/0/1] quit
[S3] interface gigabitethernet 1/0/2
[S3-GigabitEthernet1/0/2] port link-type trunk
[S3-GigabitEthernet1/0/2] port trunk allow-pass vlan 10
[S3-GigabitEthernet1/0/2] quit
```

Configure S1.

```
[S1] interface gigabitethernet 1/0/1
[S1-GigabitEthernet1/0/1] port link-type trunk
[S1-GigabitEthernet1/0/1] port trunk allow-pass vlan 10
[S1-GigabitEthernet1/0/1] quit
[S1] interface gigabitethernet 1/0/2
[S1-GigabitEthernet1/0/2] port link-type trunk
[S1-GigabitEthernet1/0/2] port trunk allow-pass vlan 10
[S1-GigabitEthernet1/0/2] quit
```

After the VLAN is configured, run the **display port vlan** command to view the VLAN configurations and types of the ports on switch. S2 is used as an example here.

```
<S2> display port vlan
Port                 Link Type    PVID   Trunk VLAN List
-------------------------------------------------------------------
GE1/0/1              access       10     -
GE1/0/2              trunk        1      1 10
...
```

From the command outputs, you can see that S2's GE1/0/1 has been configured as an Access port and added to VLAN 10, and S2's GE1/0/2 has been configured as a Trunk port and allows frames from VLAN 10 to pass through, indicating that the VLAN configuration commands have taken effect on S2's GE1/0/1 and GE1/0/2.

You can apply the same configuration example to configure VLAN 20 and VLAN 30.

5.8 GVRP

When configuring VLANs on switches, you need to create all required VLANs on each switch and manually add ports to the corresponding VLANs. However, if you need to configure a large number of VLANs frequently then manual configuration becomes a time consuming and challenging process.

The Generic Attribute Registration Protocol (GARP) defined by IEEE effectively reduces the manual workload in VLAN configuration. GARP includes two protocols: GARP Multicast Registration Protocol (GMRP) and GARP VLAN Registration Protocol (GVRP).

Manually created VLANs are called static VLANs, and VLANs created by the GVRP are called dynamic VLANs. GVRP allows VLAN attribute transmission between switches to implement dynamic VLAN registration and deregistration on switches. After configuring GVRP, you only need to manually configure VLANs on a few switches, and then these switches deliver VLAN configurations to other switches.

5.8.1 Dynamic VLAN Registration Process

Figure 5.17 illustrates the following information:

- PC 1 and PC 2 are allocated to VLAN 10, which means VLAN 10 needs to be configured on all switches.
- GVRP has been enabled globally on S1, S2, S3, and S4 and on S1's GE0/0/1, S2's GE0/0/1 and GE0/0/2, S3's GE0/0/1 and GE0/0/2, as well as S4's GE0/0/1.

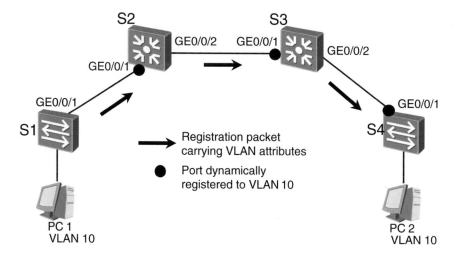

Fig. 5.17 One-way VLAN registration

- VLAN 10 has been manually created on S1, so S1's GE0/0/1 allows the frames from VLAN 10 to pass through.

The following example demonstrates the VLAN registration process:

1. S1's GE0/0/1 sends a registration packet carrying VLAN attributes.
2. After S2's GE0/0/1 receives the registration packet from S1, S2 automatically creates VLAN 10 and registers its own GE0/0/1 to VLAN 10.
3. S2's GE0/0/2 sends the registration packet out.
   (Note: Only ports receiving the registration packet can be registered to VLAN 10; therefore S2's GE0/0/2 cannot be registered to VLAN 10.)
4. After S3's GE0/0/1 receives the registration packet from S2, S3 automatically creates VLAN 10 and registers its own GE0/0/1 to VLAN 10.
5. S3's GE0/0/2 sends the registration packet out.
   (Note: S3's GE0/0/2 cannot be registered to VLAN 10.)
6. After S4's GE0/0/1 receives the registration packet from S3, S4 automatically creates VLAN 10 and registers its own GE0/0/1 to VLAN 10.

During the preceding process, VLAN 10 was automatically created on S2, S3, and S4, and S2's GE0/0/1, S3's GE0/0/1, and S4's GE0/0/1 were added to VLAN 10. This is called one-way VLAN registration. However, S2's GE0/0/2 and S3's GE0/0/2 were not added to VLAN 10. For this process, a reverse VLAN registration process is required. (Note that static VLAN 10 information will overwrite dynamic VLAN 10 information on S4.)

Figure 5.18 demonstrates the reverse VLAN registration process:

1. Manually create VLAN 10 on S4 and configure S4's GE0/0/1 to allow frames from VLAN 10 to pass through.
2. S4's GE0/0/1 sends a registration packet carrying VLAN attributes.

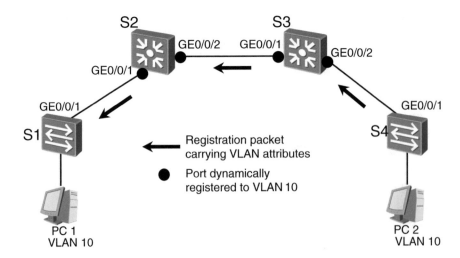

Fig. 5.18 Reverse VLAN registration

3. After S3's GE0/0/2 receives the registration packet from S4 it automatically registers its own GE0/0/2 to VLAN 10.
4. S3's GE0/0/1 sends the registration packet out.
5. After S2's GE0/0/2 receives the registration packet from S3 it automatically registers its own GE0/0/2 to VLAN 10.
6. S2's GE0/0/1 sends the registration packet out.

S1's GE0/0/1 also receives the registration packet from S2; however S1 and S1's GE0/0/1 already have static VLAN 10 information, so do not need to dynamically register VLAN 10.

5.8.2 Dynamic VLAN Deregistration Process

When the number of VLANs on a network reduces, GVRP automatically deletes and deregisters VLANs.

Figure 5.19 shows how PC 1 and PC 4 need to be excluded from VLAN 10. The VLAN deregistration process is as follows:

1. Manually delete VLAN 10 from S1.
2. S1's GE0/0/1 sends a deregistration packet carrying VLAN attributes.
3. After S2's GE0/0/1 receives the deregistration packet from S1, S2 automatically deregisters its own GE0/0/1 from VLAN 10.
4. S2's GE0/0/2 sends the deregistration packet out.
   (Note: Only ports receiving the deregistration packet can be deregistered from VLAN 10, meaning S2's GE0/0/2 has not been deregistered as it still has the dynamic VLAN 10 information.)

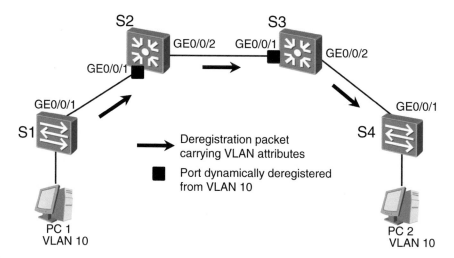

Fig. 5.19 One-way VLAN deregistration

5. After S3's GE0/0/1 receives the deregistration packet from S2, S3 automatically deregisters its own GE0/0/1 from VLAN 10.
6. S3's GE0/0/2 sends the deregistration packet out.
   (Note: S3's GE0/0/2 still has the dynamic VLAN 10 information.)

S4's GE0/0/1 receives the deregistration packet from S3 but does not deregister VLAN 10 dynamically because the VLAN 10 on S4 was created manually.

In the preceding process, S2's GE0/0/1 and S3's GE0/0/1 were deregistered from VLAN 10. This process is called one-way VLAN deregistration. However, dynamic VLAN 10 information still exists on S2 and S3, as well as S2's GE0/0/2 and S3's GE0/0/2. A reverse VLAN deregistration process is required.

Figure 5.20 demonstrates the reverse VLAN deregistration process:

1. Manually delete VLAN 10 from S4.
2. S4's GE0/0/1 sends a deregistration packet carrying VLAN attributes.
3. After S3's GE0/0/2 receives the deregistration packet from S4, S3 automatically deregisters its own GE0/0/2 from VLAN 10.
4. S3's GE0/0/1 sends the deregistration packet out, and S3 automatically deletes VLAN 10.
5. After S2's GE0/0/2 receives the deregistration packet from S3, S2 automatically deregisters its own GE0/0/2 from VLAN 10.
6. S2's GE0/0/1 sends the deregistration packet out and S2 automatically deletes VLAN 10.

After S1's GE0/0/1 receives the deregistration packet from S2, S1 does not deregister VLAN 10 dynamically because VLAN 10 does not exist on S1.

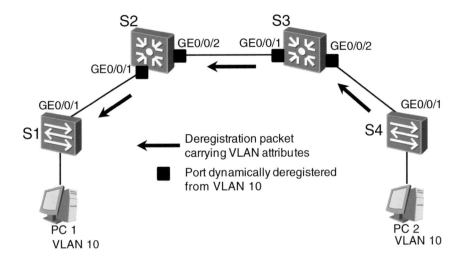

Fig. 5.20 Reverse VLAN deregistration

5.9 GVRP Configuration Example

Figure 5.21 illustrates how PC 1 and PC 2 are allocated to VLAN 1000. GVRP needs to be configured to implement automatic creation and registration of VLAN 1000.

Configuration Roadmap

1. Enable GVRP on each switch globally and on related ports.
2. Configure Layer 2 connectivity between switches by configuring required ports as Trunk ports, allowing frames from VLAN 1000 to pass through.
3. Manually create VLAN 1000 on S1 and S4.

Procedure

Run the **gvrp** command in the system view of a switch to enable GVRP globally.

Enable GVRP on S1 globally.
```
<Quidway> system-view
[Quidway] sysname S1
[S1] gvrp
```

Enable GVRP on S2 globally.
```
<Quidway> system-view
[Quidway] sysname S2
[S2] gvrp
```

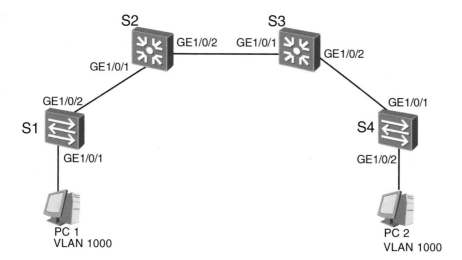

Fig. 5.21 GVRP configuration example

Enable GVRP on S3 globally.
```
<Quidway> system-view
[Quidway] sysname S3
[S3] gvrp
```

Enable GVRP on S4 globally.
```
<Quidway> system-view
[Quidway] sysname S4
[S4] gvrp
```

Configure the Related Ports

1. Enable GVRP on a port. (Note: GVRP must be globally enabled on a switch before it is enabled on a port of the switch.)
2. Configure the related ports as Trunk ports and allow frames from VLAN 1000 to pass through. (GVRP can be configured only on Trunk ports.)

Configure S1's ports.
```
[S1] interface gigabitethernet 1/0/1
[S1-GigabitEthernet1/0/1] port link-type access
[S1-GigabitEthernet1/0/1] port default vlan 1000
[S1-GigabitEthernet1/0/1] quit
[S1] interface gigabitethernet 1/0/2
[S1-GigabitEthernet1/0/2] gvrp
[S1-GigabitEthernet1/0/2] port link-type trunk
[S1-GigabitEthernet1/0/2] port trunk allow-pass vlan all
[S1-GigabitEthernet1/0/2] quit
```

Configure S2's ports.
```
[S2] interface gigabitethernet 1/0/1
[S2-GigabitEthernet1/0/1] gvrp
[S2-GigabitEthernet1/0/1] port link-type trunk
[S2-GigabitEthernet1/0/1] port trunk allow-pass vlan all
[S2-GigabitEthernet1/0/1] quit
[S2] interface gigabitethernet 1/0/2
[S2-GigabitEthernet1/0/2] gvrp
[S2-GigabitEthernet1/0/2] port link-type trunk
[S2-GigabitEthernet1/0/2] port trunk allow-pass vlan all
[S2-GigabitEthernet1/0/2] quit
```

Configure S3's ports.
```
[S3] interface gigabitethernet 1/0/1
[S3-GigabitEthernet1/0/1] gvrp
[S3-GigabitEthernet1/0/1] port link-type trunk
[S3-GigabitEthernet1/0/1] port trunk allow-pass vlan all
[S3-GigabitEthernet1/0/1] quit
[S3] interface gigabitethernet 1/0/2
[S3-GigabitEthernet1/0/2] gvrp
```

```
[S3-GigabitEthernet1/0/2] port link-type trunk
[S3-GigabitEthernet1/0/2] port trunk allow-pass vlan all
[S3-GigabitEthernet1/0/2] quit
```

Configure S4's ports.
```
[S4] interface gigabitethernet 1/0/1
[S4-GigabitEthernet1/0/1] gvrp
[S4-GigabitEthernet1/0/1] port link-type trunk
[S4-GigabitEthernet1/0/1] port trunk allow-pass vlan all
[S4-GigabitEthernet1/0/1] quit
[S4] interface gigabitethernet 1/0/2
[S4-GigabitEthernet1/0/2] port link-type access
[S4-GigabitEthernet1/0/2] port default vlan 1000
[S4-GigabitEthernet1/0/2] quit
```

Create VLAN 1000 on S1 and S4 manually to allow GVRP to automatically complete VLAN configurations on S2 and S3. View before and after VLAN configurations on S2 and S3 so that you can see what GVRP does. For example:
Run the **display vlan summary** command in the system view of S2.

```
[S2] display vlan summary
static vlan:
Total 1 static vlan.
 1

dynamic vlan:
Total 0 dynamic vlan.
```

The command output shows that S2 does not have dynamic VLAN configuration. Next, create VLAN 1000 on S1 and S4 manually.

Create VLAN 1000 on S1.
```
[S1] vlan 1000
[S1-VLAN1000] quit
```

Create VLAN 1000 on S4.
```
[S4] vlan 1000
[S4-VLAN1000] quit
```

Run the following commands to verify the configuration:

- **display gvrp status:** shows whether GVRP is globally enabled.
- **display gvrp statistics:** displays GVRP statistics on each port.

    # Run the **display gvrp status** command on S1.
    ```
    [S1] display gvrp status
    Info:GVRP is enabled
    ```

GVRP has been enabled on S1 globally.
Run the **display gvrp statistics** command on S2.

```
[S2] display gvrp statistics
GVRP statistics on port GigabitEthernet1/0/1
GVRP status                : Enabled
GVRP registrations failed  : 0
GVRP last PDU origin        : 0000-0000-0000
GVRP registration type     : Normal

GVRP statistics on port GigabitEthernet1/0/2
GVRP status                : Enabled
GVRP registrations failed  : 0
GVRP last PDU origin        : 0000-0000-0000
GVRP registration type     : Normal
```

In the command output, "GVRP status: Enabled" indicates GVRP is enabled on S2's GE1/0/1 and GE1/0/2.
Next, see the VLAN configuration changes on S2.
Run the **display vlan summary** command on S2.

```
[S2] display vlan summary
static vlan:
Total 1 static vlan.
  1

dynamic vlan:
Total 1 dynamic vlan.
  1000
```

The command output shows dynamic VLAN 1000 exists on S2.

5.10   Review Questions

1. (Choose all that apply) Which statements about VLAN are not true?

   A. VLAN technology can divide a large-sized collision domain into several small-sized collision domains.
   B. VLAN technology can divide a large-sized Layer 2 broadcast domain into several Layer 2 broadcast domains.
   C. Computers in different VLANs cannot communicate with each other.
   D. Computers in the same VLAN can communicate with each other at Layer 2.

2. (Choose all that apply) Which statements about VLAN are true?

   A. The VID in the tag of an IEEE 802.1Q frame can be 1.
   B. The VID in the tag of an IEEE 802.1Q frame can be 1024.
   C. The VID in the tag of an IEEE 802.1Q frame can be 2048.
   D. The VID in the tag of an IEEE 802.1Q frame can be 4096.

3. (Choose all that apply) Which statements about VLAN are not true?

   A. A computer can create and send a tagged IEEE 802.1Q frame.
   B. VLAN configurations must be set up on both switches and computers.
   C. Layer 3 VLAN is the most widely used in VLAN communications.

4. (Choose all that apply) Which statements about VLAN are true?

   A. On a switch, the port directly connected to computers is an Access port.
   B. On a switch, the port directly connected to computers is a Trunk port.
   C. Only tagged frames can transmit over an Access link.

5. (Choose all that apply) Which statements about GVRP are true?

   A. GVRP is short for Generic VLAN Registration Protocol.
   B. GVRP is short for GARP VLAN Registration Protocol.
   C. GVRP can reduce the manual workload in VLAN configuration.

Chapter 6
IP Basics

IP stands for Internet Protocol, which is the name of the protocol file RFC 791 originally published by the Internet Engineering Task Force (IETF) in 1981. This core protocol defines, explains, and codifies the formats of IP packets used in computer networks. However, when we use the term "IP," we are commonly referring to anything that is directly or indirectly related to the Internet Protocol, and not necessarily the Internet Protocol file itself. In this chapter, "IP" refers both to the protocol and related topics.

After completing this section, you should be able to:

- Understand the five classes of IP addresses.
- Understand the differences between network addresses and host interface addresses.
- Understand the purpose and usage of subnet masks.
- List some IP addresses that are reserved for special purposes.
- Understand how router interfaces handle packets.
- Understand the IP forwarding process.
- Understand the concepts of Layer 2 networks, Layer 3 networks, and internets.
- Understand the format of IP packets as well as the purpose of different fields in their headers.

As shown in Fig. 1.7, IP is one of the network layer protocols in the TCP/IP protocol suite. Although we often refer to the network layer as "the IP layer," it should be noted that there are many other network layer protocols aside from IP, including Internet Control Message Protocol (ICMP), Internet Group Management Protocol (IGMP), and others. The Address Resolution Protocol (ARP) that we learned about previously is also a network layer protocol.

The IP document itself has multiple versions, the most important of which are IP Version 4 (IPv4) and IP Version 6 (IPv6). Currently, most IP packets transmitted over the Internet are IPv4 packets. However, many IPv4 networks are migrating to IPv6 networks. Unless otherwise specified, this chapter covers the standards specified by IPv4.

© Springer Science+Business Media Singapore 2016
Huawei Technologies Co., Ltd., *HCNA Networking Study Guide*,
DOI 10.1007/978-981-10-1554-0_6

6.1 Classful Addressing

In Sect. 3.2.1 we learned about MAC addresses. As you'll recall, MAC addresses are not real addresses, but unique IDs assigned to the interfaces (or network adapters) on a device. In other words, a MAC address indicates the identity of a given device, but not its location.

The devices on a global network cannot use MAC addresses to communicate with each other. In order to do so, each device would need to know all of the MAC addresses in use on the network, as well as the physical locations of the devices they represent. This would be impossible.

Instead, devices communicate with each other using IP addresses. Similar to phone numbers that contain the country and city code of a fixed land line, IP addresses indicate the physical locations of devices on a network.

Like a MAC address, an IP address is also the property of the interface on a network device, not a property of the network device itself. So when we say "allocate an IP address to a device," what we're actually doing is allocating an IP address to the device's network interface. In the event that a device has multiple interfaces, each interface should have at least one IP address.

In most instances, the interfaces of routers and computers need IP addresses, whereas the interfaces (or ports) of switches do not (here we're referring to Layer 2 switches that do not support network layer forwarding). The routers and computers involved in IP address allocation are typically called hosts, and their IP addresses are simply referred to as host IP addresses.

The Structure and Classes of IP Addresses

An IP address is composed of 32 bits, which are divided into four sections (or bytes) of eight bits. IP addresses are most frequently presented in dot-decimal notation to facilitate reading and writing. For example, 11.1.0.254 is an IP address in dot-decimal notation. Refer to Table 6.1 for the binary notation of this same address.

IP addresses are uniformly allocated and managed by the Internet Corporation for Assigned Names and Numbers (ICANN). They have a strict set of procedures in place to ensure the uniqueness of all IP addresses allocated on the Internet.

In classful network architecture, there are five classes of IP addresses: A, B, C, D, and E. Special-purposes classes include Class D, which is for multicast IP addresses (not multicast MAC addresses, although they have similarities), and Class E addresses, which are reserved for experimental purposes. In this chapter, we

Table 6.1 Mapping between binary notation and decimal notation

Format	First byte	Second byte	Third byte	Fourth byte
Decimal notation	11	1	0	254
Binary notation	00001011	00000001	00000000	11111110

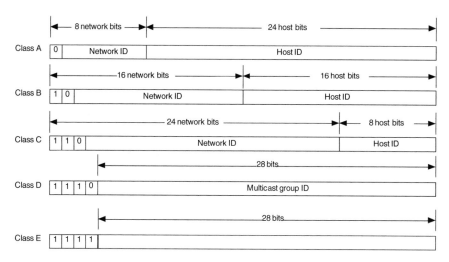

Fig. 6.1   Five classes of IP addresses

will only discuss Class A, B, and C addresses. Refer to Fig. 6.1 for a basic breakdown of these classes and the structures of their IP addresses.

For the most part, Class A, Class B, and Class C addresses are unicast IP addresses (with the exception of some special-use IP addresses within these ranges). Only addresses in these three classes can be allocated to host interfaces. The IP address of the host interface is the identity of the interface in the network layer, and reflects its physical location.

As shown in Fig. 6.1, a host IP address consists of a network ID (frequently referred to as a NetID) and a host ID (HostID). The network ID indicates the network where the host interface is located. In this way, it is similar to the structure of a postal address, such as "XX street, XX district, XX city, XX province." This is followed by a host ID that indicates a certain host interface within that network. In the postal address analogy, the host ID is similar to a house number.

Networks using Class A addresses are called Class A networks, those using Class B addresses are Class B networks, and so on. As shown in Fig. 6.1, Class A networks have fewer bits dedicated to their network ID, instead dedicating more bits to host IDs. This allocates a greater number of host IP addresses per each network. In comparison, Class C networks allow for far more network IDs, but fewer host interfaces per network. In terms of address space, Class B networks are between Class A and Class C. For details, see Table 6.2.

The "network ID + host ID" structure of classful addressing makes IP address allocation relatively simple and flexible. For example, a Class A network ID would suit a large-sized network that has 16 million host interfaces, and two Class C network IDs would suit a small-sized network with 500 host interfaces.

A network ID represents an individual network or network segment. As shown in Table 6.2, the number of usable IP addresses on a network segment is

Table 6.2 Difference between Class A, B, and C networks

	Network ID bits	Network IDs	Host ID bits	Number of host IP addresses allocated by each network ID	Address range
Class A	8	$2^7 = 128$	24	$2^{24} - 2 = 16,777,214$	0.0.0.0– 127.255.255.255
Class B	16	$2^{14} = 16,384$	16	$2^{16} - 2 = 65,534$	128.0.0.0– 191.255.255.255
Class C	24	$2^{21} = 2,097,152$	8	$2^8 - 2 = 254$	192.0.0.0– 223.255.255.255

determined by the number of leftover bits allocated for host IDs. This number can be calculated with the following formula:

$$2^{(\text{host bits})} - 2 = \# \text{ of Host IP Addresses Allocated by Each Network ID}$$

In this equation, you subtract two because, for each network ID (or network segment), two IP addresses are reserved for special purposes:

1. **The network's IP address**—Say that the network ID of an IP address is X. If every host ID bit that follows this network ID is 0 (i.e., "X.0.0.0"), then this is the IP address of the network itself. A network address cannot be allocated to a host interface.
2. **The network's broadcast address**—Say that the network of an IP address is X. If every host ID bit that follows this network ID is 1 (i.e., "X.255.255.255"— remember that eight 1's in binary is 255 in decimal notation), then this is the network's broadcast address. Broadcast addresses are used to send messages to all hosts in the network and, similar to the IP address of the network itself, a broadcast address cannot be allocated to a host interface.

Table 6.3 breaks down the structure of a Class A network, showing which values can be allocated and which are reserved. In this example, the network ID of the IP address is 01000000 in binary notation (or 64 in decimal notation), so

Table 6.3 Breakdown of a Class A network address

Network ID (binary notation)		Host ID (binary notation)	Dot-decimal notation	Type of IP address
Fixed bit	Other bits			
0	1000000	00000000 00000000 00000000	64.0.0.0	Network address
		00000000 00000000 00000001– 11111111 11111111 11111110	64.0.0.1– 64.255.255.254	Host address
		11111111 11111111 11111111	64.255.255.255	Broadcast address

64.0.0.0 is the network address. The broadcast address of this network (or segment) is 64.255.255.255. Therefore, on this particular network, the range of IP addresses that can be allocated to host interfaces is 64.0.0.1–64.255.255.254.

In the early age of network communication development, a network comprised only a few computers and therefore only required a handful of IP addresses. The classful addressing method was more than sufficient to meet network requirements at the time.

However, with the rapid growth of network communication technology, classful addressing has begun to cause problems. For example, say that a business needs to build a large-sized network that requires 1000 IP addresses. In the event that all Class B network IDs have been allocated, a Class A network ID needs to be allocated to this network. Because Class A networks have an enormous allotment of IP addresses, this means that about 16,600,000 addresses will be wasted.

Similar examples abound in recent times. As demand for greater and more numerous networks continues to increase, classful addressing has become much less flexible and has led to allocating IP addresses with unsuitable granularity. Many Class A and Class B addresses with a large number of host IDs cannot be used to their fullest extent, which has wasted countless IP addresses.

6.2   Classless Addressing

In classful addressing, the network IDs and host IDs of Class A, B, and C IP addresses have fixed numbers of bits. In classless addressing, network IDs and host IDs are of variable length, thereby improving the flexibility and efficiency of IP address allocation.

For example, if the IP addresses on Class A network segment 64.0.0.0 were allocated to a single organization, many IP addresses would be wasted. In classless addressing, we can increase the number of network bits and reduce the number of host bits as needed. As a result, the "leftover" host IP addresses on this original network segment can be allocated to the networks of different organizations, reducing the number of wasted IP addresses.

For example, if you needed to divide the IP addresses on this Class A network segment into four parts and allocate those IP addresses to four different organizations, you could do so by apportioning two bits from the host ID to serve as extended network ID bits.

Why two bits? Because in binary, two bits can be combined in four different ways:

$$00, 01, 10, 11$$

Although there are now two fewer bits used for host IDs in the network, by affixing these two bits to the end of the original network ID, we can effectively divide the original IP address into four distinct network segments. Each of these

Table 6.4 "Borrowing" host ID bits and affixing them to a network ID

	Network ID	Number of bits in host ID	Number of allocatable IP addresses per network
Classful addressing	0100 0000	24	$2^{24} - 2 = 16,777,214$
Classless addressing	0100 0000 00	22	$2^{22} - 2 = 4,194,302$
	0100 0000 01	22	$2^{22} - 2 = 4,194,302$
	0100 0000 10	22	$2^{22} - 2 = 4,194,302$
	0100 0000 11	22	$2^{22} - 2 = 4,194,302$

distinct network segments is called "subnets", which you will read more about in the next section.

As you can see in Table 6.4, each network segment (or subnet) will have fewer IP addresses, but this allows the original network to allocate IP addresses to more organizations without altering its network ID.

Based on this method, you can plan IP address allocation in this way: If an organization requires N host IP addresses, calculate the minimum powers of 2 that is greater than or equal to N + 2, and then use this exponent as the number of host bits. The remaining number will serve as network bits.

For example, say that Company X has applied for the Class C network segment 192.168.1.0. The original network ID of this network segment has 24 bits, and the host ID has 8 bits, for a total of 254 IP addresses that can be allocated ($2^8 - 2$ addresses for special purposes = 254 IP addresses ranging from 192.168.1.1 to 192.168.1.254).

Company X has three departments: X1, X2, and X3. Each department needs to have its own independent network, and they all must have different network IDs. They need 100, 50, and 30 IP addresses, respectively. You can allocate IP addresses to these three different departments following the method shown in Table 6.5.

In this instance, with network and host IDs of variable length, how do you know which bits indicate the network ID and which bits indicate the host IDs?

As we've learned, when using classful addressing we can easily discern all of information about an IP address. Take the IP address 64.1.5.0 for example. The first byte is between 0 and 127, indicating a Class A address. Therefore, 64 is its network ID, and the other three bytes are the host ID. Furthermore, we know that the IP address of the network segment itself is 64.0.0.0, the broadcast address is 64.255.255.255, and 64.1.5.0 is a host interface address on the network.

With classless addressing, you need a different method of distinguishing network IDs from host IDs. For example, the IP address 64.1.5.0 could be one of three things:

- A host interface address on a network with the network ID 64.1
- A subnet address on the network with network ID 64.1.5
- Something else entirely

Table 6.5 Classless addressing for three different-sized networks

Department	Required number of IP addresses (N)	Min powers of $2 \geq N + 2$	Host bits	Network bits	Network ID (first 24 bits omitted)	Host ID range	IP address range	Number of useable IP addresses
X1	100	$128 = 2^7$	7	$32 - 7 = 25$	0	0000000–1111111	192.168.1.0–192.168.1.127	$2^7 - 2 = 126$
X2	50	$64 = 2^6$	6	$32 - 6 = 26$	10	000000–111111	192.168.1.128–192.168.1.191	$2^6 - 2 = 62$
X3	30	$32 = 2^5$	5	$32 - 5 = 27$	110	00000–11111	192.168.1.192–192.168.1.223	$2^5 - 2 = 30$
Remaining	–	–	5	27	111	00000–11111	192.168.1.224–192.168.1. 255	$2^5 - 2 = 30$

So how can you determine the network ID of an IP address when using classless addressing? You do so with a subnet mask.

6.3 Subnet Masks

A subnet mask consists of 32 bits, which are divided into 4 bytes (like an IP address). A subnet mask is usually represented in dot-decimal notation. Although they look similar, a subnet mask is not an IP address. Subnet masks always consist of a group of consecutive 1s followed by a group of consecutive 0s. These are some examples of subnet masks:

11111100 00000000 00000000 00000000 (252.0.0.0)—subnet mask
11111111 11000000 00000000 00000000 (255.192.0.0)—subnet mask
11111111 11111111 11111111 11110000 (255.255.255.240)—subnet mask
11111111 11111111 11111111 11111111 (255.255.255.255)—subnet mask
00000000 00000000 00000000 00000000 (0.0.0.0)—subnet mask
11011000 00000000 00000000 00000000 (216.0.0.0)—not a subnet mask
00000000 11111111 11111111 11111111 (0.255.255.255)—not a subnet mask

Note that the last two examples are not subnet masks because they do not consist of a group of consecutive 1s followed by a group of consecutive 0s. Note also that you will occasionally come across subnet masks that are all 1s or all 0s, but 0s never come before 1s, nor can a group of 1s be broken up by 0s.

If you imagine physically superimposing these 32 subnet bits on top of the bits that constitute an IP address, a 1 in the subnet mask indicates that the bit it's "masking" is a network ID bit, whereas a 0 indicates a host ID bit. Working together with an IP address, the number of 1s in the subnet mask is the number of network bits in the IP address, and the number of 0s is the number of host bits in the IP address.

To determine the network address of the network in which the IP address is located, perform an AND operation between every bit in the subnet mask and its corresponding bit in the IP address. For example, 255.255.0.0 is the subnet mask of the IP address 64.1.5.0. By performing an AND operation, we can determine that the network address of the network to which this IP address belongs is 64.1.0.0. To see how this is calculated, refer to Table 6.6.

With subnet masks, classless addressing is backward compatible with classful addressing. That is, when classful addressing is used, the Class A subnet mask is always 255.0.0.0, the Class B subnet mask is always 255.255.0.0, and the Class C subnet mask is always 255.255.255.0. You can therefore consider classful addressing as a special instance of classless addressing.

When classless addressing is used, the subnet mask length is changeable according to your networking requirements; therefore, the subnet mask is also called

Table 6.6 Calculating the network address based on IP address and subnet mask

	First byte	Second byte	Third byte	Fourth byte
IP address	10000000	00000001	00000101	00000000
Subnet mask	11111111	11111111	00000000	00000000
Result of AND operation (binary)	10000000	00000001	00000000	00000000
Network address (decimal)	64	1	0	0

a Variable Length Subnet Mask (VLSM). The number of 1s in a subnet mask indicates the subnet mask length. For example, the length of subnet mask 0.0.0.0 is 0, the length of subnet mask 252.0.0.0 is 6 (252 in binary = 11111100), the length of subnet mask 255.192.0.0 is 10, and the length of subnet mask 255.255.255.255 is 32.

Classless addressing is now widely used on the Internet, so many IP addresses will have a subnet mask. When you write an IP address with a subnet mask, you first write the IP address, then a slash (/), followed by the subnet mask. For example: 64.1.5.0/255.255.0.0. There are also two different types of shorthand for referring to a subnet mask by its length. The subnet mask 255.192.0.0 is called a 10-bit subnet mask, because there are ten 1s used to indicate the network ID. This can also be called a/10 (slash 10) mask.

When written, you will most often see subnet masks referred to by their lengths. Therefore 64.1.5.0/255.255.0.0 would be written as 64.1.5.0/16, and 192.168.1.5/252.0.0.0 would be written as 192.168.1.5/6.

6.4 Special IP Addresses

As we mentioned before, IP addresses are allocated by the ICANN. This uniform allocation method ensures IP address uniqueness on the Internet. Actually, the "IP address" here refers to public IP addresses. Each network device connected to the Internet must have a public IP address allocated by the ICANN.

However, some networks do not need to connect to the Internet, for example, a closed test network used in a university's lab. The devices on such a network do not need public IP addresses. The only requirement is that each IP address on this closed network is unique.

The IP addresses used on closed networks are called private IP addresses. Private IP addresses exist among Class A, B, and C addresses:

1. **Class A**: 10.0.0.0–10.255.255.255
2. **Class B**: 172.16.0.0–172.31.255.255
3. **Class C**: 192.168.0.0–192.168.255.255

Devices on the Internet do not receive, send, or forward any packets to or from private IP addresses. Private IP addresses can only be used on private networks, and they flexibly extend networks because a private IP address can be re-used on different private networks.

Private networks using private IP addresses should not connect to the Internet. In some instances, however, a private network may need to access the Internet for one reason or another. That is, the private network needs to communicate with the Internet, or a group of private networks needs to communicate with each other through the Internet, as shown in Fig. 6.2. Network Address Translation (NAT) technology is designed to meet these requirements. We will discuss NAT technology in Chap. 11.

In addition to private IP addresses, there are other IP addresses used for special purposes, for example:

255.255.255.255

This is a Limited Broadcast Address. When used as the destination IP address of an IP packet, the packet is broadcast to all nodes on the local network. When a router receives such an IP packet, it will not forward it.

0.0.0.0

If this address is used as a network address, it can belong to any network. It can also be used as a host interface address. For example, before a host interface has been allocated an IP address, it sends a Dynamic Host Configuration Protocol (DHCP) request packet with the Limited Broadcast Address as the destination address and 0.0.0.0 as the source address to the DHCP server to apply for an IP address.

127.0.0.0/8

This is a loopback address. A loopback address can be used as the destination IP address of an IP packet. An IP packet using the loopback address as the destination address cannot be sent out of its device. Generally, a loopback address is used to test the software system in a device.

Fig. 6.2 Connecting private networks to the Internet

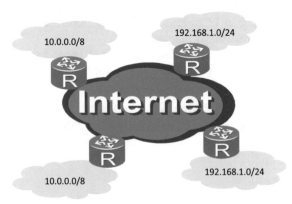

169.254.0.0/16

If a device attempts to obtain an IP address dynamically but fails to find a valid DHCP server, it temporarily uses an IP address on network segment 169.254.0.0/16.

6.5 IP Forwarding

A router has two major jobs: (1) creating and maintaining its own routing table using routing protocols, and (2) forwarding IP packets based on the contents of the table. IP packet forwarding ("IP forwarding" for short) is also called "network layer forwarding" or "Layer 3 forwarding." IP forwarding is the most important concept in this chapter.

Similar to a switch, a router has multiple interfaces (or ports) for forwarding data. The behavior of an interface is controlled by its corresponding network adapter. These network adapters have the same structure as the network adapters on switches or computers, which are the CU, OB, IB, LC, LD, TX, and RX modules. (For details, see Sects. 3.1.1 and 3.1.2) Moreover, the network adapter on each interface has its own MAC address called an interface MAC address.

Router interfaces handle packets in the following ways:

- When a **unicast frame** reaches a router interface through a line (transmission media), this interface compares the destination MAC address of the frame with its own MAC address. If the two MAC addresses are different, the interface discards this frame. If the two MAC addresses are the same, the interface extracts the payload from this frame, and sends the payload to the corresponding network layer module in the router according to the Type field of the frame.
- When a **broadcast frame** reaches a router interface through a line, the interface extracts the payload from the frame, and sends the payload to the corresponding network layer module in the router according to the Type field of the frame.
- When a **multicast frame** reaches a router interface through a line, the handling procedure is complicated. We do not cover multicast frames in this course.

A general explanation of the IP forwarding process follows. Before reading the explanation, take note of the following assumptions (used here to simplify the example):

- All interfaces on the router are Ethernet interfaces.
- An interface on the router receives a unicast frame named X through a line.
- The destination MAC address of frame X is the MAC address of this interface.
- The Type field value of frame X is 0x0800. That is, the payload of frame X is an IP packet, named P.
- P is a unicast IP packet. That is, the destination IP address of P is a unicast IP address.

Keeping these assumptions in mind, the following is a description of the IP forwarding process: ·

1. When frame X reaches a router interface through a line, the interface extracts its packet because the destination MAC address of frame X is the same as the MAC address of the interface.
2. The Type field in frame X is 0x0800, so the interface sends the packet to the IP forwarding module of the router.
3. After receiving the packet, the IP forwarding module searches its own routing table based on the packet's destination IP address. There are two possible results of a routing table search: (1) the router discards the packet, or (2) the router finds the outbound interface (through which the packet leaves the router) and the next hop address of the packet.
4. Assume that the IP forwarding module sends the packet to the outbound interface and notifies the outbound interface of the next hop address.
5. The outbound interface encapsulates the packet in a unicast frame named Y. Frame Y has the following characteristics:

   – Its payload is the original packet.
   – Its Type field is 0x0800.
   – Its source MAC address is the outbound interface MAC address.
   – Its destination MAC address matches the next hop address of the packet.

   If the router has found the MAC address matching the next hop IP address in its own ARP table (Address Resolution Protocol table—as you'll recall, this table lists the MAC addresses matching IP addresses cached from previous communications), it will use it as the destination address of frame Y. Otherwise, the outbound interface sends an ARP packet to request the MAC address that matches the next hop address. For details, see Sect. 3.4.
6. The outbound interface sends frame Y over the line.

Figure 6.3 illustrates the IP forwarding process within a router's IP forwarding module. This is a visual representation of Step 3, the core step of the IP forwarding process.

Figure 6.4 shows a detailed example of IP forwarding. In this example, PC 1 (IP address 10.0.0.2/24) needs to send a unicast packet to PC 2 (IP address 10.0.2.2/24). Therefore the source IP address of the unicast packet is 10.0.0.2/24, and its destination IP address is 10.0.2.2/24.

As you will notice in Fig. 6.4, a packet is generated by PC 1 at the network layer. PC 1 searches its own routing table based on the packet's destination IP address, 10.0.2.2/24. After searching its routing table, PC 1 determines that the packet's outbound interface is its own (PC 1's) network interface (in this example, assume that PC 1 only has one network interface). It also determines that the next hop address is the IP address of Interface 1 (10.0.0.1/24) on Router A (which is the gateway of network segment 10.0.0.0/24).

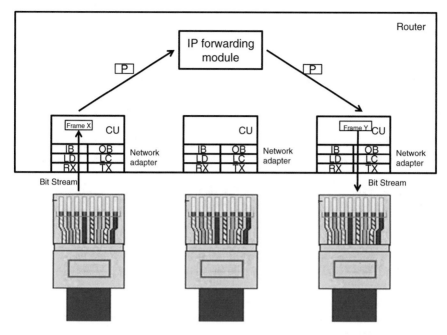

Fig. 6.3 IP forwarding process

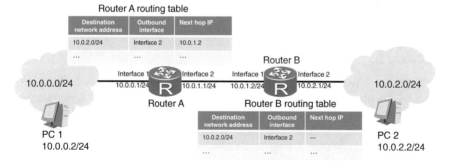

Fig. 6.4 An example of IP forwarding

PC 1 encapsulates the packet in a unicast frame. The following are details about the unicast frame:

- Payload: original packet
- Type field: 0x0800
- Source MAC address: Network interface on PC 1
- Destination MAC address: matched to IP address 10.0.0.1/24 (Interface 1 on Router A)

If PC 1 found the MAC address matching the IP address 10.0.0.1/24 in its own ARP table, then it uses this MAC address as the destination address of the frame. Otherwise, the outbound interface of PC 1 sends an ARP packet to request the MAC address that matches the IP address 10.0.0.1/24. For details on this process, see Sect. 3.4.

PC 1 then sends the unicast frame containing the packet to the switch on the network segment (a switching domain without routers), and the switch forwards the frame to Interface 1 of Router A. After receiving the frame, Interface 1 on Router A does not discard it, but extracts the frame's payload (the original packet). The Type field of the frame is 0x0800, so Interface 1 forwards the frame to the IP forwarding module.

After receiving the packet, Router A's IP forwarding module searches its own routing table based on the destination IP address, 10.0.2.2/24. The IP forwarding module finds a route destined for the network segment (IP address 10.0.2.0/24) on which the destination address resides. The outbound interface of the route is Interface 2, and the next hop address is 10.0.1.2/24. Because the packet's destination IP address (10.0.2.2/24) resides on the network segment 10.0.2.0/24, this is a viable route.

Router A's IP forwarding module sends the packet to Interface 2, and notifies Interface 2 that the packet's next hop address is 10.0.1.2/24. Then Interface 2 encapsulates the packet in a unicast frame.

The following is a summary of unicast frame created by Interface 2 on Router A:

- Payload: original packet
- Type field: 0x0800
- Source MAC address: Interface 2 on Router A
- Destination MAC address: matched to IP address 10.0.1.2/24 (Interface 1 on Router B)

If Router A found the MAC address matching the IP address 10.0.1.2/24 in its own ARP table, then it uses this MAC address as the destination address of the frame. Otherwise, Interface 2 on Router A sends an ARP packet to request the MAC address that matches the IP address 10.0.1.2/24.

Interface 2 on Router A then sends out the unicast frame. After receiving the frame, Interface 1 on Router B does not discard it, but extracts the frame's payload. The Type field of the frame is 0x0800, so Interface 1 forwards the packet to the router's IP forwarding module.

After receiving the packet, the IP forwarding module of Router B searches its own routing table based on the destination IP address, 10.0.2.2/24. The IP forwarding module finds a route destined for the network segment (10.0.2.0/24) on which the IP address resides. The outbound interface of the route is Interface 2. In this instance, there is no next hop address because Interface 2 is directly connected to the final network segment. Because the packet's destination IP address (10.0.2.2/24) is on this network segment, this is a viable route.

The IP forwarding module of Router B then sends the packet to Interface 2, and notifies Interface 2 that the packet's next hop address is not found. Interface 2 encapsulates the packet in a unicast frame. The following is a summary of the unicast frame created by Interface 2 on Router B:

- Payload: original packet
- Type field: 0x0800
- Source MAC address: Interface 2 on Router B
- Destination MAC address: matched to IP address 10.0.2.2/24 (Network interface on PC 2)

If Router B found the MAC address matching the IP address 10.0.2.2/24 in its own ARP table, it uses this MAC address as the destination address of the frame. Otherwise, the Interface 2 on Router B sends an ARP packet to request the MAC address that matches the IP address 10.0.2.2/24.

Interface 2 on Router B then sends out the unicast frame to the switch on the network segment, and the switch forwards the frame to PC 2's network interface. After receiving the frame, the network interface on PC 2 does not discard it, but extracts the payload from the frame. The Type field of the frame is 0x0800, so the network interface forwards the frame to the IP module.

The packet is thereby successfully sent from the network layer of PC 1 to the network layer of PC 2. The Layer 3 forwarding of the packet is complete.

In the example above, you'll notice the following:

- Unicast frame sent by PC 1

  - Source MAC address: MAC address of network interface on PC 1
  - Destination MAC address: MAC address of Interface 1 on Router A

- Unicast frame sent by Router A

  - Source MAC address: MAC address of Interface 2 on Router A
  - Destination MAC address: MAC address of Interface 1 on Router B

- Unicast frame sent by Router B

  - Source MAC address: MAC address of Interface 2 on Router B
  - Destination MAC address: MAC address of network interface on PC 2

This indicates that the frame received by PC 2 is not the frame sent by PC 1—PC 1 and PC 2 cannot exchange frames with one another. Layer 2 (data link layer) communication between PC 1 and PC 2 is blocked by the router. However, the IP packet received by the network layer of PC 2 is the original IP packet sent by the network layer of PC 1, so these two PCs are able to exchange IP packets. In other words, Layer 3 (network layer) communication is implemented between PC 1 and PC 2.

Routers and internets

The development of routers led to the development of internets, or interconnected networks (note that our use of the word "internet" here is deliberately spelled with a lower-case letter I, not to be confused with "the Internet"). Figure 6.5 shows the same network in Fig. 6.4, reconfigured to illustrate the concept of an internet.

Figure 6.5 shows an example of a typical internet. In the figure, each Layer 2 network connected to this internet is called a net. On a Layer 2 network, network interfaces can implement Layer 2 (data link layer) communication; that is, the network interfaces can exchange frames. If the Layer 2 network is an Ethernet (i.e., all network interfaces on the network are Ethernet interfaces) or token ring network (i.e., all network interfaces on the network are token ring interfaces), then the Layer 2 network is actually a Layer 2 broadcast domain.

An internet connects multiple Layer 2 networks (each of which must have at least one router) into a Layer 3 network. As shown in Fig. 6.5, three Layer 2 networks are connected by two routers to form an internet.

On an internet, routers are the boundaries and junctions of the Layer 2 networks. Routers block Layer 2 communication between the Layer 2 networks, but allow Layer 3 (network layer) communication between them. In Fig. 6.5, Interface 1 of Router A belongs to Net 1, and Interface 2 of Router A belongs to Net 2. Net 1 and Net 2 communicate with each other through the Layer 3 forwarding module in Router A.

Net 1 comprises all interfaces on network segment 10.0.0.0/24, the network interface of PC 1, and Interface 1 on Router A. Net 2 comprises Interface 2 of Router A and Interface 1 of Router B. Net 3 comprises Interface 2 of Router B, the network interface of PC 2, and all interfaces on network segment 10.0.2.0/24.

On an internet, switches and routers have different functions. The switches forward frames within the same Layer 2 network, whereas the routers forward packets between different Layer 2 networks. Frames are Layer 2 (data link layer)

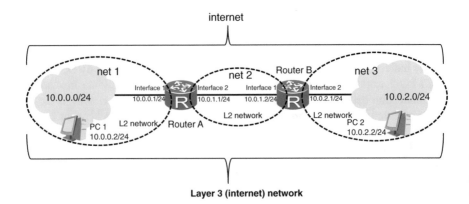

Fig. 6.5 Example of an internet

Smallest internet   **Largest internet**

Fig. 6.6 Smallest and largest internets

data units, so the switches perform Layer 2 forwarding. IP packets are Layer 3 (network layer) data units, so the routers perform Layer 3 forwarding.

You can set up your own internet by using several routers, switches, and PCs. There are small-sized internets and large-sized internets. The largest internet in the world is *the Internet* (note here the use of the upper-case letter I). Figure 6.6 shows the smallest possible internet and the largest internet ("the Internet").

6.6   IP Packet Format

IETF RFC 791 also defines the format of IP packets, as shown in Fig. 6.7.

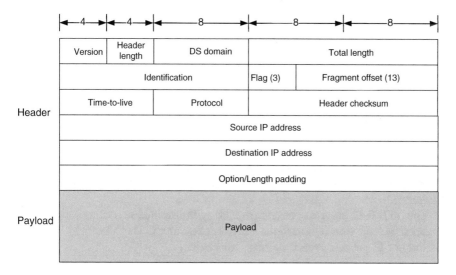

Fig. 6.7 IP packet format

Version

This 4-bit field indicates the version of an IP packet. The value 0x4 indicates an IPv4 packet. The value 0x6 indicates an IPv6 packet. It should be noted that the IPv6 packet format is incompatible with the IPv4 packet format. Figure 6.7 shows the IPv4 packet format.

Packet header length

This 4-bit field indicates the length of an IP packet header. An IP packet header contains variable-length options, so its length is unfixed but must be a multiple of 4.

$$\text{IP packet header length} \times 4 = \text{Number of bytes in header}$$

DS domain

This 8-bit field is called the Type of Service (ToS) domain in RFC 791, and Differentiated Services Code Point (DSCP) in RFC 2474. This field indicates the Quality of Service (QoS) level of a packet, which indicates the forwarding priority of the packet.

Total length

This 16-bit field indicates the length of an IP packet, including IP packet header and payload. The maximum length of an IP packet is 65536 (2^{16}) bytes.

Identification

This 16-bit field is used to fragment and reassemble an IP packet. This chapter does not discuss the fragmentation and reassembling of IP packets.

Flag

This 3-bit field is used to fragment and reassemble an IP packet, which is not discussed in this chapter.

Fragment offset

This 13-bit field is also used to fragment and reassemble an IP packet, which is not discussed in this chapter.

Time To Live (TTL)

This is an 8-bit field. The TTL value of an IP packet is decremented by one by every router that handles the packet. When this field reaches 0, the IP packet is discarded.

The TTL field prevents packets from being transmitted in routing loops on the internet forever, thereby consuming network resources. The TTL field limits the lifetime of IP packets even if routing loops exist.

Protocol

This 8-bit field indicates the payload type of an IP packet. The value 0x01 indicates an ICMP packet; the value 0x02 indicates an IGMP packet; the value 0x06 indicates a TCP segment; the value 0x11 indicates a UDP packet; and the value 0x59 indicates an OSPF packet. Other values are not discussed here.

Header checksum

This 16-bit field is used to carry out checksum on IP packet headers. It is similar to the Frame Checksum (FCS) or CRC field in Ethernet frames. This chapter does not discuss this field.

Source IP address

This 32-bit field indicates the IP address of the interface that sends the IP packet.

Destination IP address

This 32-bit field indicates the IP address of the interface that receives the IP packet.

Option/Length padding

This field has a variable length for options that provide different extended functions. If the length of an IP packet header is not a multiple of 4 after an option is inserted to the IP packet, 0s must be added to the header.

6.7 Review Questions

1. Which are not host interface IP addresses? (Choose all that apply)

   A. 12.3.4.5.6
   B. 12.3.4.567
   C. 12.3.4.5
   D. 224.5.6.7

2. Which IP addresses cannot be used on the Internet? (Choose all that apply)

   A. 0.0.0.0
   B. 255.255.255.255
   C. 10.1.1.1
   D. 168.254.1.1
   E. 172.18.1.1
   F. 192.1.1.1
   G. 192.168.1.1

3. An IP address is 192.168.7.53 and its subnet mask is 255.255.255.192. Which is the network address of the network segment where the IP address resides? (Choose one)

A. 192.168.7.0
B. 192.168.7.128
C. 192.168.7.192
D. 192.168.7.224

4. An IP address is 192.168.7.53 and its subnet mask is 255.255.255.192. Which is the broadcast address of the network segment where the IP address resides? (Choose one)

A. 192.168.7.255
B. 192.168.7.127
C. 192.168.7.63
D. 192.168.7.31

5. How many host interface IP addresses are supported by the network to which 192.168.7.53/18 belongs? (Choose one)

A. 256
B. 254
C. 16384
D. 16382
E. 262144
F. 262142

6. Which statements are not true? (Choose all that apply)

A. After receiving a broadcast frame, a router interface discards the frame, but does not forward it at Layer 3.
B. After receiving a broadcast frame, a router interface floods the frame on the network.
C. After receiving a unicast frame, a router interface may discard the frame.

7. Which statements about IP packets are true? (Choose all that apply)

A. IP packets do not have tails.
B. The length of an IP packet cannot exceed 65536 bytes.
C. An IP packet header contains at least 20 bytes.

Chapter 7
TCP and UDP

As shown in Fig. 1.7, the Transmission Control Protocol (TCP) and User Datagram Protocol (UDP) are transport layer protocols in the TCP/IP protocol suite. TCP is a connection-oriented protocol, whereas UDP is a connectionless protocol.

After completing this section, you should be able to:

- Understand the differences between connectionless and connection-oriented communication.
- Understand how a TCP session is created and terminated.
- Understand the acknowledgement and retransmission mechanisms of TCP.
- Be familiar with the meanings and purposes of important fields (such as SeqNo and AckNo) in TCP segments.
- Be familiar with the purposes of application ports.
- Understand the use scenarios of TCP and UDP.

7.1 Connectionless and Connection-Oriented Communication

To help you understand the two communication methods, imagine two people, Player A and Player B, are playing a ball game.

Player A has a box containing many red, yellow, and blue balls. The different colors represent different words:

- Red = I
- Yellow = love
- Blue = you

Player A wants to express "I love you" by throwing balls in Player B's box. They cannot talk with each other. Player B knows what word each color represents.

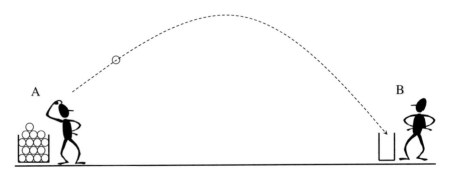

Fig. 7.1 Visual representation of connectionless communication

Player A throws the corresponding balls at Player B's box. However, Player A has no way of knowing if Player B was ready to receive the balls, if all the balls landed in the box or if they landed in the correct order.

Player B doesn't know when to expect the balls, if he has received all of the balls thrown or whether the ones that landed did so in right order. There are many ways that the message can be incorrectly received.

This is an example of connectionless communication. Figure 7.1 shows a visual representation of this example.

To improve communication reliability, the players are allowed to talk with each other during the game, but they are not allowed to tell each other the colors of the balls.

Player A writes the same number on all balls of the same color. For example, reds are five, yellows are six and blues are seven.

The Players are now able to discuss which balls will be thrown, whether Player B is ready to receive the balls, which balls have been received, and when they are both ready to stop playing because Player B has received the correct balls. Player B then arranges the balls in sequence, and gets the information "I love you."

This is connection-oriented communication. A visual representation is shown in Fig. 7.2.

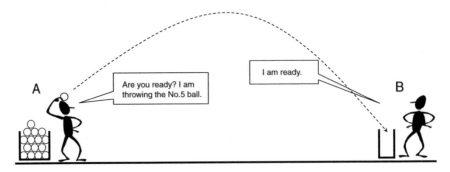

Fig. 7.2 Connection-oriented communication

Connection-oriented communication is more reliable than connection-less communication. The players control the start time, end time, and progress of the game. It also allows for extra information to be passed such as Player B requesting Player A to throw balls faster or slower, or asking Player A to re-throw the missing ball.

If we consider the game to be a session, the balls can be considered data packets, and the conversations control packets. Players A and B exchange control packets to control the data packet transmission process.

Now, let's discuss Layer 2 (Ethernet) communication. Within a Layer 2 network, interfaces exchange frames to communicate with each other. The sender's network adapter does not notify the receiver's network adapter that it will send a frame, or know whether the receiver's network adapter has received all the frames in sequence. Frames do not contain sequence numbers, so the receiver's network adapter does not know whether any frame is missing. There is no mechanism to allow the receiver's network adapter to communicate with the sender's network adapter. The Layer 2 functional modules of sender and receiver cannot control the frame exchange process. Therefore, Layer 2 (Ethernet) communication is connectionless.

However, in Layer 3 (the network or IP layer) communication, the IP modules of sender and receiver exchange IP packets to communicate with each other. The sender's IP module does not notify the receiver's IP module that it will send a packet or know whether the receiver's IP module has received all the packets in sequence. IP packets do not contain sequence numbers, so the receiver's IP module does not know whether any packet is missing. There is no mechanism to allow the receiver's IP module to communicate with the sender's IP module. The Layer 3 IP modules of sender and receiver cannot control the packet exchange process. Therefore, Layer 3 (network layer or IP layer) communication is also a connectionless method.

7.2 TCP

Transmission Control Protocol (TCP) is one of the transport layer protocols in the TCP/IP protocol suite. The suite contains several different transport layer protocols, but TCP is the most important and most commonly used.

Within a network, frames are exchanged at the data link layer (Layer 2), IP packets are exchanged at the network or IP layer (Layer 3), and TCP segments are exchanged at the transport layer (Layer 4).

When the sender's TCP module receives data from the application layer, it encapsulates data into TCP segments. Before the sender's TCP module sends TCP segments to the IP module, it exchanges TCP control segments with the receiver's

TCP module to set up a TCP session. After the TCP session is set up, the TCP modules of sender and receiver start to transmit TCP segments. The TCP modules keep exchanging TCP control segments until they exchange TCP control segments to end the TCP session. This exchange of control segments means that TCP communication is reliable and connection-oriented.

TCP also compensates for unreliability in Layer 2 and Layer 3 communication. Frames and packets can be lost through network congestion, but neither Layer 2 nor Layer 3 technology can detect frame or packet loss. However, TCP was designed to detect frame and packet loss and also perform retransmission to ensure reliable messaging. This is possible through encapsulation: a Layer 2 frame is encapsulated into an IP packet as a payload which is then encapsulated into a TCP segment as a payload.

7.2.1 TCP Session Setup

When a computer wants to communicate with another through TCP, the computer must begin a three-way handshake to create a TCP session.

Figure 7.3 shows how a TCP session is created through a three-way handshake. The TCP session creation process is:

1. Computer A's TCP module sends a SYN segment to Computer B's TCP module to request the creation of a TCP session. This TCP connection will allow Computer A to send control data to Computer B.
2. Computer B's TCP module returns a single SYN+ACK segment to Computer A. This contains an acknowledgement of Computer A's request as well as Computer B's request to create its own TCP connection

Fig. 7.3 A TCP session created through a three-way handshake

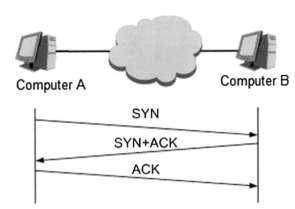

3. Computer A's TCP module sends an ACK segment to Computer B to confirm
   that the creation of the second TCP connection.

Note that this process creates two separate TCP connections: one from
Computer A to Computer B and the other from B to A.

7.2.2 TCP Session Termination

After the TCP session is created through the three-way handshake, Computer A and
Computer B can start to exchange TCP segments and TCP control segments. When
the TCP segment exchange is complete, the computers exchange FIN and ACK
segments to terminate the TCP session. This is done through a four-way handshake.
Figure 7.4 shows a TCP session terminated through four-way handshake.
Termination of a TCP session follows the following process:

- Computer A sends a FIN segment to Computer B to request termination of the
  TCP connection.
- Computer B replies with an ACK segment to accept Computer A's request, and
  terminates the connection.
- When Computer A receives the ACK segment, it terminates the connection.
- This process is then repeated from Computer B to Computer A. It is important to
  note that these are two separate processes as there are two separate TCP
  connections.

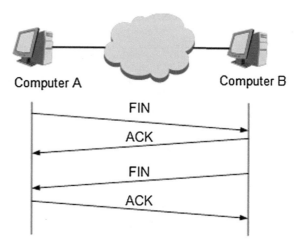

Fig. 7.4 Terminating a TCP
session through a four-way
handshake

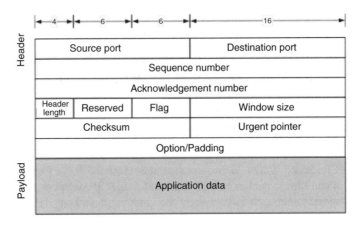

Fig. 7.5 TCP segment structure

7.2.3 TCP Segment Structure

As you can see in Fig. 7.5, there are many fields in a TCP segment. This chapter discusses only the major fields in a TCP segment.

Source port

This 16-bit field indicates the application module that generates and sends the TCP segment payload.

Destination port

This 16-bit field indicates the application module that receives the payload of the TCP segment.

Sequence number

The short form is SeqNo. This 32-bit field indicates the sequence number of the TCP segment. According to this sequence number, the receiver can determine whether any segment is repeatedly received or missing.

Acknowledgement number

The short form is AckNo. The usage of this field will be explained later.

Header length

This 4-bit field indicates the length of a TCP segment header. Because the header may contain options, the header length is variable; however, the header length must be a multiple of 4.

Value of the **Header length** field × 4 = Number of bytes in header

Flag

This is a 6-bit field. Each bit has its own name and meaning: URG, ACK, PSH, RST, SYN, and FIN. The ACK bit value for the ACK and ACK+SYN segments is 1. The SYN bit value for the SYN and ACK+SYN segments is 1. The FIN bit value for the FIN segment is 1.

Checksum

This 16-bit field is used for error-check of the header and data.

Option/Padding

This field has a variable length for options that provide different extended TCP functions. If the length of a segment header is not a multiple of 4 after an option is inserted to the segment, 0s must be added to the header.

SeqNo and AckNo values in different segments

As shown in Fig. 7.6, before Computer A initiates a TCP session, it generates a random integer x, which is an Initial Sequence Number (ISN). The first TCP segment sent by Computer A is a SYN segment. The SeqNo value in the SYN segment is x.

After receiving the SYN segment, Computer B also generates an ISN (signified here by y). When Computer B sends to Computer A a SYN+ACK segment, the SeqNo is y while the AckNo is x+1.

Computer A then replies with an ACK segment. In this ACK segment, the value of SeqNo is x+1 and the value of AckNo is y+1.

The TCP session is now created.

Fig. 7.6 SeqNo and AckNo values in the TCP session creation process

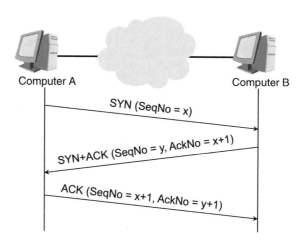

7.2.4   TCP Acknowledgement and Retransmission

Figure 7.7 shows the TCP acknowledgement and retransmission process.

Assume that Computers A and B have set up TCP connections. Computer A needs to transmit three TCP segments (with 400, 500, and 800 bytes in length respectively) to Computer B. The ISN of Computer A is 1367.

The SeqNo of the first TCP segment is 1369, because 1367 and 1368 were used by Computer A during the three-way handshake. 1369 is then the sequence number of the first byte in the first TCP segment. The sequence number of the last byte in the first TCP segment is 1768 (1369 + 400 − 1). After sending the first TCP segment, Computer A waits for the message from Computer B.

Computer B replies with an ACK segment. The AckNo of this ACK segment is 1769 (1369 + 400), which means that the SeqNo of the next byte is 1769 and all the bytes before 1768 have been received.

After receiving the ACK segment from Computer B, Computer A sends the second segment. The SeqNo of the second segment is 1769, the sequence number of the first byte in the second TCP segment. The sequence number of the last byte in the second TCP segment is 2268 (1769 + 500 − 1). After sending the second TCP segment, Computer A waits for the message from Computer B.

Computer B replies with another ACK segment. The AckNo of this ACK segment is 2269 (1769 + 500), which means that the SeqNo of the next byte is 2269 and all the bytes before 2268 have been received.

Fig. 7.7 TCP acknowledgement and retransmission example 1

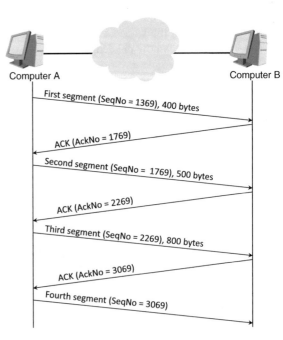

Fig. 7.8 TCP
acknowledgement and
retransmission example 2

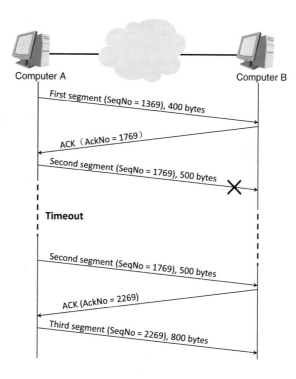

After receiving the ACK segment from Computer B, Computer A starts to send the third segment. The SeqNo of the third segment is 2269, the sequence number of the first byte in the third TCP segment. The sequence number of the last byte in the third TCP segment is 3068 ($2269 + 800 - 1$). After sending the third TCP segment, Computer A waits for the message from Computer B.

Computer B replies with the third ACK segment. The AckNo of this ACK segment is 3069 ($2269 + 800$), which means that the SeqNo of the next byte is 3069 and all the bytes before 3068 have been received.

After receiving the ACK segment from Computer B, Computer A starts to send the fourth segment. The SeqNo of the fourth segment is 3069.

If the second segment sent by Computer A is lost, Computer B will not send an ACK segment to respond to the second segment. Computer A will not send the third segment because it does not receive a response to the second segment. Computer A will wait until the waiting time to expire and then resend the second segment. Computer A will wait again for a response.

Figure 7.8 shows this process.

In this example, Computer A must wait for the response from Computer B every time it sends a segment. Because of this, TCP transmission is considered inefficient. To improve transmission efficiency, TCP uses sliding window. The slide window mechanism is not discussed in this chapter.

Table 7.1 Well-known TCP port samples

Port number	Application	Description
20	File Transfer Protocol (FTP) data	Allows two network devices to exchange files
21	FTP control	Uses port 20 to transfer files and port 21 to transfer control data
23	Telnet	Controls network devices remotely
25	Simple Mail Transfer Protocol (SMTP)	Sends emails
53	Domain Name System (DNS)	Translates domain names into IP addresses
80	Hypertext Transfer Protocol (HTTP)	Browses websites and web pages
110	Post Office Protocol 3 (POP3)	Receives emails

7.2.5 Application Port

As we've learned, a TCP segment contains source and destination ports. The ports refer to logical "application ports", but not physical ports on devices. The application ports in TCP segments identify the application modules matching the payloads in TCP segments.

Application ports include well-known ports and unknown ports. Well-known port numbers range from 0 to 1023. These ports are allocated to certain application modules so that all network devices can identify the applications to which the payloads in TCP segments belong. Table 7.1 lists samples of well-known ports. Unknown port numbers range from 1024 to 65535. These ports are dynamically allocated to the application programs that need to communicate through network devices.

7.3 UDP

The User Datagram Protocol (UDP) is a connectionless protocol provided at the transport layer (Layer 4).

In network communication, information transmission reliability and efficiency conflict with each other. Sometimes, reliability is improved at the expense of efficiency or vice versa.

For example, acknowledgement and retransmission improves reliability, but reduces efficiency. With the increased development of network technologies, transmission media provide higher speeds, anti-interference capabilities, so network connections are now more reliable. There is a low possibility of errors. In addition, for some applications, low transmission reliability is tolerable. For example, users

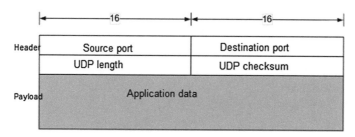

Fig. 7.9 UDP datagram structure

cannot detect the loss of a small amount of data in video transfer, but cannot tolerate the time retransmission takes.

UDP was developed for time-sensitive applications. For these types of applications, dropping packets is preferable to waiting for delayed packets.

Figure 7.9 breaks down the UDP datagram structure. The source and destination ports in a UDP header are the same as those in TCP segment header. The UDP header does not contain a sequence number field.

Because UDP is connectionless, UDP datagrams are not classified into data packets and control packets. The UDP modules of sender and receiver do not set up UDP sessions nor do they take acknowledgement or retransmission measures. The sender's UDP module encapsulates the data delivered by the application layer into UDP datagrams and sends the UDP datagrams to the IP module. The receiver's UDP module extracts the payloads from the UDP datagrams and sends the payloads to the application module matching the destination port.

UDP does not resolve the packet loss, repetition, delay, or sequencing problems because the reliability of UDP datagrams is guaranteed by the application layer. If an application program requires highly reliable transmission, the program itself will provide acknowledgement and retransmission.

The Internet Engineering Task Force (IETF) has specified which applications must use TCP, which applications must use UDP, which applications can use both TCP and UDP, and which applications cannot use TCP or UDP (only IP protocols). For more information, refer to the related RFC recommendations.

7.4   Review Questions

1. What is the full name of UDP? (Choose one)

    A. User Delivery Protocol
    B. User Datagram Procedure
    C. User Datagram Protocol
    D. Unreliable Datagram Protocol

2. When a TCP module sends a TCP segment, which layer will subsequently process the TCP segment to be sent? (Choose one)

    A. Application layer
    B. Transport layer
    C. Network layer
    D. Data link layer

3. Which numbers can be used as UDP port numbers? (Choose all that apply)

    A. 1
    B. 80
    C. 2048
    D. 65536

4. Which TCP segments will not be used in TCP three-way handshake? (Choose all that apply)

    A. SYN
    B. SYN+ACK
    C. ACK
    D. FIN
    E. FIN+ACK

5. Which TCP segments will be used in TCP session termination? (Choose all that apply)

    A. SYN
    B. SYN+ACK
    C. ACK
    D. FIN
    E. FIN+ACK

6. Which port is used by FTP? (Choose one)

    A. 20
    B. 21
    C. 20 and 21

Chapter 8
Routing Protocol Basics

Learning about routing and routing protocols is essential to your understanding of networking. They are fundamental to your network technology knowledge.

After completing this section, you should be able to:

- Understand a route's composition and how it is generated
- Distinguish between a computer's routing table and a router's routing table
- Classify routing protocols
- Understand the basics of RIP
- Understand the basics of OSPF and its differences with RIP

8.1 Routing

8.1.1 Routes and Routing Tables

Essentially, a route is a network-layer path from a network device to a destination, and a routing table stores information about routes. Routing tables are stored on routers, computers, and Layer 3 switches (not Layer 2 switches) and function like a database, in which information specific to each route is called a routing entry.

The following shows a routing table and some of the entries stored within.

```
<R1> display ip routing-table
-------------------------------------------------------------------------
Destination/Mask Proto    Pre Cost Flags   NextHop       Interface
1.0.0.0/8        Direct   0   0    D       1.0.0.1       GigabitEthernet1/0/0
1.0.0.1/32       Direct   0   0    D       127.0.0.1     InLoopBack0
2.0.0.0/8        Static   60  0    D       12.0.0.2      GigabitEthernet1/0/1
2.1.0.0/16       RIP      100 1    D       12.0.0.2      GigabitEthernet1/0/1
12.0.0.0/30      Direct   0   0    D       12.0.0.1      GigabitEthernet1/0/1
12.0.0.1/32      Direct   0   0    D       127.0.0.1     InLoopBack0
...
```

© Springer Science+Business Media Singapore 2016
Huawei Technologies Co., Ltd., *HCNA Networking Study Guide*,
DOI 10.1007/978-981-10-1554-0_8

The preceding routing table is that of an Internet-connected Huawei AR series router (named R1). To check the routing table, run the **display ip routing-table** command on R1.

Each line is a routing entry, and each routing entry must contain three important elements: a destination address/mask (**Destination/Mask**), an outbound interface (**Interface**), and a next-hop IP address (**NextHop**). In addition to these elements, a routing entry may contain attributes such as a route preference (**Pre**), route cost (**Cost**), and protocol (**Proto**) that generated the routing entry. These attributes are described in subsequent sections.

Take the routing entry 2.0.0.0/8 (destination address/mask) as an example. R1 is aware that a network exists at 2.0.0.0/8, as 2.0.0.0 is a network address and 8 is the mask length. This entry specifies that, for all IP packets destined to 2.0.0.0/8, R1 must send them through its outbound interface GigabitEthernet1/0/1 to the next-hop IP address 12.0.0.2.

Assume that R1 receives a packet whose destination IP address is 2.1.0.1. R1 performs an AND operation on 2.1.0.1 and each routing entry to determine which of the entries match this packet. The result of this operation is that two routing entries, 2.0.0.0/8 and 2.1.0.0/16, match the IP packet. If an IP packet matches more than one routing entry, R1 uses the longest match rule to determine the optimal route for forwarding the packet. (The longest match rule is an algorithm used to ascertain which of the routing entries that match the packet's destination address is the most specific.) 2.1.0.0/16 is the optimal route because it is the most specific; its mask length is greater than that of 2.0.0.0/8. Therefore, R1 sends this received packet to 2.1.0.0/16.

Computers also send packets through the optimal route. After a computer constructs IP packets to be sent out at the network layer, it searches its routing table for entries that match the packets' destination address. The process is the same for both routers and computers, and once the computer identifies the optimal route, it sends the packets out through this route.

In some routing entries, the IP address is the same for both the next-hop and outbound interface. In such a routing entry, the outbound interface resides on the destination network—the outbound interface directly connects to the destination network specified in the routing entry, and resides on the same Layer 2 network or in the same Layer 2 broadcast domain as the host interface of the next hop.

8.1.2   Routing Information Source

Routing information—the information that forms routing entries in a routing table—is generated by automatic discovery, manual configuration, or a dynamic routing protocol; routes are therefore known as direct, static, or dynamic, respectively. Note that, of the attributes mentioned in Sect. 8.1.1, the protocol (**Proto**) column specifies the protocol of each route, and may contain **Direct** (indicates direct routing information discovered by R1), **Static** (indicates static routing information manually configured), or **RIP** (indicates dynamic routing information that R1 has learned using RIP).

Direct route

After you power on a network device and its interfaces go Up, the device can discover routes to the networks that are directly connected to its interfaces. A network is deemed directly connected to an interface (and therefore the device) if the interface resides on that network and the network is a Layer 2 network or Layer 2 broadcast domain.

Figure 8.1 provides an example showing how direct routes are automatically discovered.

On the network shown in Fig. 8.1, R1's GE 1/0/0 and GE 2/0/0 are each directly connected to a network. When GE 1/0/0 goes Up, R1 learns that the address of the network where GE 1/0/0 resides is 1.0.0.0/24. R1 then creates and saves to its routing table a routing entry that contains the destination address/mask 1.0.0.0/24, outbound interface GE 1/0/0, and next-hop IP address 1.0.0.1 (IP address of the outbound interface). Because this is a direct route, its protocol is **Direct**. The cost of direct routes is fixed at 0.

Similarly, when R1's GE 2/0/0 goes Up, R1 automatically discovers the direct route destined for 2.0.0.0/24. R1 then stores a routing entry that contains the destination address/mask 2.0.0.0/24, outbound interface GE 2/0/0, and next-hop IP address 2.0.0.1. The protocol is **Direct**, and the cost is 0.

PC1 also discovers the direct route destined for 1.0.0.0/24 and uses the following routing information to generate a routing entry: destination address/mask 1.0.0.0/24, outbound interface being PC1's network interface (assume that PC1 has only one network interface), next-hop IP address 1.0.0.2, protocol being **Direct**, and cost being 0.

PC2, in the same way, discovers the direct route destined for 2.0.0.0/24.

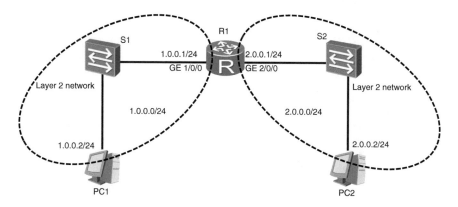

Fig. 8.1 Direct routes automatically discovered

Static route

On the network shown in Fig. 8.2, R1 and R2 can automatically discover some routes but not other routes. You can configure the routes that cannot be automatically discovered—these routes are known as static routes.

In Fig. 8.2, R1 can automatically discover the two direct routes 1.0.0.0/8 and 12.0.0.0/30, but not the route 2.0.0.0/8. You can configure this route and specify the destination address/mask 2.0.0.0/8, outbound interface GE 1/0/1 (R1's interface), next-hop IP address 12.0.0.2 (IP address of R2's GE 1/0/1), and cost of 0 or any desired value. Then, R1 saves this route to its routing table, with the protocol being **Static**.

Similarly, R2 cannot automatically discover the route 1.0.0.0/8. You can configure this route on R2 also as a static route and specify the destination address/mask 1.0.0.0/8, outbound interface GE 1/0/1 (R2's interface), next-hop IP address 12.0.0.1 (IP address of R1's GE 1/0/1), and a cost of 0 or any desired value.

Dynamic route

In addition to automatically discovering and manually configuring routes (direct and static routes, respectively), a network device can also discover routes by using routing protocols.

Imagine how time-consuming and laborious it would be to configure static routes for a network device that indirectly connects to many networks. You would

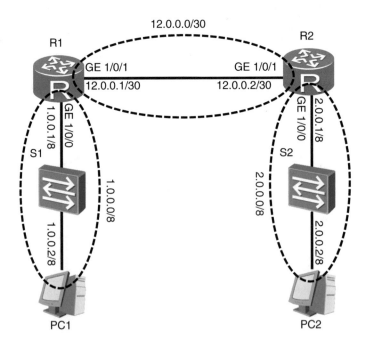

Fig. 8.2 Manually configuring static routes

need to configure each route one at a time. In addition, the static routes that you configure may become invalid if a fault occurs or the network structure changes. On a live network, where time is of the essence, configuring so many static routes that may potentially become invalid is not a viable option.

Dynamic routing protocols (also simply referred to as routing protocols because no static routing protocol exists) alleviate the aforementioned problems. Protocols such as the Routing Information Protocol (RIP) and Open Shortest Path First (OSPF) are a few examples of routing protocols. A network device can have one or more such protocols, separately or in combination, to enable it to dynamically learn routes and update its routing table if network changes occur.

Note that a router running both RIP and OSPF will create and maintain a RIP routing table and an OSPF routing table in addition to an IP routing table. The RIP routing table stores all routes discovered by RIP, and the OSPF routing table stores all routes discovered by OSPF. Although routing tables of routing protocols exist, the router only uses routing entries in the IP routing table to forward IP packets. However, some routing entries in the RIP and OSPF routing tables can be injected into the IP routing table based on specific rules.

Unlike a router, a computer does not run any routing protocol even though it has an IP routing table.

8.1.3 Route Preference

A device running both RIP and OSPF may discover two routes to the same destination/mask, for example, 1.0.0.0/24. If a static route has also been configured for 1.0.0.0/24, the device potentially knows three different routes to 1.0.0.0/24. Deciding which of the three routes is to be injected into the IP routing table for packet forwarding depends on route preferences.

Routes generated from different information sources are assigned different preferences. The smaller the preference value, the higher the preference. The device selects as the optimal route the one assigned the highest preference among all routes with the same destination/mask but generated from different information sources, and then injects this route into its IP routing table. The other routes remain in the deactivated state and do not appear in the IP routing table.

Routes generated from different information sources have different default preference values. These values may differ between devices of different vendors. Table 8.1 lists the default preference values of some routes on Huawei AR devices.

So, if the device mentioned at the start of this section was a Huawei AR device, which route would it select from the RIP, OSPF, and static routes to the same destination/mask? (If you said OSPF, well done, you're right.)

Table 8.1 Route preferences

Route	Default preference value
Direct route	0
OSPF route	10
Static route	60
RIP route	100
BGP route	255

8.1.4 Route Cost

Each route to a destination/mask is attributed a cost. If a routing protocol discovers multiple routes to the same destination/mask, the route with the smallest cost is selected and injected into this protocol's routing table.

Different routing protocols calculate the cost based on different metrics. For example, RIP calculates the cost based on the number of routers that a packet must traverse to reach its destination/mask. This number is known as a hop count. Figure 8.3 provides an example to illustrate how route costs determine route selection.

On the network shown in Fig. 8.3, R1, R2, and R3 all run RIP. R1 uses RIP to discover two routes to 2.0.0.0/8. The first route has the outbound interface being R1's GE 1/0/0, next-hop IP address being the IP address of R2's GE 1/0/0, and cost being 3. This route's cost is 3 because the route passes through R1, R2, and R3 (a hop count of 3) before arriving at 2.0.0.0/8. The second route has the outbound interface being R1's GE 2/0/0, next-hop IP address being the IP address of R3's GE 1/0/0, and cost being 2. Because this route passes through only R1 and R3 (a hop count of 2) before arriving at 2.0.0.0/8, its cost is 2. Therefore, the second route is determined to be the optimal route (because its cost is less than that of the first route) and is injected into R1's RIP routing table.

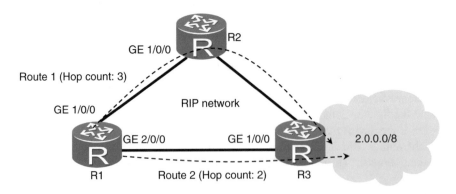

Fig. 8.3 RIP using a hop count as the route cost

Figure 8.4 provides another example of RIP using a hop count, but in this example, multiple routes have the same cost (routes with the same cost are called equal-cost routes).

In Fig. 8.4, R1, R2, R3, and R4 all run RIP. R1 uses RIP to discover two routes to 2.0.0.0/8. The first route has the outbound interface being R1's GE 1/0/0, next-hop IP address being the IP address of R2's GE 1/0/0, and cost being 3. The second route has the outbound interface being R1's GE 2/0/0, next-hop IP address being the IP address of R4's GE 1/0/0, and cost also being 3. These two routes are added to R1's RIP routing table, and are classified as equal-cost routes because they both pass through an identical number of hops (the first passes through R1, R2, and R3, and the second passes through R1, R4, and R3). If both routes are selected and injected into the IP routing table, R1 balances traffic destined for 2.0.0.0/8 between the two routes. This implementation is called load balancing.

The preceding examples used RIP to describe route costs. However, because different routing protocols calculate costs differently, costs are specific to each protocol and cannot be compared or converted.

If a router concurrently runs multiple routing protocols and each one discovers one or more routes to the same destination/mask (for example, z/y), each routing protocol will select an optimal route based on the cost and inject the optimal route into the protocol's routing table. Then, the optimal route with the highest preference among the optimal routes of all routing protocols is injected into the router's IP routing table. If the router also has direct and static routes to z/y, these routes are included in the route selection process together with the optimal routes discovered by routing protocols. Only the route with the highest preference is injected into the IP routing table.

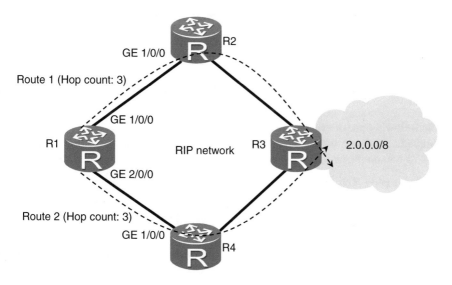

Fig. 8.4 Equal-cost routes

8.1.5   Default Route

The default route 0.0.0.0/0 is used for IP packets destined to an unknown destination/mask. 0.0.0.0/0 is the least specific routing entry in a routing table and used for forwarding packets that do not match any other routing entry. A packet that matches no routing entry other than the default route is forwarded to an address mapped to the default route. The mapped address can be generated by a routing protocol or manually configured, and is known as a dynamic default route or static default route, respectively.

Routers and computers may or may not have a default route stored in their IP routing table. If no default route is available, IP packets that do not match any routing entry will be silently discarded.

8.1.6   Comparison Between Routing Tables on a Computer and Router

A computer's IP routing table generally contains about 20 routing entries, whereas a router's IP routing table can contain anything from a few to millions of entries, depending on the routing protocols the router is running and its network position.

Because computers do not run any routing protocol, their routing tables are comprised of direct routes, static routes manually configured, and routes configured by the computer's OS. Routers, on the other hand, do run routing protocols and so their IP routing tables include dynamic routes in addition to direct and static routes (dynamic routes account for the majority of entries in a router's IP routing table). Routers also create and maintain routing tables of each routing protocol they run, in addition to their IP routing tables.

8.1.7   Static Route Configuration Example

The following provides an example of configuring static routes. Figure 8.5 shows a simple network, on which static routes must be configured on R1 and R2 to allow PCs to communicate.

Configuration Roadmap

- Configure a static route on R1, with the destination/mask being 2.0.0.0/8, next-hop IP address being 12.0.0.2 (IP address of R2's GE 1/0/1), and outbound interface being R1's GE 1/0/1.
- Configure a static route on R2, with the destination/mask being 1.0.0.0/8, next-hop IP address being 12.0.0.1 (IP address of R1's GE 1/0/1), and outbound interface being R2's GE 1/0/1.

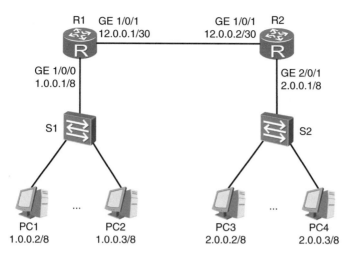

Fig. 8.5 Example network for configuring static routes

Procedure

Run the **ip route-static** *ip-address* {*mask* | *mask-length*} {*nexthop-address* | *interface-type interface-number* [*nexthop-address*]} [**preference** *preference*] command in the system view to configure a static route. *ip-address* {*mask* | *mask-length*} specifies a destination IP address and mask or mask length; *nexthop-address* specifies a next-hop IP address; *interface-type interface-number* specifies the type and number of an outbound interface; and *preference* specifies a route preference.

\# Configure R1.

```
<R1> system-view
[R1] ip route-static 2.0.0.0 8 12.0.0.2 gigabitethernet
1/0/1
```

\# Configure R2.

```
<R2> system-view
[R2] ip route-static 1.0.0.0 8 12.0.0.1 gigabitethernet
1/0/1
```

After completing the configuration, check the configured routes. Run the **display ip routing-table** command to check the IP routing table. The following example shows information about R1's IP routing table.

```
<R1> display ip routing-table
Route Flags: R - relay, D - download to fib
------------------------------------------------------------------------------
Routing Tables: Public
         Destinations : 5          Routes : 5
Destination/Mask Proto   Pre Cost  Flags  NextHop        Interface
    1.0.0.0/8        Direct  0   0      D     1.0.0.1        GigabitEthernet1/0/0
    1.0.0.1/32       Direct  0   0      D     127.0.0.1      InLoopBack0
    2.0.0.0/8        Static  60  0      D     12.0.0.2       GigabitEthernet1/0/1
    12.0.0.0/30      Direct  0   0      D     12.0.0.1       GigabitEthernet1/0/1
    12.0.0.1/32      Direct  0   0      D     127.0.0.1      InLoopBack0
```

The command output shows that R1's IP routing table has a static route to 2.0.0.0/8 and the route preference is 60 (the route preference is set to 60, by default, because no preference was specified).

8.1.8   Default Route Configuration Example

Figure 8.6 shows an expansion of the network shown in Fig. 8.5. On this network, R3 belongs to an Internet Service Provider (ISP) and has a route to the Internet. To allow PCs to communicate and access the Internet, configure default routes.

Configuration Roadmap

- Configure a static route on R1, with the destination/mask being 2.0.0.0/8, next-hop IP address being 12.0.0.2 (IP address of R2's GE 1/0/1), and outbound interface being R1's GE 1/0/1. Configure a default route on R1, with the next-hop IP address being 23.0.0.1 (IP address of R3's GE 2/0/0) and the outbound interface being R1's GE 2/0/0.
- Configure a static route on R2, with the destination/mask being 1.0.0.0/8, next-hop IP address being 12.0.0.1 (IP address of R1's GE 1/0/1), and outbound interface being R2's GE 1/0/1. Configure a default route on R2, with the next-hop IP address being 12.0.0.1 (IP address of R1's GE 1/0/1) and the outbound interface being R2's GE 1/0/1.
- Configure a static route to 1.0.0.0/8 and one to 2.0.0.0/8 on R3, both with the next-hop IP address being 23.0.0.2 (IP address of R1's GE 2/0/0) and outbound interface being R3's GE 2/0/0.

Procedure

Configure R1.

```
<R1> system-view
[R1] ip route-static 2.0.0.0 8 12.0.0.2 gigabitethernet
1/0/1
```

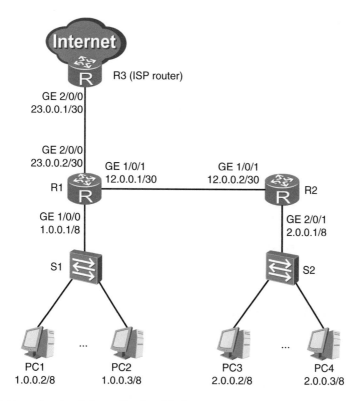

Fig. 8.6 Example network for configuring default routes

```
[R1] ip route-static 0.0.0.0 0 23.0.0.1 gigabitethernet
2/0/0
```

Configure R2.

```
<R2> system-view
[R2] ip route-static 1.0.0.0 8 12.0.0.1 gigabitethernet
1/0/1
[R2] ip route-static 0.0.0.0 0 12.0.0.1 gigabitethernet
1/0/1
```

Configure R3.

```
<R3> system-view
[R3] ip route-static 1.0.0.0 8 23.0.0.2 gigabitethernet
2/0/0
[R3] ip route-static 2.0.0.0 8 23.0.0.2 gigabitethernet
2/0/0
```

After completing the configuration, check the configured routes. Run the **display ip routing-table** command to check the IP routing table. The following example shows information about R1's IP routing table.

```
<R1> display ip routing-table
Route Flags: R - relay, D - download to fib
--------------------------------------------------------------------------------

Routing Tables: Public
          Destinations : 8        Routes : 8
Destination/Mask Proto   Pre Cost Flags   NextHop        Interface
0.0.0.0/0        Static  60  0    RD      23.0.0.1       GigabitEthernet2/0/0
1.0.0.0/8        Direct  0   0    D       1.0.0.1        GigabitEthernet1/0/0
1.0.0.1/32       Direct  0   0    D       127.0.0.1      InLoopBack0
2.0.0.0/8        Static  60  0    D       12.0.0.2       GigabitEthernet1/0/1
12.0.0.0/30      Direct  0   0    D       12.0.0.1       GigabitEthernet1/0/1
12.0.0.1/32      Direct  0   0    D       127.0.0.1      InLoopBack0
23.0.0.0/30      Direct  0   0    D       23.0.0.2       GigabitEthernet2/0/0
23.0.0.2/32      Direct  0   0    D       127.0.0.1      InLoopBack0
```

The command output shows that R1's IP routing table has a default static route 0.0.0.0/0.

8.1.9 Review Questions

1. Which of the following static routes will a router select from its IP routing table to forward IP packets whose destination IP address is 8.1.1.1? (Choose one)

   A. 0.0.0.0/0
   B. 8.0.0.0/8
   C. 8.1.0.0/16
   D. 18.0.0.0/16

2. What are the sources for routing information? (Choose all that apply)

   A. Direct routes automatically discovered
   B. Static routes manually configured
   C. Dynamic routes discovered by routing protocols
   D. None of the above

3. A router runs both RIP and OSPF. It has four routes to 9.0.0.0/8, one direct route automatically discovered, one discovered using RIP, one discovered using OSPF, and one manually configured. By default, which of these four routes will be injected into the router's IP routing table? (Choose one)

   A. Direct route automatically discovered
   B. Static route manually configured

    C. Route discovered by RIP

    D. Route discovered by OSPF

4. What is the default preference of a static route? (Choose one)

    A. 0

    B. 60

    C. 100

    D. 120

5. A router runs both RIP and OSPF. RIP discovers two routes to 9.0.0.0/8, one with the cost being 5 and the other with the cost being 7. OSPF discovers a route to 9.0.0.0/8 with the cost being 100. In addition, a static route to 9.0.0.0/8 is manually configured, with the cost being 60. By default, which of these four routes will be injected into the router's IP routing table? (Choose one)

    A. Static route with the cost 60

    B. RIP route with the cost 5

    C. RIP route with the cost 7

    D. OSPF route with the cost 100

6. Which of the following static routes will a router select from its IP routing table to forward IP packets whose destination IP address is 8.1.1.1? (Choose one)

    A. 0.0.0.0/0

    B. 8.2.0.0/16

    C. 8.1.2.0/24

    D. 18.1.0.0/16

8.2   RIP

8.2.1   Routing Protocols

To understand what a routing protocol is, you must first understand the basics of autonomous systems (ASs). In network communications, an AS is a set of Layer 2 networks and routers administered by a single entity. An internetwork can contain one or more ASs. For example, the internetwork shown in Fig. 8.7 contains three ASs: X, Y, and Z.

    Routing protocols are classified as interior gateway protocols (IGPs) or exterior gateway protocols (EGPs). IGPs are used to exchange routing information with routers in the same AS. IGPs include Routing Information Protocol (RIP), Open Shortest Path First (OSPF), and Intermediate System to Intermediate System (IS-IS). EGPs are used between routers in different ASs. An example of an EGP is Border Gateway Protocol (BGP), which is the only EGP currently used.

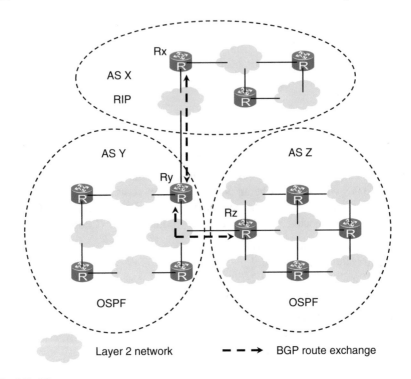

Fig. 8.7 ASs

In an AS, all routers generally run one IGP specified by the AS's administrative entity; however, running multiple IGPs in an AS is possible. Each router running an IGP is able to discover routes to all destination networks within this AS. In scenarios where multiple ASs comprise an internetwork, BGP enables the exchange of routing information between different ASs. The exchange of routing information allows each router to discover routes to destinations both inside and outside the AS in which it resides.

For example, on the internetwork shown in Fig. 8.7, all routers (including Rx) in AS X run RIP, and all routers (including Ry and Rz) in AS Y and AS Z run OSPF. Rx, Ry, and Rz must also run BGP to enable the exchange of routing information between ASs, which thereby allows each router to discover routes to all destinations on the internetwork.

8.2.2 Basic Principles of RIP

RIP is a distance-vector IGP and has a preference of 100. Compared with other routing protocols, RIP is simple and easy to implement.

RIP uses a hop count as the route cost. A hop count is the number of routers through which a packet passes to reach its destination. On the network shown in Fig. 8.8, R1 uses 1 hop to reach Network A, 2 hops to Network B, 3 hops to Network C, and 4 hops to Network D. RIP defines as unreachable any route whose hop count is greater than or equal to 16. Due to this hop limit, RIP is applicable only to small-scale networks.

To explain the workings of RIP, let's use an analogy. Imagine that a number of children join hands to form a circle. This circle can be thought of as a RIP network. At the beginning, each child knows the name only of the person with whom they are holding hands. Periodically, each child tells their neighbors the names of the people they know. As time progresses, all of the children will come to discover the names of all those forming the circle. RIP works in a similar manner, whereby routers send to their neighbors the routing information of which they are aware.

A router that runs RIP is called a RIP router. If RIP is used as the IGP within an AS, all routers in this AS are RIP routers and this AS is called a RIP network. In addition to its IP routing table, each RIP router also has a RIP routing table that stores routes discovered by RIP.

When a RIP router initially creates a RIP routing table, this table is in the initial state and contains only the direct routes that the router has automatically discovered. Once every 30 s, each RIP router sends to all of its neighbors an update message that contains all routing information stored in its updated RIP routing table. The RIP routers then use the routing information they receive to update their RIP routing tables. After RIP route convergence is complete, RIP routing tables no longer change and, instead, enter the stable state. A RIP routing table in the stable state contains routes to all destinations on the RIP network; however, the exchange of routing information continues so that, if the network topology changes, each RIP routing table is updated accordingly. Upon RIP routing convergence after an update, each RIP routing table again enters the stable state.

8.2.3 RIP Routing Table

A RIP routing table stores routes discovered by RIP. The following example describes how a RIP router uses the routing information it receives from its neighbors to update its RIP routing table. Assume that Ry's RIP routing table

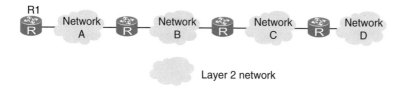

Fig. 8.8 Hops

contains a route with the destination/mask z/y and cost n $(1 \le n \le 16)$. Ry sends this route to Rx through its Interface-y, and Rx receives this route through Interface-x. Rx's Interface-x and Ry's Interface-y reside on the same Layer 2 network. After Rx receives the route, it uses the distance-vector algorithm (also called the Bellman-Ford algorithm) to update its RIP routing table. In the algorithm implementation, if $n + 1 < 16$, then $m = n + 1$; if $n + 1 \ge 16$, then $m = 16$.

1. If Rx's RIP routing table does not have a routing entry to the destination/mask z/y, Rx injects a routing entry into its RIP routing table, with the destination/mask z/y, outbound interface being Rx's Interface-x, next-hop IP address being the IP address of Ry's Interface-y, and cost being m.
2. If Rx's RIP routing table has a routing entry to the destination/mask z/y with the next-hop IP address being the IP address of Ry's Interface-y, Rx updates the outbound interface to Rx's Interface-x, next-hop IP address to the IP address of Ry's Interface-y, and cost to m.
3. If Rx's RIP routing table has a routing entry to the destination/mask z/y but the next-hop IP address is not the IP address of Ry's Interface-y and the cost is greater than m, Rx updates the outbound interface of the routing entry to Rx's Interface-x, next-hop IP address to the IP address of Ry's Interface-y, and cost to m.
4. If Rx's RIP routing table has a routing entry to the destination/mask z/y but the next-hop IP address is not the IP address of Ry's Interface-y and the cost is less than or equal to m, Rx does not update the routing entry; specifically, it retains the outbound interface, next-hop IP address, and cost of this routing entry.

Figure 8.9 shows how RIP routing tables are generated. As a practice exercise, see if you can determine what the RIP routing table is in the stable state. To check whether you are right, see Fig. 8.10.

8.2.4 RIP Message Format

RIP routers exchange two types of RIP messages: request and response messages. When a RIP router starts up, it sends a RIP request to all of its neighbors to request routing information of the entire RIP network. A running RIP router can also send such a message. Upon receipt of a RIP request, a RIP router immediately replies with a RIP response that contains the routing information of which the router is aware. In addition, each RIP router sends to all of its neighbors, every 30 s, a RIP response messages that contains its updated RIP routing information.

RIP is available in two versions, RIP version 1 (RIP-1) and RIP version 2 (RIP-2), which are compared in subsequent sections. This section describes the RIP-1 message format.

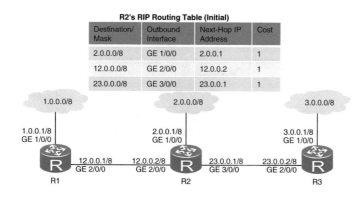

Fig. 8.9 RIP routing table in the initial state

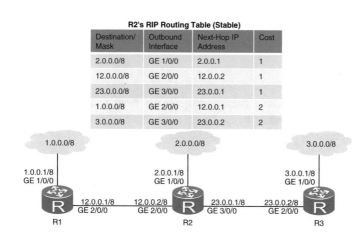

Fig. 8.10 RIP routing table in the stable state

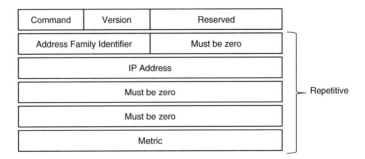

Fig. 8.11 RIP-1 message format

The fields in a RIP-1 message, shown in Fig. 8.11, are described as follows:

Command
This 8-bit field specifies whether the message is a request or response. The value 1 indicates a request, and the value 2 indicates a response.

Version
This 8-bit field specifies the RIP version. The value 1 indicates a RIP-1 message, and the value 2 indicates a RIP-2 message.

Address Family Identifier
This 16-bit field specifies the protocol suite in use. The value 2 indicates the TCP/IP protocol suite.

IP Address
This 32-bit field specifies the destination network address of a routing entry. The 14 bytes following the address family identifier are used to identify the destination network address of a routing entry. Because the protocol suite used is TCP/IP, only 4 bytes are used to identify the network address, and the others are set to 0.

Metric
This 32-bit field specifies the hop count (cost). The cost has a value ranging from 1 to 16. The value 16 indicates that the route is unreachable.

In Fig. 8.11, the portion from the Address Family Identifier through Metric can be repeated up to 25 times, which means that a RIP message can contain up to 25 routes.

A RIP router can send a RIP request to request some or all routing information of a RIP network. Figure 8.12 shows the difference between the RIP-1 requests.

The following is an example of a RIP response. On the network shown in Fig. 8.13, R1, R2, and R3 all run RIP-1 and are in the route convergence state. R1's RIP routing table contains four routing entries. R1 periodically sends a RIP response containing these entries.

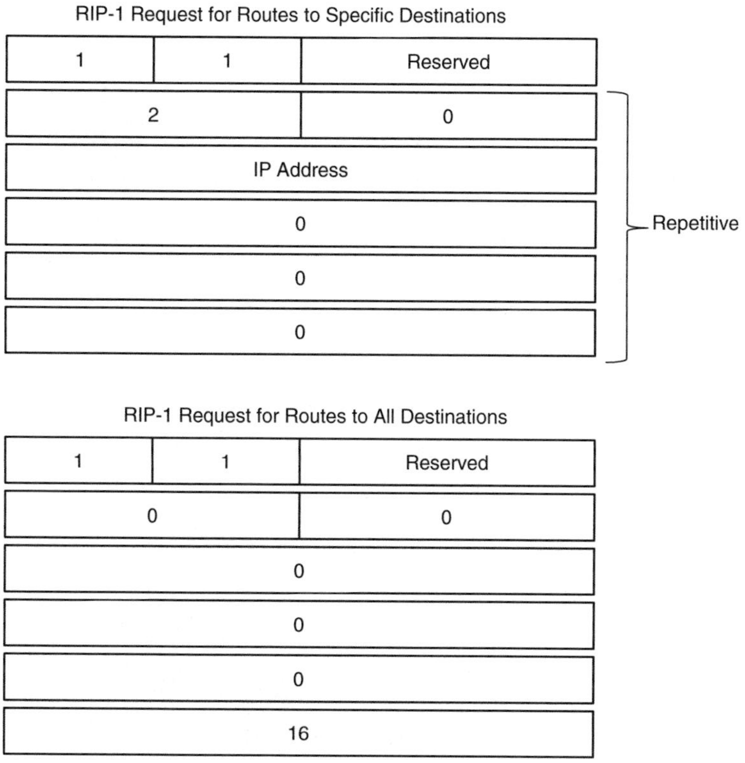

RIP-1 Request for Routes to Specific Destinations

1	1	Reserved
2		0
IP Address		
0		
0		
0		

— Repetitive

RIP-1 Request for Routes to All Destinations

1	1	Reserved
0		0
0		
0		
0		
16		

Fig. 8.12   Two RIP-1 requests

8.2.5   *RIP-1 and RIP-2*

As mentioned above, RIP has two versions: RIP-1 and RIP-2. Figure 8.14 shows the RIP-2 message format.

Command
This 8-bit field specifies whether the message is a request or response, identical to RIP-1.

Version
This 8-bit field specifies the RIP version, identical to RIP-1. The value 2 indicates a RIP-2 message.

Address Family Identifier
This 16-bit field specifies the protocol suite in use, identical to RIP-1.

Route Flag
This 16-bit field carries AS numbers to receive BGP information. The usage scenario and method of this field is beyond the scope of this book.

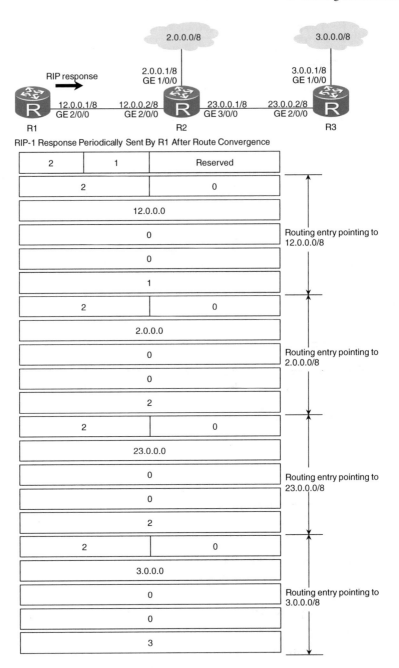

Fig. 8.13 RIP response

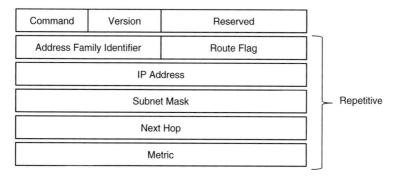

Fig. 8.14 RIP-2 message format

IP Address
This 32-bit field specifies the destination network address of a routing entry, identical to RIP-1.

Subnet Mask
This 32-bit field contains the subnet mask applied to the IP address.

Next Hop
This 32-bit field specifies the next-hop IP address of the destination network. The usage scenario and method of this field is beyond the scope of this book.

Metric
This 32-bit field specifies the hop count or cost, identical to RIP-1.

RIP-2 extends the message format of RIP-1, allowing RIP routers to share additional information. Most importantly, RIP-2 messages can carry subnet mask information, whereas RIP-1 message cannot. Therefore, RIP-2 supports classless routing and variable length subnet mask (VLSM) and classless inter-domain routing (CIDR), whereas RIP-1 applies only to classful addressing scenarios in which the default mask is used to implement classful routing.

In addition, RIP-2 provides an authentication mechanism, which is lacking in RIP-1. The authentication mechanism is used to prevent false information being advertised by malicious routers. Figure 8.15 shows the RIP-2 format with the authentication mechanism.

Message encapsulation

Both RIP-1 and RIP-2 messages are encapsulated into UDP packets, which are sent and received on the port numbered 520. The UDP packets are then encapsulated into IP packets. In RIP-1 implementation, an IP packet that contains a RIP-1 request or periodic response (update message) has the destination address being the broadcast address 255.255.255.255, the source address being the IP address of the interface that sends the request or response, and the Protocol field value 0x11. An IP packet that contains a RIP response sent in reply to a request has the

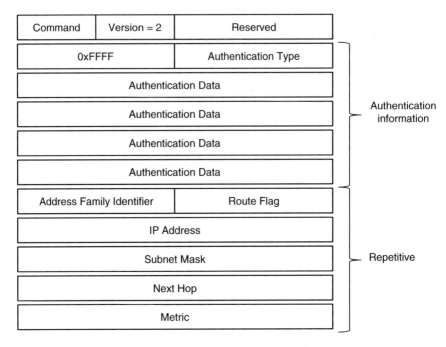

Fig. 8.15 RIP-2 message format with the authentication mechanism

destination address being the IP address of the interface that sent the request, the source address being the IP address of the interface that sent the response, and the Protocol field value being 0x11.

Suppose that all interfaces on a router are Ethernet interfaces. For an IP packet that contains a RIP-1 request or periodic response, the packet is encapsulated into an Ethernet frame, which has the destination address being the broadcast MAC address ff-ff-ff-ff-ff-ff, the source address being the MAC address of the interface that sent the RIP-1 request or periodic response, and the Type field value being 0x0800. For an IP packet that contains a RIP-1 response sent in reply to a request, the packet is encapsulated into an Ethernet frame, which has the destination address being the MAC address of the interface that sent the request, the source address being the MAC address of the interface that sent the response, and the Type field value being 0x0800.

In RIP-2 implementation, an IP packet that contains a RIP-2 request or periodic response (update message) has the destination address being the multicast address 224.0.0.9 (which points to all RIP-2 routers) or the broadcast address 255.255.255.255, the source address being the IP address of the interface that sent the request or response, and the Protocol field value 0x11. An IP packet that contains a RIP response sent in reply to a request has the destination address being the IP address of the interface that sent the request, the source address being the IP address of the interface that sent the response, and the Protocol field value being 0x11.

Again, suppose that all interfaces on a router are Ethernet interfaces. For an IP packet that contains a RIP-2 request or periodic response, the packet is encapsulated into an Ethernet frame, which has the destination address being the broadcast MAC address ff-ff-ff-ff-ff-ff or a specific multicast MAC address, the source address being the MAC address of the interface that sent the request or periodic response, and the Type field value being 0x0800. For an IP packet that contains a RIP-2 response sent in reply to a request, the packet is encapsulated into an Ethernet frame, which has the destination address being the MAC address of the interface that sent the request, the source address being the MAC address of the interface that sent the response, and the Type field value being 0x0800.

The encapsulation procedures differ for RIP-1 and RIP-2 messages. This difference allows RIP-2 to consume fewer resources than RIP-1. On the network shown in Fig. 8.16, if R1 and R2 both run RIP-1, they periodically send RIP-1 responses (update messages) through their GE 1/0/0. Upon receipt of these RIP-1 responses, the switch floods the broadcast frames to the PC. After the PC receives the broadcast frames, it determines the frames' Type field value 0x0800 and sends the IP packets (the payload of the frames) to its network-layer IP module. The IP module determines that the destination address of the received packets is the broadcast IP address 255.255.255.255 and that the Protocol field value is 0x11. Then, the IP module sends the UDP packets (the payload of the IP packets) to the PC's transport-layer UDP module, which determines that the port specified in the packets is UDP port 520 (used by RIP). However, because the PC does not run RIP, its application layer does not have the RIP module and therefore the UDP module discards the UDP packets.

If R1 and R2 both run RIP-2, they periodically send RIP-2 responses through their GE 1/0/0. Assume that the RIP-2 responses are encapsulated into broadcast frames. After the switch receives the broadcast frames, it floods the broadcast frames to the PC. Upon receipt of the broadcast frames, the PC determines the frames' Type field value 0x0800 and sends the IP packets (the payload of the frames) to its network-layer IP module. If the IP packets' destination address is the multicast address 224.0.0.9 but the PC does not run RIP-2, the PC's IP module discards these IP packets.

Despite the PC not running RIP, RIP consumes the PC's resources. However, because the PC discards packets that contain RIP-2 messages sooner than those

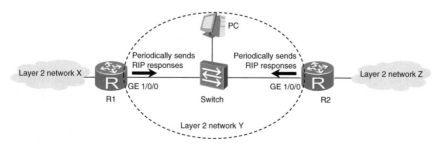

Fig. 8.16 RIP networking

containing RIP-1 messages (specifically, RIP-2 messages are discarded at the network layer, RIP-1 at the transport layer), RIP-2 consumes fewer resources than RIP-1 does.

Compared with RIP-1, RIP-2 has the following advantages:

- Added functions. RIP-2 supports classless routes and VLSM and CIDR, whereas RIP-1 supports only classful routes.
- Enhanced security. RIP-2 supports authentication, whereas RIP-1 does not.
- Consumption of fewer processing resources. RIP-2 can use multicast to advertise messages, whereas RIP-1 cannot.

Further differences exist between RIP-1 and RIP-2, but RIP-2 is backward compatible with RIP-1. How RIP-1 and RIP-2 are used together on live networks is beyond the scope of this book.

8.2.6   RIP Timers

RIP uses three timers: update timer, invalid timer, and garbage-collection timer.

Update timer

Each RIP router has a RIP update timer, which periodically triggers the transmission of update messages. The update timer, also called the periodic timer, counts down from 30 s by default. After the update timer expires, the router sends a RIP response to all of its neighbors. In addition to sending a RIP response upon receipt of a request, the router periodically sends RIP responses each time the update timer expires.

Invalid timer

Each RIP router creates and maintains an invalid timer for each routing entry in the RIP routing table. The invalid timer, also called the age timer, counts down from 180 s by default, which is 6 times the update timer value. Each time a routing entry is created or updated, the invalid timer is reset and starts over. A routing entry is updated every 30 s. If a routing entry is not updated for 180 s, specifically, the invalid timer of a routing entry becomes 0, the router considers the routing entry invalid and the destination unreachable. Then, the router sets the cost of the route to 16.

Garbage-collection timer

When the invalid timer of a routing entry expires, the entry becomes invalid and the cost of the route is set to 16. However, the router does not immediately delete the invalid route; instead, the router starts a garbage-collection timer for this route. The garbage-collection timer has an initial value of 120 s. Before the garbage-collection timer expires, the route is included in all updates sent by the router to inform its neighbors of the route's invalidity. Once the garbage-collection timer expires, the router deletes the invalid route as well as the invalid and garbage-collection timers for the route. If the invalid route is updated to a valid route with the cost less than 16 before the garbage-collection timer expires, the invalid timer will be reset and starts again, and the garbage-collection timer is deleted.

Now, assume that the RIP routing table of a RIP router contains 30 routing entries. Of these entries, 23 have a cost less than 16, and 7 have a cost of 16. How many RIP timers are running?

Let's analyze the question. Among the 30 invalid timers (the RIP router creates such a timer for each routing entry), 23 are running and 7 have expired. Therefore, 7 garbage-collection timers and 1 update timer, in addition to the 23 invalid timers, are running. As a result, 31 (23 + 7 + 1 = 31) RIP timers are running.

8.2.7 Routing Loops

The distance-vector algorithm (the Bellman-Ford algorithm) is easy to implement but susceptible to routing loops. The following example describes this susceptibility.

On the RIP network shown in Fig. 8.17, route convergence is complete. R3's RIP routing table contains a route to the destination network 3.0.0.0/8, with the outbound interface being R3's GE 1/0/0, next-hop IP address being 3.0.0.1, and cost being 1. R2's RIP routing table also has a route to the destination 3.0.0.0/8, with the outbound interface being R2's GE 3/0/0, next-hop IP address being 23.0.0.2, and cost being 2.

Assume that R3's physical link to 3.0.0.0/8 is broken. As a result, R3's GE 1/0/0 cannot forward packets through this link. After detecting the fault, R3 sets to 16 the cost of the route to the destination 3.0.0.0/8 in its RIP routing table, indicating that the route is unreachable (invalid route). Before this invalid route is sent to R2 in the next periodic routing update, R3 receives from R2 the routing information about 3.0.0.0/8. R3 then updates the invalid route to 3.0.0.0/8 as a valid route in the RIP routing table, with the outbound interface updated to R3's GE 2/0/0, next-hop IP address to 23.0.0.1, and cost to 3. Therefore, despite the link failure between R3 and 3.0.0.0/8, R3 assumes it can reach 3.0.0.0/8 through R2. R2 and R3 each have a valid route to 3.0.0.0/8, with the next hop of the route being the other device. If R2

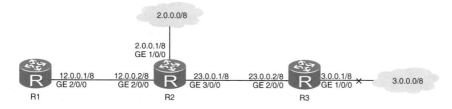

Fig. 8.17 RIP routing loop

or R3 forwards an IP packet destined for 3.0.0.0/8, the IP packet is looped between R2 and R3, resulting in a routing loop between the two devices.

Routing loops disrupt network operation. To address this problem, RIP provides triggered update, split horizon, and poison reverse.

Triggered update

Triggered update allows a router to advertise RIP responses upon changes to routing information in an attempt to speed up route convergence and reduce the probability of routing loops. To decrease consumption of bandwidth and router resources, the triggered updates contain only routing entries with changed routing information.

On the network shown in Fig. 8.18, triggered update is enabled on R3. After route convergence, R3's RIP routing table contains a route to the destination network 3.0.0.0/8, with the outbound interface being R3's GE 1/0/0, next-hop IP address being 3.0.0.1, and cost being 1. R2's RIP routing table also contains a route to the destination network 3.0.0.0/8, with the outbound interface being R2's GE 3/0/0, next-hop IP address being 23.0.0.2, and cost being 2.

Assume that R3's physical link to 3.0.0.0/8 is broken. As a result, R3's GE 1/0/0 cannot forward packets through this link. After detecting the fault, R3 sets to 16 the cost of the route to the destination 3.0.0.0/8 in its RIP routing table, indicating that the route is unreachable (invalid route). Because the routing entry to 3.0.0.0/8 has changed in R3's RIP routing table, R3 sends a triggered update about 3.0.0.0/8 to R2. Upon receipt of the update, R2 uses the distance-vector algorithm to update to 16 the cost of the route to 3.0.0.0/8 in its RIP routing table. R2 and R3 continue to send RIP responses periodically; however, they retain the cost of the route to 3.0.0.0/8 in their RIP routing tables. Therefore, R2 and R3 consider the routes to 3.0.0.0/8 unreachable. After R2 or R3 receives an IP packet destined for 3.0.0.0/8, it directly discards the packet.

Split horizon

Split horizon prevents routes being sent from a RIP interface back to the interface from which the routes were learned, thereby preventing routing loops.

In the preceding example (describing triggered update), if R3 receives a periodic response from R2 before R2 receives the triggered update from R3, a routing loop

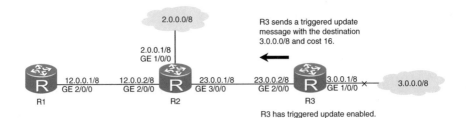

Fig. 8.18 Triggered update

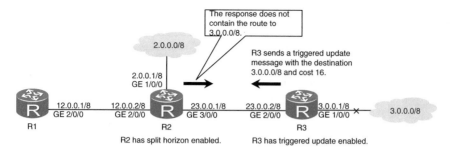

Fig. 8.19 Split horizon networking

occurs. Triggered update cannot prevent routing loops from occurring; it only reduces the probability that routing loops occur. In split horizon, if a router's RIP routing table contains a route with the destination/mask z/y and the route is learned from the router's Interface-x, split horizon prevents the router from sending out this route through Interface-x.

On the network shown in Fig. 8.19, R3 has triggered update enabled, and R2 has split horizon enabled. After route convergence, R3's RIP routing table contains a route to the destination network 3.0.0.0/8, with the outbound interface being R3's GE 1/0/0, next-hop IP address being 3.0.0.1, and cost being 1. R2's RIP routing table also contains a route to the destination network 3.0.0.0/8, with the outbound interface being R2's GE 3/0/0, next-hop IP address being 23.0.0.2, and cost being 2. Because the routing entry for 3.0.0.0/8 in R2's RIP routing table has the outbound interface being R2's GE 3/0/0 (indicating that this routing entry was learned by R2's GE 3/0/0), information about the route to 3.0.0.0/8 is not sent when R2 sends out RIP responses through GE 3/0/0.

Assume that R3's physical link to 3.0.0.0/8 is broken. As a result, R3's GE 1/0/0 cannot forward packets through this link. After detecting the fault, R3 sets to 16 the cost of the route to 3.0.0.0/8 and sends R2 a triggered update message about the route to 3.0.0.0/8. Even if R3 receives a periodic response from R2 before R2 receives a triggered update message from R3, no routing loop will occur. Upon receipt of the update, R2 uses the distance-vector algorithm to update to 16 the cost of the route to 3.0.0.0/8 in its RIP routing table. R2 and R3 continue to send RIP responses periodically; however, they retain the cost of the route to 3.0.0.0/8 in their RIP routing tables. When the garbage-collection timer expires, the routing entry is deleted from the RIP routing table.

Poison reverse

Poison reverse allows a RIP interface to set the cost of a route learned from a neighbor to 16 (indicating that the route is unreachable) and then send this route back to the neighbor. If a router's RIP routing table contains a route with the destination/mask z/y and the route is learned from the router's Interface-x, poison reverse allows the router to set the cost of the route to 16 before sending responses that contain the route with the destination/mask z/y through Interface-x.

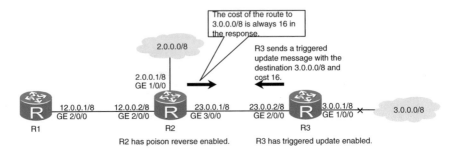

Fig. 8.20 Poison reverse

On the network shown in Fig. 8.20, R3 has triggered update enabled, and R2 has poison reverse enabled. After route convergence, R3's RIP routing table contains a route to the destination network 3.0.0.0/8, with the outbound interface being R3's GE 1/0/0, next-hop IP address being 3.0.0.1, and cost being 1. R2's RIP routing table also contains a route to the destination network 3.0.0.0/8, with the outbound interface being R2's GE 3/0/0, next-hop IP address being 23.0.0.2, and cost being 2. The routing entry for 3.0.0.0/8 in R2's RIP routing table has the outbound interface being R2's GE 3/0/0, indicating that this routing entry was learned by R2's GE 3/0/0. When R2 sends RIP responses through GE 3/0/0, the responses must contain the routing entry for 3.0.0.0/8, but the cost is always 16.

Assume that R3's physical link to 3.0.0.0/8 is broken. As a result, R3's GE 1/0/0 cannot forward packets through this link. After detecting the fault, R3 sets to 16 the cost of the route to 3.0.0.0/8 and sends R2 a triggered update message about the route to 3.0.0.0/8. Even if R3 receives a periodic response from R2 before R2 receives a triggered update message from R3, no routing loop will occur.

Poison reverse and split horizon prevent routing loops; however, they are incompatible with each other and only one can be enabled on a RIP router. Generally, either split horizon or poison reverse is enabled after triggered update is enabled on a RIP router.

8.2.8 RIP Configuration Example

On the network shown in Fig. 8.21, an enterprise has three routers. R2 resides in the HQ, and R1 and R3 reside in branches A and B, respectively. R1, R2, and R3 all run RIP to implement connectivity.

Configuration Roadmap

Start RIP processes on the routers and enable the routers to advertise network segment information.

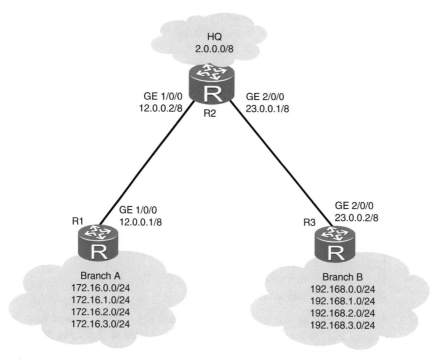

Fig. 8.21 RIP configuration example

Procedure

Step 1   Run the **rip** [*process-id*] command in the system view to create a RIP
process and enter the RIP view. If *process-id* is not specified, RIP process
1 is created by default.
Configure R1.

```
<R1> system-view
[R1] rip
[R1-rip-1]
```

Configure R2.

```
<R2> system-view
[R2] rip
[R2-rip-1]
```

Configure R3.

```
<R3> system-view
[R3] rip
[R3-rip-1]
```

Step 2 Run the **network** *network-address* command to advertise a specified network segment. *network-address* must be a natural network segment address.
Configure R1.

```
[R1-rip-1] network 12.0.0.0
[R1-rip-1] network 172.16.0.0
```

Configure R2.

```
[R2-rip-1] network 12.0.0.0
[R2-rip-1] network 23.0.0.0
[R2-rip-1] network 2.0.0.0
```

Configure R3.

```
[R3-rip-1] network 23.0.0.0
[R3-rip-1] network 192.168.0.0
[R3-rip-1] network 192.168.1.0
[R3-rip-1] network 192.168.2.0
[R3-rip-1] network 192.168.3.0
```

Step 3 After completing the configuration, check the configurations. Run the **display rip** [*process-id*] command on each router to check the RIP configurations. The following example uses the command output on R1.

```
<R1> display rip
  Public VPN-instance
    RIP process : 1
      RIP version : 1
      Preference : 100
  …
        Update time   : 30 sec  Age time  : 180 sec
        Garbage-collect time : 120 sec
  …
        Networks :
        12.0.0.0      172.16.0.0
  …
```

In the command output:

RIP process: 1 indicates that the RIP process ID is 1.
RIP version: 1 indicates that RIPv1 is running.
Preference: 100 indicates that the RIP preference value is 100.
Update time: 30 s indicates that the update timer value is 30 s.
Age time: 180 s indicates that the invalid timer value is 180 s.
Garbage-collect time: 120 s indicates that the garbage-collection timer is 120 s.

Run the **display rip** *process-id* **route** command on R1 to check RIP routes learned from other routers.

```
<R1> display rip 1 route
Route Flags: R - RIP
             A - Aging, G - Garbage-collect
----------------------------------------------------------------------
Destination/Mask     Nexthop      Cost     Tag Flags     Sec
 2.0.0.0/8           12.0.0.2     1        0   RA        15
 23.0.0.0/8          12.0.0.2     1        0   RA        15
 192.168.0.0/24      12.0.0.2     2        0   RA        15
 192.168.1.0/24      12.0.0.2     2        0   RA        15
 192.168.2.0/24      12.0.0.2     2        0   RA        15
 192.168.3.0/24      12.0.0.2     2        0   RA        15
```

The command output shows that R1 has learned routes to 2.0.0.0/8, 23.0.0.0/8, 192.168.0.0/24, 192.168.1.0/24, 192.168.2.0/24, 192.168.3.0/24, all of which are indirect routes.

8.2.9 Review Questions

1. Which of the following statements are true? (Choose all that apply)

   A. RIP is a static routing protocol.
   B. RIP is an exterior gateway protocol (EGP).
   C. OSPF is an interior gateway protocol (IGP).
   D. RIP is a distance-vector routing protocol.

2. How many routing entries can a RIP response contain at most? (Choose one)

   A. 1
   B. 15
   C. 25
   D. 35

3. Which of the following options are not used to prevent RIP routing loops? (Choose all that apply)

   A. Triggered update
   B. Split horizon
   C. Poison reverse
   D. Distance vector algorithm

4. What is the maximum allowable length of a RIP response before it is encapsulated into a UDP packet? (Choose one)

   A. 204 bytes
   B. 304 bytes
   C. 404 bytes
   D. 504 bytes

5. Which of the following statements are RIP-2 advantages over RIP-1? (Choose all that apply)

   A. RIP-2 can send RIP messages in multicast mode
   B. RIP-2 supports authentication.
   C. RIP-2 can use the hop count as well as bandwidth as a route cost.
   D. RIP-2 supports classless routing.

6. Which of the following statements are true? (Choose all that apply)

   A. A RIP router can have both triggered update and split horizon configured.
   B. A RIP router can have both triggered update and poison reverse configured.
   C. A RIP router can have both poison reverse and split horizon configured.
   D. A RIP router can have triggered update, split horizon, and poison reverse all configured.

8.3   OSPF

Open Shortest Path First (OSPF) is a link-state Interior Gateway Protocol (IGP). An AS running OSPF as its IGP is an OSPF network.

OSPF is far more complex and, consequently, far more difficult to learn than RIP. The following sections describe the basic concepts and terms used in OSPF.

8.3.1   Basic Principles of OSPF

To explain the workings of OSPF, let's use an analogy based on that used for RIP in Sect. 8.2.2 "Basic Principles of RIP."

Similar to the RIP analogy, imagine that a number of children join hands to form a circle, with each child knowing the name only of the person with whom they are holding hands. This OSPF analogy differs in that, instead of each child periodically telling their neighbor the names of the people they know, each child tells the entire circle. This circle can be thought of as an area on an OSPF network. After all of the children have told each other the names of the people they know, the entire circle knows all of these names.

The key differences between the RIP and OSPF analogies are:

1. In RIP, each child speaks to and hears from only their neighbor. In OSPF, each child speaks to and hears from everyone.
2. In RIP, each child tells their neighbor the updated names of the people they know. In OSPF, each child tells everyone only the names of their neighbors.
3. In RIP, each child periodically and repeatedly tells their neighbor the names of the people they know. In OSPF, each child tells everyone the names of the people they know only once.

OSPF works in a similar manner, whereby routers flood their link state information to all routers all at once.

8.3.2 Comparison Between OSPF and RIP

OSPF is a link-state routing protocol, whereas RIP is a distance-vector routing protocol. (Link state is described in Sect. 8.3.5 "Link State and LSA.")

RIP allows routers to transfer routing information one after another. OSPF allows routers to advertise routing information to all. Therefore, OSPF route convergence takes less time than RIP route convergence.

After route convergence, RIP may continue to generate a large amount of RIP traffic, whereas OSPF generates little OSPF traffic. The less the protocol packet traffic, the less network bandwidth resources are consumed.

RIP uses UDP as the transport layer protocol, and RIP messages are encapsulated into UDP packets. OSPF does not have any transport layer protocol, and OSPF packets are encapsulated into IP packets. UDP and IP are both connectionless and unreliable; however, both RIP and OSPF provide reliable transmission.

RIP messages are classified as RIP requests or responses. OSPF packets are classified as Hello, Database Description (DD), Link State Request (LSR), Link State Update (LSU), or Link State Acknowledgment (LSAck) packets.

RIP uses a hop count as the route cost. OSPF can use one or more parameters as a route cost. For example, OSPF can use the link bandwidth, link delay, or link cost as the route cost. The most commonly used route cost for OSPF is the link bandwidth.

RIP and OSPF are both open standards defined by the Internet Engineering Task Force (IETF). OSPF has two versions: OSPFv1 and OSPFv2. However, OSPFv2 is the only version currently in use. Similar to RIPv2, OSPF is a classless routing protocol that supports VLSM and CIDR as well as authentication.

An OSPF network allows for area partitioning, whereas a RIP network does not. On an OSPF network, routers are assigned different roles and have different functions. On a RIP network, routers are not assigned roles. Each OSPF router has a unique router ID, whereas a RIP router does not.

Both RIP and OSPF are widely applied. However, RIP applies to small-scale networks, whereas OSPF applies to networks of any scale.

Despite the protocol complexity, OSPF is advantageous over RIP.

8.3.3 OSPF Areas

OSPF networks can be partitioned into different areas. An OSPF network with only one area is a single-area OSPF network, and an OSPF network with multiple areas is a multi-area OSPF network.

Each OSPF area is identified by an area ID, which can be a 32-bit binary number or a decimal number. Area 0 is the backbone area, and all other areas are non-backbone areas. The single area that a single-area OSPF network contains must be the backbone area. A multi-area OSPF network has one backbone area and several non-backbone areas directly connecting to the backbone area. Non-backbone areas cannot directly connect to each other. When virtual links are used, non-backbone areas and the backbone area are directly connected logically but not physically. In other words, non-backbone areas must communicate through the backbone area.

The OSPF network shown in Fig. 8.22 consists of four areas, in which Area 0 is the backbone area. On R9, the upper interface belongs to Area 2, and the lower interface belongs to Area 0. Similarly, R10 has its two interfaces in Area 3 and two interfaces in Area 0. R1 has one interface in Area 0 and three interfaces in Area 1.

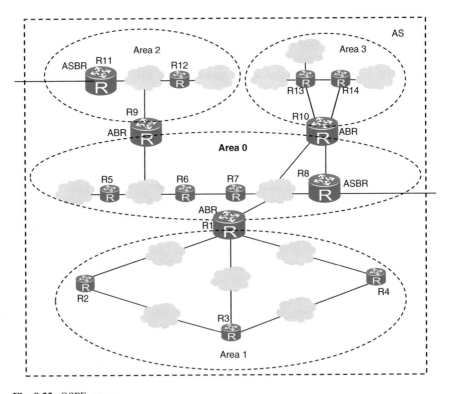

Fig. 8.22 OSPF areas

On an OSPF network, if all interfaces on a router belong to the same area, the router is an internal router. For example, Area 0 has four internal routers: R5, R6, R7, and R8. Area 1 has three internal routers: R2, R3, and R4. Area 2 has two internal routers: R11 and R12. Area 3 has two internal routers: R13 and R14.

If at least one interface on a router belongs to Area 0, the router is a backbone router. The example OSPF network has seven backbone routers: R5, R6, R7, R8, R1, R9, and R10.

If a router has some interfaces in Area 0 and the other interfaces in other areas, the router is an area border router (ABR). The example OSPF network has three ABRs: R1, R9, and R10.

If a router exchanges routing information with other ASs, the router is an autonomous system boundary router (ASBR). The example OSPF network has two ASBRs: R8 and R11. An ASBR can be an internal router or an ABR.

8.3.4 OSPF Network Types

OSPF supports the following types of Layer 2 networks:

- Broadcast network (An Ethernet network is a typical broadcast network.)
- Non-broadcast multi-access (NBMA) network
- Point-to-point (P2P) network
- Point-to-multipoint (P2MP) network

The type of an OSPF router interface must be the same as the type of the Layer 2 network directly connected to the interface. For example, if an interface connects to a broadcast network, the interface must be a broadcast interface; if an interface connects to a P2P network, the interface must be a P2P interface.

On a broadcast or NBMA network, a designated router (DR) and a backup designated router (BDR) must be elected. For details on the DR and BDR, see Sect. 8.3.10 "DR and BDR."

8.3.5 Link State and LSA

OSPF is a link-state routing protocol. The link state is the router interface state, which contains the following information:

- IP address and mask of the interface
- Area ID
- Router ID of the router on which the interface resides
- Interface type, which is also the connected Layer 2 network type (broadcast, NBMA, P2P, or P2MP)

- Interface cost (The interface bandwidth is commonly used as the interface cost. The higher the bandwidth, the lower the cost.)
- Router Priority (for DR and BDR election)
- DR on the connected Layer 2 network
- BDR on the connected Layer 2 network
- HelloInterval (interval at which Hello packets are sent)
- RouterDeadInterval (If a router does not receive any Hello packets from its neighbors within a specified dead interval, the neighbors are considered Down.)
- All neighbors
- Authentication type
- Key

OSPF allows each router to advertise the interface or link state to other routers. Then, each router is able to calculate the routes to the destinations based on the interface states of its own and other routers.

There are more than 10 types of link state advertisements (LSAs). This section describes the following LSAs:

- Type 1 LSA (router-LSA)
- Type 2 LSA (network-LSA)
- Type 3 LSA (network-summary-LSA)
- Type 4 LSA (ASBR-summary-LSA)
- Type 5 LSA (AS-external-LSA)

Link state information is carried in LSAs and shared after LSAs are flooded. Routers that perform different roles generate different types of LSAs. Different types of LSAs carry different link state information and have different functions and advertisement scope. For example:

- Type 1 LSA: is originated by any router. This LSA describes the type, IP address, and cost of every interface on the router. Type 1 LSAs are flooded only within the area where they are originated.
- Type 2 LSA: is originated by a DR. This LSA describes the network masks and all routers on the Layer 2 network where the DR resides. Type 2 LSAs are flooded only within the area where they are originated.
- Type 3 LSA: is originated by an ABR. An ABR converts Type 1 and Type 2 LSAs in the areas to which it belongs into Type 3 LSAs that describe inter-area routing information. Type 3 LSAs can be flooded in the entire AS, but not to totally stub areas or totally not-so-stubby areas (NSSAs). The totally stub areas and totally NSSAs are beyond the scope of this book.
- Type 4 LSA: is originated by an ABR in an area where an ASBR resides. This LSA describes routes to the ASBR. Type 4 LSAs can be flooded in the entire AS, but not to stub areas, totally stub areas, NSSAs, or totally NSSAs. These area types are beyond the scope of this book.

- Type 5 LSA: is originated by an ASBR. This LSA describes AS external routes, which are flooded to the entire AS but not to stub areas, totally stub areas, NSSAs, or totally NSSAs.

8.3.6 OSPF Packet Types

OSPF packets are encapsulated into IP packets, with the OSPF protocol number 89 in the IP header. Figure 8.23 shows the encapsulation.

OSPF packets are classified as Hello, DD, LSR, LSU, or LSAck packets, as shown in Fig. 8.24. LSU packets carry all types of LSAs. Other types of OSPF packets do not carry LSAs, but carry link state information as well as other protocol information.

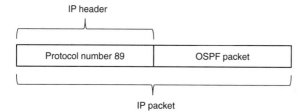

Fig. 8.23 OSPF packet encapsulated in an IP packet

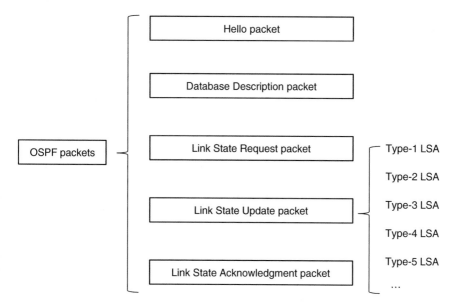

Fig. 8.24 Five types of OSPF packets

This chapter does not describe the five types of OSPF packets in detail. However, knowing what information a Hello packet contains is vital.

A router interface sends a Hello packet that contains (but not limited to) the following information:

1. OSPF version number
2. Router ID of the router on which the interface resides
3. Area ID
4. Authentication type
5. Key
6. Subnet mask of the interface's IP address
7. HelloInterval (interval at which Hello packets are sent)
8. Router Priority (for DR and BDR election)
9. RouterDeadInterval (If a router does not receive any Hello packets from its neighbors within a specified dead interval, the neighbors are considered Down.)
10. DR on the connected Layer 2 network
11. BDR on the connected Layer 2 network
12. All neighbors

8.3.7   Single-Area OSPF Network

A single-area OSPF network has only Area 0, which represents an AS. This OSPF network is shown in Fig. 8.25 and does not contain an ABR. This section describes the OSPF working process on this network, with the assumption that no ASBR exists.

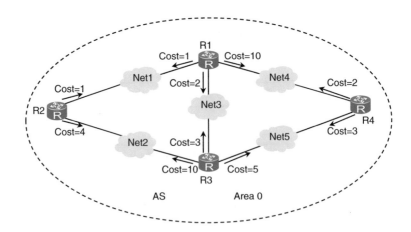

Fig. 8.25 Single-area OSPF network

Link state database (LSDB)

On this single-area OSPF network, each router generates Type 1 LSAs and floods them to Area 0. The DR generates Type 2 LSAs and also floods them to Area 0. Area 0 has only Type 1 and Type 2 LSAs.

Each router combines all LSAs it has generated and received to form an LSDB. An LSDB is a collection of LSAs. Because LSAs are flooded in Area 0, each router can receive the LSAs originated by other routers in Area 0. Eventually, all routers in Area 0 contain the same LSDB.

An LSDB is a map of Area 0, presenting the routers, router interfaces, interface types and costs, and router connections.

Shortest path tree (SPT)

After every router in Area 0 has the same LSDB, each router can find paths to all destinations in Area 0. Because loops exist, a router can reach a destination through different paths. The router must select from all available paths an optimal path with the least cost, which results in SPT generation.

Each router uses the shortest path first (SPF) algorithm to calculate a loop-free SPT, with the router itself as the root. The path from the root to a destination is the optimal path.

The SPF algorithm is also called the Dijkstra algorithm, named after its creator Edsger W. Dijkstra. This chapter does not describe the SPF algorithm in detail. Figure 8.26 shows R1's SPT and R4's SPT.

OSPF routing table

After an OSPF router generates an SPT, it calculates routes to all destinations based on the SPT. These routes form an OSPF routing table. Figure 8.27 shows route calculation for R1.

After route calculation, R1's OSPF routing table should contain (but not limited to) the following routing information:

- Destination: Net1; outbound interface: Intf-11; next-hop IP address: Intf-11's IP address; cost: 1
- Destination: Net2; outbound interface: Intf-11; next-hop IP address: Intf-21's IP address; cost: 5
- Destination: Net3; outbound interface: Intf-12; next-hop IP address: Intf-12's IP address; cost: 2
- Destination: Net4; outbound interface: Intf-12; next-hop IP address: Intf-31's IP address; cost: 9
- Destination: Net5; outbound interface: Intf-12; next-hop IP address: Intf-31's IP address; cost: 7

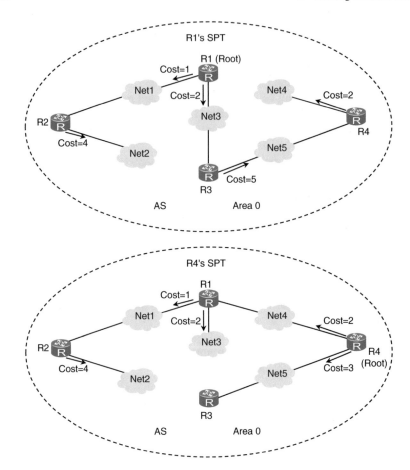

Fig. 8.26 SPTs

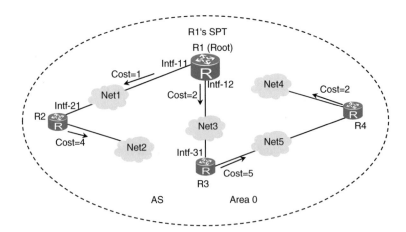

Fig. 8.27 SPT-based route calculation

8.3.8 Multi-area OSPF Network

This chapter briefly describes the OSPF working process on a multi-area OSPF network.

A multi-area OSPF network has both ABRs and ASBRs, and therefore has Type 3, Type 4, and Type 5 LSAs in addition to Type 1 and Type 2 LSAs. This means that the LSDB of a router has all types of LSAs. A router uses the SPF algorithm to calculate an SPT for the local area based on Type 1 and Type 2 LSAs, and then uses the SPT to calculate routes to all destinations in the local area. This process is the same as that on a single-area OSPF network. The router then uses the distance vector algorithm both to calculate routes to destinations in other areas based on Type 3 LSAs and to calculate AS external routes based on Type 4 and Type 5 LSAs.

In the OSPF areas shown in Fig. 8.22, R3 uses the SPF algorithm to calculate the SPT of Area 1 based on Type 1 and Type 2 LSAs, and then uses the SPT to calculate routes to all destinations in Area 1. R3 then uses the distance vector algorithm to calculate routes to destinations in Area 0, Area 2, and Area 3 based on Type 3 LSAs. R3 also uses the distance vector algorithm to calculate routes to destinations outside the OSPF network based on Type 4 and Type 5 LSAs.

The OSPF working process on a multi-area OSPF network is more complex than that on a single-area OSPF network.

8.3.9 Neighbor Relationship and Adjacency

RIP uses the concept of neighbors. A RIP router sends its updated RIP routing information to all of its neighbors every 30 s and also receives updated routing information from its neighbors. Then, the RIP router uses the received routing information to update its RIP routing table. If an interface on RIP router A resides on the same Layer 2 network with an interface on RIP router B, A and B have a neighbor relationship and are neighbors to each other.

OSPF is more complicated. If an interface on OSPF router A resides on the same Layer 2 network with an interface on OSPF router B, A and B are neighboring. This relationship is neither a neighbor relationship nor an adjacency.

Each router uses its OSPF interface to send Hello packets at a specific interval (HelloInterval). If two neighboring routers receive Hello packets with the same parameters as the packets they sent to each other, they establish a neighbor relationship.

If two OSPF neighbors reside on a Layer 2 P2P or P2MP network, they exchange DD, LSR, and LSU packets to synchronize the LSDBs. After LSDB synchronization is complete, the two OSPF neighbors establish an adjacency. LSDB synchronization allows two OSPF neighbors to have the same LSDB. This chapter does not describe the LSDB synchronization process in detail.

If two OSPF neighbors reside on a Layer 2 broadcast or NBMA network, they can synchronize the LSDBs only if either of them is a DR or BDR.

Differentiating an OSPF neighbor relationship from an adjacency is important. Two OSPF routers that have established an adjacency must be neighbors to each other, whereas two OSPF routers that are neighbors may not necessarily establish an adjacency. The number of adjacencies on an OSPF network is always less than or equal to the number of neighbor relationships. LSA flooding is allowed only between OSPF routers that have established an adjacency.

8.3.10 DR and BDR

On a broadcast or NBMA network, a DR and a BDR must be elected. After a DR and a BDR are elected, they establish adjacencies with all other routers, but the other routers cannot establish adjacencies between themselves.

This implementation reduces the number of adjacencies established between routers on a broadcast or NBMA network. If the DR fails, the BDR immediately takes over.

The Layer 2 Ethernet network shown in Fig. 8.28 is a broadcast network that consists of six routers and one Ethernet switch. If any two neighbors establish an adjacency, 15 [6 x (6 − 1)/2] adjacencies will be established.

After a DR and a BDR are elected, only 9 adjacencies must be established. Figure 8.29 shows these adjacencies. The greater the number of routers on the Ethernet network, the more effective a DR and a BDR will be.

To elect a DR, routers on a broadcast or NBMA network exchange Hello packets, each of which contains the priority and ID of the router that has sent the packet. The router priority can be an 8-bit binary number or a decimal number. The value ranges from 0 to 255. The larger the value, the higher the priority. Any router

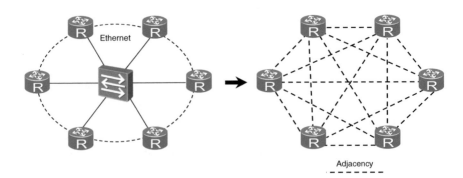

Fig. 8.28 Broadcast network

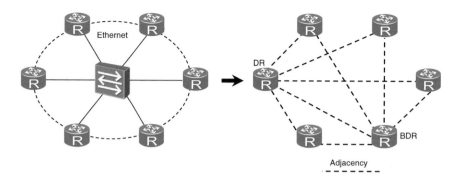

Fig. 8.29 Number of adjacencies reduced

that has a router priority value greater than 0 is eligible for DR and BDR elections. During a DR election, all eligible routers compare the router priority value of each other and elect as the DR the router with the largest router priority value. If two routers have the same largest router priority value, the one with the larger router ID is elected as the DR.

If a broadcast or NBMA network has a DR but no BDR and the DR fails, routers must reselect a DR, which takes time. The use of a BDR shortens the process because the BDR backs up the DR and is ready to take over.

A BDR is elected after a DR is elected, in the same process as the DR election. Note that the DR and BDR cannot be the same router.

The DR or BDR functionality is an interface attribute; it is not a router attribute. A router may be a DR on one Layer 2 network but not a DR on another Layer 2 network.

For example, if R1 in Fig. 8.30 has the router priority value of 10, it will become a DR on Ethernet 2 but cannot be a DR on Ethernet 1.

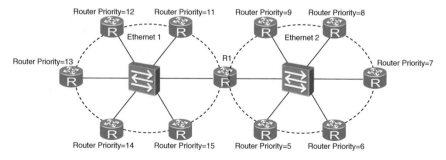

Fig. 8.30 DR/BDR on a router interface

8.3.11 OSPF Configuration Example

On the network shown in Fig. 8.31, an enterprise has three routers. R2 resides in the HQ, and R1 and R3 reside in branches in Area 1 and Area 3, respectively. It is required that OSPF run on the network and multiple areas be used.

Configuration Roadmap

1. Create an OSPF process on each router.
2. Specify an area for each router interface.

Procedure

Step 1   Run the **ospf** [*process-id* | **router-id** *router-id*] command in the system view to create an OSPF process and enter the OSPF view.

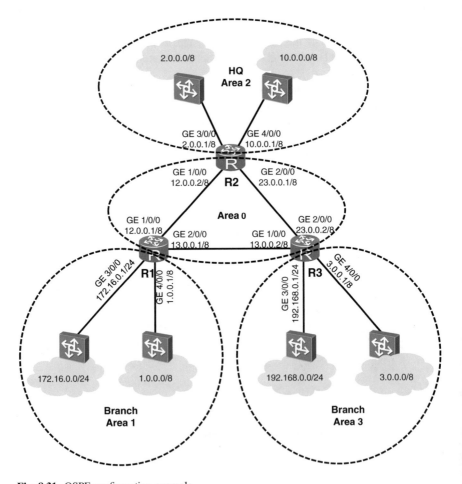

Fig. 8.31 OSPF configuration example

If *process-id* is not specified, OSPF process 1 is created by default. *router-id* can be 32-bit binary number or a dotted decimal number. If *router-id* is not specified, a value is automatically generated based on a specific rule to be used as the router ID.

\# Configure R1.

```
<R1> system-view
[R1] ospf router-id 11.1.1.1//Enable an OSPF process on R1
```
and specify the router ID as 11.1.1.1 for R1.
```
[R1-ospf-1]
```

\# Configure R2.

```
<R2> system-view
[R2] ospf router-id 22.2.2.2
[R2-ospf-1]
```

\# Configure R3.

```
<R3> system-view
[R3] ospf router-id 33.3.3.3
[R3-ospf-1]
```

Step 2 Specify an area for each router interface. Specifically, run the **area** *area-id* command in the OSPF view to create an area and enter the area view. Run the **network** *address wildcard-mask* command in the area view to specify the area for interfaces on a network segment. The end of this chapter describes the wildcard mask.

\# Configure R1.

```
[R1-ospf-1] area 0
[R1-ospf-1-area-0.0.0.0]  network  12.0.0.0  0.255.
255.255
[R1-ospf-1-area-0.0.0.0]  network  13.0.0.0  0.255.
255.255
[R1-ospf-1-area-0.0.0.0] quit
[R1-ospf-1] area 1
[R1-ospf-1-area-0.0.0.1]  network  1.0.0.0  0.255.
255.255
[R1-ospf-1-area-0.0.0.1] network 172.16.0.0 0.0.0.
255
```

\# Configure R2.

```
[R2-ospf-1] area 0
[R2-ospf-1-area-0.0.0.0]  network  12.0.0.0  0.255.
255.255
[R2-ospf-1-area-0.0.0.0]  network  23.0.0.0  0.255.
255.255
```

```
[R2-ospf-1-area-0.0.0.0] quit
[R2-ospf-1] area 2
[R2-ospf-1-area-0.0.0.2]   network   2.0.0.0   0.255.
255.255
[R2-ospf-1-area-0.0.0.2]   network  10.0.0.0   0.255.
255.255
```

Configure R3.

```
[R3-ospf-1] area 0
[R3-ospf-1-area-0.0.0.0]   network  13.0.0.0   0.255.
255.255
[R3-ospf-1-area-0.0.0.0]   network  23.0.0.0   0.255.
255.255
[R3-ospf-1-area-0.0.0.0] quit
[R3-ospf-1] area 3
[R3-ospf-1-area-0.0.0.3]   network   3.0.0.0   0.255.
255.255
[R3-ospf-1-area-0.0.0.3] network 192.168.0.0 0.0.0.
255
```

Step 3   After completing the configuration, check the configurations. Run the
display ospf [*process-id*] **peer** command to check OSPF neighbor information. The following example uses the command output on R1.

```
<R1> display ospf peer
                    OSPF Process 1 with Router ID 11.1.1.1
                                  Neighbors
    Area 0.0.0.0 interface 12.0.0.1(GigabitEthernet1/0/0)'s neighbors
    Router ID: 22.2.2.2        Address: 12.0.0.2
      State: Full  Mode:Nbr is Master  Priority: 1
      DR: 12.0.0.2 BDR: 12.0.0.1 MTU: 0
    ...

                                  Neighbors
    Area 0.0.0.0 interface 13.0.0.1(GigabitEthernet2/0/0)'s neighbors
    Router ID: 33.3.3.3        Address: 13.0.0.2
      State: Full  Mode:Nbr is Master  Priority: 1
      DR: 13.0.0.2 BDR: 13.0.0.1 MTU: 0
    ...
```

In the command output, "State: Full" is displayed, indicating that R1 has
established an adjacency with R2 (whose router ID is 22.2.2.2) and with R3 (whose
router ID is 33.3.3.3).

"DR: 12.0.0.2 BDR: 12.0.0.1" is displayed, indicating that R2 has been elected
as the DR and R1 elected as the BDR on the Ethernet between R1 and R2. "DR:

13.0.0.2 BDR: 13.0.0.1" is displayed, indicating that R3 has been elected as the DR and R1 elected as the BDR on the Ethernet between R1 and R3.

Run the **display ospf** [*process-id*] **routing** command to check the OSPF routing table. The following example uses the command output on R1.

```
[R1] display ospf routing
                    OSPF Process 1 with Router ID 11.1.1.1
                             Routing Tables
 Routing for Network
 Destination      Cost Type       NextHop      AdvRouter    Area
 1.0.0.0/8        1    Stub       1.0.0.1      11.1.1.1     0.0.0.1
 12.0.0.0/8       1    Transit    12.0.0.1     11.1.1.1     0.0.0.0
 13.0.0.0/8       1    Transit    13.0.0.1     11.1.1.1     0.0.0.0
 172.16.0.0/24    1    Stub       172.16.0.1   11.1.1.1     0.0.0.1
 2.0.0.0/8        2    Inter-area 12.0.0.2     22.2.2.2     0.0.0.0
 3.0.0.0/8        2    Inter-area 13.0.0.2     33.3.3.3     0.0.0.0
 10.0.0.0/8       2    Inter-area 12.0.0.2     22.2.2.2     0.0.0.0
 23.0.0.0/8       2    Transit    13.0.0.2     33.3.3.3     0.0.0.0
 23.0.0.0/8       2    Transit    12.0.0.2     22.3.3.3     0.0.0.0
 192.168.0.0/24   2    Inter-area 13.0.0.2     33.3.3.3     0.0.0.0
 Total Nets: 10
 Intra Area: 6  Inter Area: 4  ASE: 0  NSSA: 0
```

The command output shows that R1's OSPF routing table has routes to all destinations.

In the **network** *address wildcard-mask* command, *address* can be a 32-bit binary number or a dotted decimal number. *wildcard-mask* can also be a 32-bit binary number or a dotted decimal number. *address* and *wildcard-mask* both specified represent a collection of IP addresses that meet the following condition: If a bit in *wildcard-mask* is set to 0, the corresponding bit in an IP address must have the same value as this bit in *address*.

For example, if *address* is 12.0.0.0 and *wildcard-mask* is 0.0.0.0, the IP address collection contains only one IP address 12.0.0.0. If *address* is 12.0.0.0 and *wild-card-mask* is 8.0.0.1, the IP address collection contains four IP addresses: 12.0.0.0, 12.0.0.1, 4.0.0.0, and 4.0.0.1. If *address* is 12.0.0.0 and *wildcard-mask* is 0.255.255.255, the IP address collection contains 16777216 IP addresses ranging from 12.0.0.0 to 12.255.255.255.

In the following example:

```
[R5-ospf-4-area-0.0.0.3] network address wildcard-mask
```

If the IP address of one of R5's interfaces belongs to the IP address collection specified by *address* and *wildcard-mask*, then this interface belongs to Area 3 of OSPF process 4.

In another example:

```
[R1-ospf-1-area-0.0.0.0] network 12.0.0.0 0.255.255.255
```

If the IP address of one of R1's interfaces belongs to the IP address range 12.0.0.0 to 12.255.255.255, then this interface belongs to Area 0 of OSPF process 1. This configuration command is derived from the configuration example. Figure 8.31 shows that R1's GE 1/0/0 has the IP address 12.0.0.1, which belongs to the range 12.0.0.0–12.255.255.255. The **network** *12.0.0.0 0.255.255.255* command specifies R1's GE1/0/0 belongs to Area 0.

8.3.12   Review Questions

1. What is the major difference between OSPF and RIP principles? (Choose one)

   A. RIP is a slow convergence routing protocol, whereas OSPF is a fast convergence routing protocol.
   B. RIP is a distance-vector routing protocol, whereas OSPF is a link-state routing protocol.
   C. RIP can only use a hop count as the route cost, whereas OSPF does not have this limitation.
   D. RIP applies only to small-scale networks, whereas OSPF does not have this limitation.

2. Which of the following statements are true about OSPF areas? (Choose all that apply)

   A. A multi-area OSPF network can only have one backbone area.
   B. A multi-area OSPF network has at least one ABR.
   C. An ABR is also a backbone router.
   D. A backbone router is also an ABR.
   E. An ASBR exists only on the backbone area.
   F. A multi-area OSPF network has only one ASBR.
   G. Non-backbone areas must communicate through the backbone area.

3. Which of the following networks running OSPF need a DR and a BDR? (Choose all that apply)

   A. Broadcast network
   B. Non-broadcast multi-access (NBMA) network
   C. P2P network
   D. P2MP network

4. How many types of OSPF packets are available? (Choose one)

   A. 3
   B. 4
   C. 5
   D. 6

5. Which of the following statements are true about link state advertisements (LSAs)? (Choose all that apply)

   A. An OSPF Hello packet carries at least one LSA.
   B. An LSA is an OSPF protocol packet.
   C. If two LSDBs are synchronized on an OSPF network, they have the same number of Type 1 LSAs.
   D. On a multi-area OSPF network, router-LSAs can be flooded across areas.
   E. On a multi-area OSPF network, network-LSAs can be flooded across areas.
   F. On a multi-area OSPF network, network-summary-LSAs can be flooded across areas.
   G. Network-summary-LSAs are generated by an ASBR.
   H. ASBR-summary-LSAs are generated by an ABR.

6. Which of the following statements are true about OSPF neighbor relationships and adjacencies? (Choose all that apply)

   A. The number of OSPF neighbor relationships may be the same as the number of OSPF adjacencies.
   B. The number of neighbors of an OSPF router is always less than or equal to the number of adjacent routers.
   C. The DR and BDR on a broadcast network must establish an adjacency.
   D. On a multi-area OSPF network, an ABR cannot establish an adjacency with other routers.

7. Which of the following statements are true about DR and BDR elections? (Choose all that apply)

   A. On a broadcast network, if the router priority value of a router is 255, the router will surely be elected as the DR.
   B. On a broadcast network, if the router priority value of a router is 0, the router will surely be elected as the DR.
   C. On a broadcast network, the DR and BDR cannot have the same router priority value.
   D. None of the above.

Chapter 9
Inter-VLAN Layer 3 Communication

As explained in Chap. 5, computers on the same VLAN can communicate over Layer 2, whereas computers on different VLANs cannot. However, computers on different VLANs can communicate over Layer 3. This chapter further describes the principles of inter-VLAN Layer 3 communication.

After completing this chapter, you should be able to:

- Understand the working principles of inter-VLAN Layer 3 communication via a multi-armed router.
- Understand the working principles of inter-VLAN Layer 3 communication via a one-armed router.
- Understand the differences between the attributes of Layer 2 ports and Layer 3 interfaces.
- Understand the working principles of Layer 3 switches.
- Understand the working principles of intra-VLAN Layer 2 communication via a Layer 3 switch.
- Understand the working principles of inter-VLAN Layer 3 communication via a Layer 3 switch.

9.1 Inter-VLAN Layer 3 Communication via a Multi-armed Router

In Fig. 9.1, three switches and four PCs form a switched network that is divided into two port-based VLANs: VLAN 10 and VLAN 20. PC 1 and PC 2 belong to VLAN 10. PC 3 and PC 4 belong to VLAN 20.

Considering that PCs belonging to different VLANs cannot communicate over Layer 2 and that no Layer 3 channel has been established, PC 1 and PC 4 cannot communicate.

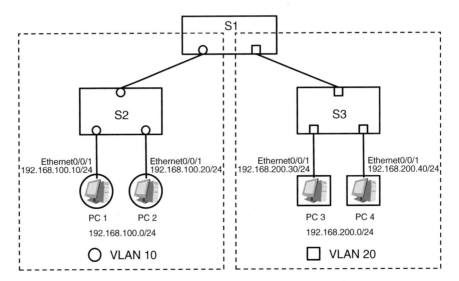

Fig. 9.1 Switched network where PC 1 and PC 4 cannot communicate

One way to allow PC 1 and PC 4 to communicate is to introduce a router. Routers can establish a Layer 3 channel between Layer 2 networks (Layer 2 broadcast domains). In this example, a router can be used to establish a Layer 3 channel between the two VLANs, because VLANs are actually separate Layer 2 networks.

The network shown in Fig. 9.2 is formed by adding router R to the network shown in Fig. 9.1. Interface GE1/0/0 on router R is connected to port D1 on switch S1, and interface GE2/0/0 on router R is connected to port D2 on switch S1. D1 belongs to VLAN 10, and D2 belongs to VLAN 20. Like interfaces on PCs, GE1/0/0 and GE2/0/0 on router R cannot send or receive tagged VLAN frames. GE1/0/0 and GE2/0/0 on router R connect to a physical link that can be considered an arm of router R. Therefore, router R is a two-armed router or, broadly, a multi-armed router.

With a Layer 3 channel in place between PC 1 and PC 4, PC 1 can send IP packets to PC 4. In Fig. 9.2, D1 and D2 on switches S1, S2, and S3 are access ports, whereas D3 on switches S1, S2, and S3 as well as D4 on switch S1 are trunk ports.

First, an IP packet is constructed on the network layer of PC 1, with the destination IP address set to 192.168.200.40 and source IP address set to 192.168.100.10. Then, PC 1 queries the IP routing table for a route that matches the IP packet's destination IP address. (Figure 9.2 shows the simplified IP routing tables on router R, PC 1, and PC 4.) The IP routing table on PC 1 includes two routes, one of which is the default route. In this example, the destination IP address 192.168.200.40 in the IP packet can only match the default route. The outgoing interface of the default route is Ethernet0/0/1 on PC 1, and the next-hop IP address is the IP address of interface GE1/0/0 on router R, namely, 192.168.100.1. (That is

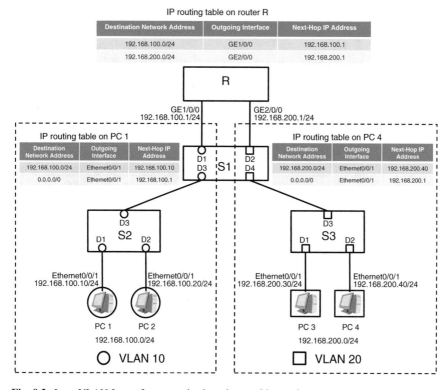

Fig. 9.2 Inter-VLAN Layer 3 communication via a multi-armed router

why interface GE1/0/0 on router R is also called the default gateway of 192.168.100.0/24 or the default gateway of VLAN 10.)

Based on the information of the default route, the IP packet will be sent to interface Ethernet0/0/1 on PC 1 and encapsulated into a frame. In this example frame, the payload data is the IP packet, the value of the type field is 0x0800, the source MAC address is the MAC address of interface Ethernet0/0/1 on PC 1, and the destination MAC address is the MAC address of interface GE1/0/0 on router R. (If PC 1 fails to obtain the MAC address corresponding to IP address 192.168.100.1 from the local ARP cache table, PC 1 must obtain the MAC address using the ARP mechanism.) Note that the frame does not carry a VLAN tag at this point.

Then, PC 1 sends the untagged frame through interface Ethernet0/0/1. After the frame arrives at S2 through port D1, S2 adds the VLAN 10 tag to the frame and forwards the tagged frame to S1. Then, S1 removes the tag and forwards the untagged frame through its port D1.

After receiving the untagged frame, interface GE1/0/0 on router R compares the destination MAC address in the frame with its own MAC address. Because the two MAC addresses are the same, GE1/0/0 sends the payload data (the IP packet) contained in the frame to the Layer 3 IP module of router R based on the value of the type field (namely, 0x0800). Upon receiving the IP packet, the Layer 3 IP module queries the local IP routing table for a route that matches 192.168.200.40, the destination IP address in the IP packet. 192.168.200.40 only matches the second route in the IP routing table. The outgoing interface of the second route is GE2/0/0, and the next-hop IP address is the IP address of GE2/0/0 (indicating that the destination network to which the IP packet should be delivered is directly connected to GE2/0/0).

Based on the information of the route, the IP packet will be sent to interface GE2/0/0 on router R and encapsulated into another frame. In the new frame, the payload data is the IP packet, the value of the type field is 0x0800, the source MAC address is the MAC address of GE2/0/0, and the destination MAC address is the MAC address corresponding to 192.168.200.40, the destination IP address in the IP packet. (If router R fails to obtain the MAC address corresponding to 192.168.200.40 from the local ARP cache table, R must send ARP requests through interface GE2/0/0 to obtain the MAC address.) Note that the new frame does not carry a VLAN tag at this point.

Router R sends the untagged frame through interface GE2/0/0. After the untagged frame arrives at S1 through port D2, S1 adds the VLAN 20 tag to the frame and forwards the tagged frame to S3. Then, S3 removes the tag and forwards the untagged frame through its port D2.

After receiving the untagged frame, interface Ethernet0/0/1 on PC 4 compares the destination MAC address in the frame with its own MAC address. Because the two MAC addresses are the same, Ethernet0/0/1 sends the payload data (the IP packet) contained in the frame to the Layer 3 IP module of PC 4 based on the value of the type field (namely, 0x0800).

The IP packet sent from the Layer 3 IP module of PC 1 reaches the Layer 3 IP module of PC 4, successfully establishing Layer 3 communication between PC 1 in VLAN 10 and PC 4 in VLAN 20.

9.2   Inter-VLAN Layer 3 Communication via a One-Armed Router

Inter-VLAN Layer 3 communication that is implemented via a multi-armed router faces the following issue: Each VLAN consumes a physical interface on the router, that is, each VLAN requires the router to provide an arm from a physical interface. If a large number of VLANs exist, many router interfaces are needed. However, the number of physical interfaces on a router is typically limited, without the capability to support numerous VLANs. In actual network deployment, inter-VLAN Layer 3 communication is seldom implemented using a multi-armed router.

To use physical interfaces on a router more efficiently, we can implement inter-VLAN Layer 3 communication via a one-armed router. In such a scenario, a physical interface on a router must be divided into subinterfaces. These subinterfaces correspond to different VLANs. The MAC address of a subinterface is the same as that of the physical interface on which it resides. However, each subinterface has a unique IP address. The IP address of a subinterface must be set to the default gateway address of the VLAN corresponding to the subinterface. Subinterfaces are logical interfaces. Therefore, subinterfaces are also called virtual interfaces.

As shown in Fig. 9.3, physical interface GE1/0/0 on router R is divided into two subinterfaces: GE1/0/0.1 and GE1/0/0.2. GE1/0/0.1 corresponds to VLAN 10, and GE1/0/0.2 corresponds to VLAN 20. The IP address of GE1/0/0.1 is 192.168.100.1/24, namely, the default gateway address of VLAN 10. The IP address of GE1/0/0.2 is 192.168.200.1/24, namely, the default gateway address of VLAN 20. GE1/0/0.1 and GE1/0/0.2 have the same MAC address, namely, the MAC address of GE1/0/0.

In Fig. 9.3, D1 and D2 on switches S2 and S3 are access ports, whereas D3 on switches S1, S2, and S3 as well as D1 and D2 on switch S1 are trunk ports. Frames that belong to VLANs 10 and 20 must be allowed to pass through port D1 on S1. The link between S1 and R is a VLAN trunk link. Frames transmitted over the link

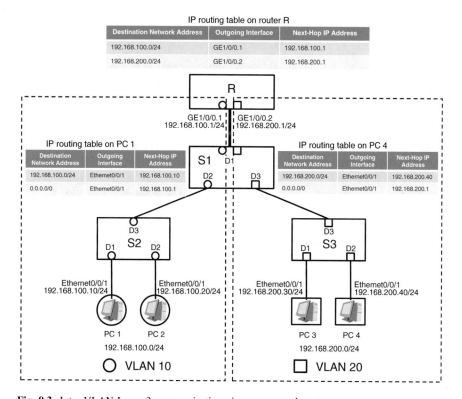

Fig. 9.3 Inter-VLAN Layer 3 communication via a one-armed router

must contain a VLAN tag. This means that frames sent by subinterfaces GE1/0/0.1 and GE1/0/0.2 must carry a VLAN tag.

With a Layer 3 channel in place between PC 1 and PC 4, PC 1 can send IP packets to PC 4.

First, an IP packet is constructed on the network layer of PC 1, with the destination IP address set to 192.168.200.40 and source IP address set to 192.168.100.10. Then, PC 1 queries the IP routing table for a route that matches the IP packet's destination IP address. The IP routing table on PC 1 includes two routes, one of which is the default route. The destination IP address 192.168.200.40 in the IP packet can only match the default route. The outgoing interface of the default route is Ethernet0/0/1 on PC 1, and the next-hop IP address is the IP address of subinterface GE1/0/0.1 on router R, namely, 192.168.100.1. (That is why subinterface GE1/0/0.1 on router R is also called the default gateway of 192.168.100.0/24 or the default gateway of VLAN 10.)

Based on the information of the default route, the IP packet will be sent to interface Ethernet0/0/1 on PC 1 and encapsulated into a frame. In this example frame, the payload data is the IP packet, the value of the type field is 0x0800, the source MAC address is the MAC address of interface Ethernet0/0/1 on PC 1, and the destination MAC address is the MAC address of subinterface GE1/0/0.1 on router R. (If PC 1 fails to obtain the MAC address corresponding to IP address 192.168.100.1 from the local ARP cache table, PC 1 must obtain the MAC address using the ARP mechanism.) Note that the frame does not carry a VLAN tag at this point.

Then, PC 1 sends the untagged frame through interface Ethernet0/0/1. After the frame arrives at S2 through port D1, S2 adds the VLAN 10 tag to the frame and forwards the tagged frame to S1. Then, S1 forwards the tagged frame to physical interface GE1/0/0 on router R.

After receiving the tagged frame, GE1/0/0 on router R finds that the tagged frame belongs to VLAN 10 and then sends it to subinterface GE1/0/0.1. GE1/0/0.1 finds that the destination MAC address in the tagged frame is its MAC address and the value of the type field is 0x0800. Therefore, GE1/0/0.1 sends the payload data (the IP packet) contained in the frame to the Layer 3 IP module of router R.

Upon receiving the IP packet, the Layer 3 IP module queries the local IP routing table for a route that matches 192.168.200.40, the destination IP address in the IP packet. 192.168.200.40 only matches the second route in the IP routing table. The outgoing interface of the second route is subinterface GE1/0/0.2, and the next-hop IP address is the IP address of GE1/0/0.2 (indicating the destination network to which the IP packet should be delivered is directly connected to GE1/0/0.2).

Based on the information of the route, the IP packet will be sent to subinterface GE1/0/0.2 on router R and encapsulated into another frame. In the new frame, the payload data is the IP packet, the value of the type field is 0x0800, the source MAC address is the MAC address of GE1/0/0.2, and the destination MAC address is the MAC address corresponding to 192.168.200.40, the destination IP address in the IP packet. (If router R fails to obtain the MAC address corresponding to 192.168.200.40 from the local ARP cache table, R must send ARP requests through

GE1/0/0.2 to obtain the MAC address.) Note that the new frame must carry the VLAN 20 tag.

Router R sends the tagged frame through its subinterface GE1/0/0.2 (physically, through interface GE1/0/0). Then, the tagged frame arrives at port D2 on switch S3. After that, S3 removes the tag from the frame and forwards the untagged frame through port D2.

After receiving the untagged frame, interface Ethernet0/0/1 on PC 4 compares the destination MAC address in the frame with its own MAC address. Because the two MAC addresses are the same, Ethernet0/0/1 sends the payload data (the IP packet) contained in the frame to the Layer 3 IP module of PC 4 based on the value of the type field (namely, 0x0800).

The IP packet sent from the Layer 3 IP module of PC 1 reaches the Layer 3 IP module of PC 4, successfully establishing Layer 3 communication between PC 1 in VLAN 10 and PC 4 in VLAN 20.

9.3   Inter-VLAN Layer 3 Communication via a Layer 3 Switch

Inter-VLAN Layer 3 communication can be implemented via a one-armed or multi-armed router. The use of a one-armed router helps save physical interface resources; however, there are still disadvantages. For example, if numerous VLANs are involved and there is heavy traffic being sent between the VLANs, the bandwidth provided by a one-armed link may be insufficient. In addition, if the one-armed link is broken, the VLANs cannot communicate. To avoid these disadvantages, a network device called a Layer 3 switch is used to implement inter-VLAN Layer 3 communication more economically, quickly, and reliably.

Before describing how to establish a connection through a Layer 3 switch, the convention in this book for referring to Layer 2 ports and Layer 3 interfaces should be discussed.

As used in this book, network ports on switches are called ports, and those on routers and computers are called interfaces. The terms port and interface are often used interchangeably, but we make a distinction here. The differences between Layer 2 ports and Layer 3 interfaces are as follows:

- A Layer 2 port has a MAC address but no IP address. A Layer 3 interface has both a MAC address and an IP address.
- Upon receiving a broadcast frame through a Layer 2 port, a device floods the frame through all the other Layer 2 ports on that device.
- Upon receiving a broadcast frame through a Layer 3 interface, a device sends the payload data in the frame to the corresponding Layer 3 module of the device based on the value of the type field in the frame.
- Upon receiving a unicast frame through a Layer 2 port, a device searches its MAC address table for the destination MAC address contained in the frame.

If the destination MAC address cannot be found, the device floods the frame through all the other Layer 2 ports. If the destination MAC address is found, the device determines whether the Layer 2 port indicated by the MAC address entry is the port through which the frame entered the device. If it is, the device discards the frame. If it is not, the device forwards the frame through the Layer 2 port indicated by the MAC address entry.

- Upon receiving a unicast frame through a Layer 3 interface, a device determines whether the destination MAC address contained in the frame is the MAC address of that Layer 3 interface. If it is, the device sends the payload data in the frame to the corresponding Layer 3 module of the device based on the value of the type field in the frame. If it is not, the device discards the frame.

This book does not describe scenarios where a Layer 2 port or Layer 3 interface receives a multicast frame.

The differences between the attributes of Layer 2 ports and Layer 3 interfaces lead to the following differences between switches and routers:

- Ports on a switch are Layer 2 ports, between which there is a Layer 2 forwarding channel but no Layer 3 forwarding channel. A switch has a MAC address table used for Layer 2 forwarding, but does not have an IP routing table.
- Interfaces on a router are Layer 3 interfaces, between which there is a Layer 3 forwarding channel but no Layer 2 forwarding channel. A router has an IP routing table used for Layer 3 forwarding, but does not have a MAC address table.

Layer 3 switches are described as follows:

A Layer 3 switch is defined as an integration of a Layer 2 switch and a router. In addition to Layer 2 ports, a Layer 3 switch can have hybrid ports. A hybrid port acts as both a Layer 2 port and a Layer 3 interface. On a Layer 3 switch, both Layer 2 and Layer 3 forwarding channels are established between hybrid ports, but only Layer 2 forwarding channels are established between Layer 2 ports as well as between a hybrid port and a Layer 2 port. A Layer 3 switch has a MAC address table used for Layer 2 forwarding and an IP routing table used for Layer 3 forwarding. A Layer 3 switch can have hybrid ports without Layer 2 ports. A Layer 3 switch can also have only Layer 2 ports (in this case, the switch is degraded into a Layer 2 switch).

Next, examples will be provided to explain how a Layer 3 switch implements intra-VLAN Layer 2 communication and inter-VLAN Layer 3 communication.

As shown in Fig. 9.4, PC 1 and PC 3 are assigned to VLAN 10, and PC 2 and PC 4 are assigned to VLAN 20. S1 is a Layer 3 switch. S2 and S3 are Layer 2 switches. To allow Layer 3 communication between VLAN 10 and VLAN 20, we must configure two logical VLAN interfaces (VLANIF 10 and VLANIF 20 in this example) on S1. VLANIF is short for VLAN interface. VLANIF 10 and VLANIF 20 have their own IP addresses and the attributes of a Layer 3 interface. The IP address of VLANIF 10 is set to 192.168.100.1/24, and that of VLANIF 20 is set to 192.168.200.1/24. The two IP addresses are actually the default gateway addresses

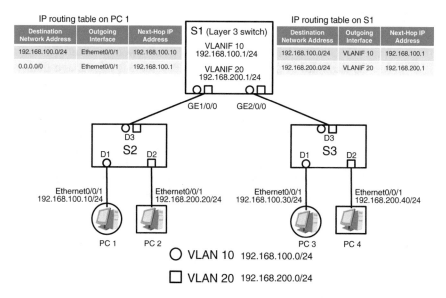

Fig. 9.4 Forwarding principle implemented by a Layer 3 switch

of VLAN 10 and VLAN 20, respectively. Then, GE1/0/0 and GE2/0/0 on S1 become hybrid ports that have the attributes of a Layer 2 port and Layer 3 interface.

In Fig. 9.4, D1 and D2 on switches S2 and S3 are access ports, whereas D3 on S2 and S3 as well as GE1/0/0 and GE2/0/0 on S1 are trunk ports.

First, let's see how a Layer 3 switch implements intra-VLAN Layer 2 communication. In this example, PC 1 shown in Fig. 9.4 sends an ARP request to query the MAC address of PC 3, namely, the MAC address corresponding to IP address 192.168.100.30. How this ARP request arrives at PC 3 is described as follows:

First, the data link layer (Layer 2) of PC 1 prepares a broadcast frame. In the frame, the destination MAC address is ff-ff-ff-ff-ff-ff, the source MAC address is the MAC address of interface Ethernet0/0/1 on PC 1, the value of the type field is 0x0806, and the payload data is an ARP request packet that is used to obtain the MAC address corresponding to IP address 192.168.100.30. Note that the frame does not carry a VLAN tag at this point.

Then, PC 1 sends the untagged frame through interface Ethernet0/0/1. After the frame arrives at S2 through its port D1, S2 adds the VLAN 10 tag to the frame. Then, the tagged frame reaches hybrid port GE1/0/0 on S1.

GE1/0/0 on S1 has the attributes of a Layer 3 interface, and the tagged frame received by GE1/0/0 is a broadcast frame. Therefore, based on the value of the type field (namely, 0x0806), GE1/0/0 sends the payload data (an ARP request packet) contained in the frame to the Layer 3 ARP module. When processing the ARP request packet, the Layer 3 ARP module detects that the packet is used to request the MAC address corresponding to IP address 192.168.100.30. However, the IP address of the Layer 3 ARP module, namely, the IP address of VLANIF 10, is

192.168.100.1. Therefore, the Layer 3 ARP module does not return an ARP response but discards the ARP request packet.

Meanwhile, GE1/0/0 on S1 floods the tagged frame through GE2/0/0 because GE1/0/0 has the attributes of a Layer 2 port and the frame is a broadcast frame.

Then, the frame arrives at port D1 on S3. D1 removes the tag and sends the untagged frame to PC 3.

Ethernet0/0/1 on PC 3 is a Layer 3 interface, and the untagged frame is a broadcast frame. Therefore, based on the value of the type field (namely, 0x0806) in the frame, Ethernet0/0/1 sends the payload data (an ARP request packet) contained in the frame to the Layer 3 ARP module. When processing the ARP request packet, the Layer 3 ARP module detects that the packet is used to request the MAC address corresponding to IP address 192.168.100.30. The IP address of the Layer 3 ARP module is 192.168.100.30. Therefore, the Layer 3 ARP module returns an ARP reply.

Intra-VLAN Layer 2 communication is now successfully implemented between PC 1 and PC 3 that reside in VLAN 10. The Layer 2 communication uses the Layer 2 forwarding channel between hybrid ports GE1/0/0 and GE2/0/0 on S1.

Next, let's learn about how a Layer 3 switch implements inter-VLAN Layer 3 communication. How PC 1 successfully sends an IP packet to PC 4 is described as follows:

First, an IP packet is constructed on the network layer of PC 1, with the destination IP address set to 192.168.200.40 and source IP address set to 192.168.100.10. Then, PC 1 queries the IP routing table for a route that matches the destination IP address. The IP routing table on PC 1 includes two routes, one of which is the default route. The destination IP address 192.168.200.40 in the IP packet can only match the default route. The outgoing interface of the default route is Ethernet0/0/1 on PC 1, and the next-hop IP address is the IP address of VLANIF 10 on S1, namely, 192.168.100.1. (That is why VLANIF 10 on S1 is also called the default gateway of 192.168.100.0/24 or the default gateway of VLAN 10.)

Based on the information of the default route, the IP packet will be sent to interface Ethernet0/0/1 on PC 1 and encapsulated into a unicast frame. In the frame, the payload data is the IP packet, the value of the type field is 0x0800, the source MAC address is the MAC address of interface Ethernet0/0/1 on PC 1, and the destination MAC address is the MAC address corresponding to the IP address of VLANIF 10. (If PC 1 fails to obtain the MAC address corresponding to IP address 192.168.100.1 from the local ARP cache table, PC 1 must obtain the MAC address using the ARP mechanism.) Note that the frame does not carry a VLAN tag at this point.

Then, PC 1 sends the untagged frame through interface Ethernet0/0/1. After the frame arrives at S2 through port D1, S2 adds the VLAN 10 tag to the frame and forwards the tagged frame to GE1/0/0 on S1.

GE1/0/0 on S1 has the attributes of a Layer 3 interface, and the tagged frame received by GE1/0/0 is a unicast frame. Therefore, GE1/0/0 compares the destination MAC address in the frame with its own MAC address. Because the two

MAC addresses are the same, GE1/0/0 sends the payload data (the IP packet) contained in the frame to the Layer 3 IP module based on the value of the type field (namely, 0x0800).

Upon receiving the IP packet, the Layer 3 IP module queries the local IP routing table for a route that matches 192.168.200.40, the destination IP address in the IP packet. 192.168.200.40 only matches the second route in the IP routing table. The outgoing interface of the second route is VLANIF 20, and the next-hop IP address is the IP address of VLANIF 20 (indicating the destination network to which the IP packet should be delivered is directly connected to VLANIF 20, but it is unclear whether the destination network is directly connected to GE1/0/0 or GE2/0/0).

Based on the information of the route, the IP packet is delivered to VLANIF 20 (but it is unclear whether the IP packet should be delivered to GE1/0/0 or GE2/0/0) and encapsulated into a unicast frame. In the unicast frame, the payload data is the IP packet, the value of the type field is 0x0800, and the destination MAC address is the MAC address corresponding to 192.168.200.40, the destination IP address in the IP packet. However, it remains unclear whether the source MAC address in the unicast frame is the MAC address of GE1/0/0 or GE2/0/0.

Assuming that S1 does not know the MAC address corresponding to 192.168.200.40, S1 must send ARP broadcast requests through both GE1/0/0 and GE2/0/0 to obtain the MAC address. Note that the ARP broadcast requests sent from GE1/0/0 and GE2/0/0 must carry the VLAN 20 tag. The final result is that GE2/0/0 receives an ARP reply (thereby learning the MAC address corresponding to 192.168.200.40) and GE1/0/0 will not receive an ARP reply. Then, it is confirmed that the source MAC address in the unicast frame is the MAC address of GE2/0/0. The outgoing interface for sending the unicast frame should be GE2/0/0. In addition, the destination MAC address in the unicast frame is the MAC address learned based on the ARP mechanism. Note that the unicast frame must carry the VLAN 20 tag.

S1 sends the tagged unicast frame through GE2/0/0. Then, the frame arrives at port D2 on switch S3. After that, S3 removes the tag and forwards the untagged frame through port D2.

After receiving the untagged frame, interface Ethernet0/0/1 on PC 4 compares the destination MAC address in the frame with its own MAC address. Because the two MAC addresses are the same, Ethernet0/0/1 sends the payload data (the IP packet) contained in the frame to the Layer 3 IP module of PC 4 based on the value of the type field (namely, 0x0800).

The IP packet sent from the Layer 3 IP module of PC 1 reaches the Layer 3 IP module of PC 4, successfully establishing Layer 3 communication between PC 1 in VLAN 10 and PC 4 in VLAN 20.

However, you should not miss the following point: After the tagged frame forwarded by S2 arrives at GE1/0/0 on S1, GE1/0/0 should process the frame based on the attributes of a Layer 2 port because GE1/0/0 has such attributes. Two processing modes are available and are described as follows:

- Processing mode 1
  After the tagged frame arrives at GE1/0/0, the Layer 3 interface of GE1/0/0 discovers that it is a unicast frame. Therefore, the Layer 3 interface of GE1/0/0 compares the destination MAC address in the frame with its own MAC address. Because the two MAC addresses are the same, the Layer 3 interface of GE1/0/0 sends the payload data (namely, the IP address packet) contained in the frame to the Layer 3 IP module and instructs the Layer 2 port of GE1/0/0 not to process the tagged frame. That is, the attributes of the Layer 2 port of GE1/0/0 are suppressed for the tagged frame.
- Processing mode 2
  After the tagged frame arrives at GE1/0/0, the Layer 3 interface of GE1/0/0 discovers that it is a unicast frame. Therefore, the Layer 3 interface of GE1/0/0 compares the destination MAC address in the frame with its own MAC address. Because the two MAC addresses are the same, the Layer 3 interface of GE1/0/0 sends the payload data (the IP packet) contained in the frame to the Layer 3 IP module, without instructing the Layer 2 port of GE1/0/0 not to process the tagged frame. As a result, S1 searches its MAC address table for the destination MAC address in the tagged frame. The destination MAC address in the tagged frame cannot be found in the MAC address table. After that, S1 floods the frame through GE2/0/0. After the frame arrives at D1 on S3 (the frame will not be sent to D2 on S3 because the frame contains the VLAN 10 tag whereas D2 belongs to VLAN 20), D1 removes the tag from the frame and sends the untagged frame to Ethernet0/0/1 on PC 3. Ethernet0/0/1 on PC 3 compares its MAC address with the destination MAC address in the untagged frame. Because the two MAC addresses are different, Ethernet0/0/1 on PC 3 discards the untagged frame.

9.4   VLANIF Configuration Example

Enable the Layer 3 switching function and configure VLANIFs on Layer 3 switch S1 to implement Layer 3 communication between users that reside in different VLANs. See Fig. 9.5.

Configuration Roadmap

1. Create VLANs on S1. (Do not create VLANs on S2 or S3.)
2. Configure ports on S1.
3. Create VLANIFs on S1 and assign an IP address for each VLANIF to implement inter-VLAN Layer 3 communication.

Procedure
Create VLAN 10 and VLAN 20 on S1.

```
<S1> system-view
[S1] vlan batch 10 20
```

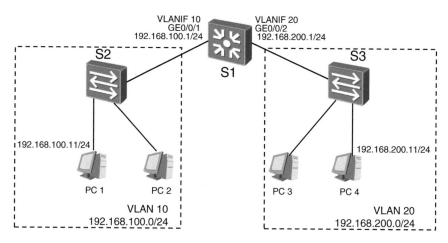

Fig. 9.5 VLANIF configuration example

Configure ports on S1.

```
[S1] interface gigabitethernet 0/0/1
[S1—GigabitEthernet0/0/1] port link-type access
[S1—GigabitEthernet0/0/1] port default vlan 10
[S1—GigabitEthernet0/0/1] quit
[S1] interface gigabitethernet 0/0/2
[S1—GigabitEthernet0/0/2] port link-type access
[S1—GigabitEthernet0/0/2] port default vlan 20
[S1—GigabitEthernet0/0/2] quit
```

Run **display vlan** *vlan-id* **verbose** to confirm the configuration. For example, run the following command to view information about VLAN 10 on S1.

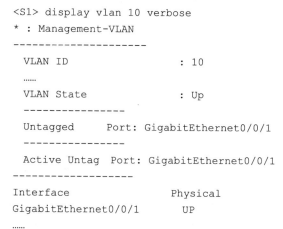

The command output verifies that GigabitEthernet0/0/1 is added to VLAN 10 on S1.

Then, run **display port vlan** to view port information about all VLANs configured on S1.

```
<S1> display port vlan
Port                    Link Type    PVID  Trunk VLAN List
-----------------------------------------------------------------
GigabitEthernet0/0/1    access        10   -
GigabitEthernet0/0/2    access        20   -
......
```

The command output verifies that GigabitEthernet0/0/1 and GigabitEthernet0/0/2 are configured as access ports and that the PVIDs are correct. This indicates that the command is in effect on the device.

Next, create VLANIFs on S1 and assign IP addresses. Run **interface vlanif** *vlan-id* to create VLANIFs. Enter the VLANIF view, and then run **ip address** *ip-address* {*mask*|*mask-length*} to assign an IP address for each VLANIF.

Configure VLANIFs on S1.

```
[S1] interface vlanif 10
[S1—Vlanif10] ip address 192.168.100.1 24
[S1-Vlanif10] quit
[S1] interface vlanif 20
[S1—Vlanif20] ip address 192.168.200.1 24
[S1-Vlanif20] quit
```

Run **display ip interface brief vlanif** *vlan-id* to confirm the VLANIF configuration. For example, run the following command to view information about VLANIF 10:

```
<S1> display ip interface brief vlanif 10
*down: administratively down
!down: FIB overload down
^down: standby
(l): loopback
(s): spoofing
Interface              IP Address/Mask     Physical   Protocol
Vlanif10               192.168.100.1/24       up         up
```

The command output verifies that the interface status and link-layer protocol status of VLANIF 10 are up, and an IP address is assigned for VLANIF 10. This indicates that VLANIF 10 is correctly configured.

All configurations on S1 are complete. Next, assign IP addresses and default gateway addresses for PC 1 and PC 4. After that, check whether PC 1 can successfully ping PC 4 to determine whether the Layer 3 switch can implement inter-VLAN Layer 3 communication.

Set the IP address of PC 1 to 192.168.100.11/24 and the default gateway address of PC 1 to 192.168.100.1/24, which is the IP address of VLANIF 10 on S1. Set the IP address of PC 4 to 192.168.200.11/24 and the default gateway address of PC 4 to 192.168.200.1/24, which is the IP address of VLANIF 20 on S1.

After the configuration is complete, run **ping** 192.168.200.11 on PC 1.

```
C:\>ping 192.168.200.11

Ping 192.168.200.11: 32 data bytes, Press Ctrl_C to break
From 192.168.200.11: bytes=32 seq=1 ttl=127 time=62 ms
From 192.168.200.11: bytes=32 seq=2 ttl=127 time=47 ms
From 192.168.200.11: bytes=32 seq=3 ttl=127 time=62 ms
From 192.168.200.11: bytes=32 seq=4 ttl=127 time=63 ms
From 192.168.200.11: bytes=32 seq=5 ttl=127 time=62 ms

--- 192.168.200.11 ping statistics ---
  5 packet(s) transmitted
  5 packet(s) received
  0.00% packet loss
  round-trip min/avg/max = 47/59/63 ms
```

The command output verifies that PC 1 has received response packets from PC 4. This indicates that PC 1 has successfully pinged PC 4, and S1 has successfully implemented Layer 3 communication between VLAN 10 and VLAN 20.

9.5   Review Questions

1. Which of the following devices can implement inter-VLAN communication? (Choose all that apply)

   A. Routers
   B. Layer 2 switches
   C. Layer 3 switches

2. Which of the following statements are true? (Choose all that apply)

   A. A router can have a MAC address table.
   B. A router does not have a MAC address table.
   C. A Layer 3 switch can have a routing table.
   D. A Layer 3 switch can have a MAC address Table

3. Which of the following statements are true? (Choose all that apply)

   A. Subinterfaces on a router must be assigned IP addresses.
   B. Subinterfaces on a router do not need an IP address.
   C. VLANIFs on a Layer 3 switch must be assigned IP addresses.
   D. VLANIFs on a Layer 3 switch do not need an IP address.

4. Which of the following statements are true? (Choose all that apply)

   A. A Layer 2 forwarding channel can be established between Layer 3 interfaces on a router.
   B. A Layer 3 forwarding channel can be established between Layer 3 interfaces on a router.
   C. A Layer 2 forwarding channel can be established between Layer 2 ports on a Layer 2 switch.
   D. A Layer 3 forwarding channel can be established between Layer 2 ports on a Layer 2 switch.
   E. A Layer 2 forwarding channel can be established between Layer 2 ports on a Layer 3 switch.
   F. A Layer 3 forwarding channel can be established between hybrid ports on a Layer 3 switch.
   G. A Layer 2 forwarding channel can be established between hybrid ports on a Layer 3 switch.

Chapter 10
Link Technologies

This chapter describes three link technologies: link aggregation, Smart Link, and Monitor Link. After completing this chapter, you should be able to:

- Understand the functions and working principles of link aggregation, Smart Link, and Monitor Link.
- Be familiar with the application scenarios of link aggregation, Smart Link, and Monitor Link.

10.1 Link Aggregation

10.1.1 Background

What are the meanings of such terms as standard Ethernet port, FE port, GE port, 10GE port, and 100GE port? These expressions are related to Ethernet standards, particularly information transmission rates. In the standards defined by IEEE, information transmission rates increase by a factor of approximately 10 per step: 10 Mbit/s, 100 Mbit/s, 1000 Mbit/s (1 Gbit/s), 10 Gbit/s, and 100 Gbit/s.

The ten-fold increase per step in evolution suits the progressions in microelectronics and optics, ensuring the standardization of Ethernet information transmission rates. Without such standards, Ethernet network interface card (NIC) manufacturers would find it difficult to match up port rates at both ends of an Ethernet link (imagine if IEEE were to release a 415 Mbit/s transmission rate standard today and a 624 Mbit/s transmission rate standard tomorrow). The naming conventions for different types of Ethernet ports are as follows:

- 10 Mbit/s: standard Ethernet port, 10 Mbit/s Ethernet port, or 10 Mbit/s port.
- 100 Mbit/s: Fast Ethernet port, 100 Mbit/s Ethernet port, 100 Mbit/s port, or FE port.

© Springer Science+Business Media Singapore 2016

Huawei Technologies Co., Ltd., *HCNA Networking Study Guide*,

DOI 10.1007/978-981-10-1554-0_10

- 1000 Mbit/s: Gigabit Ethernet port, 1000 Mbit/s port, 1 Gbit/s port, or GE port.
- 10 Gbit/s: 10 Gigabit Ethernet port, 10 Gbit/s port, or 10GE port.
- 100 Gbit/s: 100 Gigabit Ethernet port, 100 Gbit/s port, or 100GE port.

The naming of Ethernet links matches the rates of the Ethernet ports. For example, if the ports at both ends of a link are GE ports, the link is called a GE link; if the ports at both ends of a link are FE ports, the link is called an FE link.

10.1.2   Basic Concepts

Now that we have a clear understanding of Ethernet ports and links, let's talk about link aggregation. Figure 10.1 shows an example network structure in which 10 users are each connected to switch S1 through an FE link, and S1 is connected to core switch S2 through a GE link. In this scenario, traffic congestion is unlikely to occur in the GE link between S1 and S2. However, if the number of users connected to S1 were to increase to 20 and S1 and S2 continue to communicate through only one GE link, traffic congestion may occur because up to 2 Gbit/s bandwidth could be required (the single GE link is restricted to a maximum bandwidth of 1 Gbit/s).

To resolve the insufficiency in bandwidth, we can replace the link between S1 and S2 with a 10GE link if S1 and S2 both have 10GE ports. If S1 or S2 does not have or support 10GE ports, the switch must be replaced. Generally speaking, this approach is not cost-effective, and it is a waste of bandwidth resources.

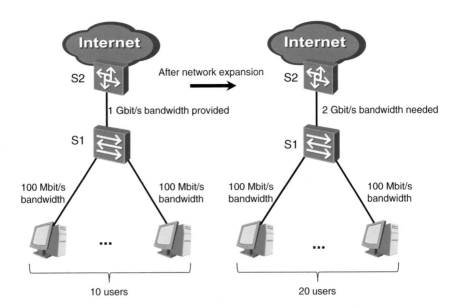

Fig. 10.1 Network before and after expansion

Fig. 10.2 Link aggregation
between two switches

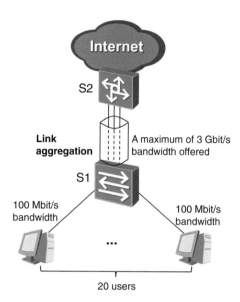

Furthermore, if there is only one link between S1 and S2 and the link goes down, none of the users will be able to access the Internet (low network reliability).

Implementing link aggregation makes the connection between S1 and S2 more reliable and meets the need for higher bandwidth in a cost-effective way. For example, if S1 and S2 each have at least three GE ports, three GE links can be established between S1 and S2, as shown in Fig. 10.2. Link aggregation can then be used to aggregate the three GE links into a single logical link that can provide up to 3 Gbit/s in bandwidth. Accordingly, the three GE ports on each switch are aggregated into a single logical port. The logical link can meet the need for 2 Gbit/s in bandwidth and help ensure link reliability if one physical GE link goes down. Although the logical link with one physical GE link down provides lower bandwidth, the situation where none of the users can access the Internet is unlikely to occur.

Link aggregation can accomplish the following:

- Flexible increase in bandwidth between network devices
- Improved connection reliability between network devices
- Reduced costs.

10.1.3 Application Scenarios

Link aggregation is also known as link trunking and link bonding. For the purposes of this book, link aggregation is specific to Ethernet links.

In the example described in Sect. 10.1.2, link aggregation is implemented between two switches. Link aggregation can also be implemented between a switch

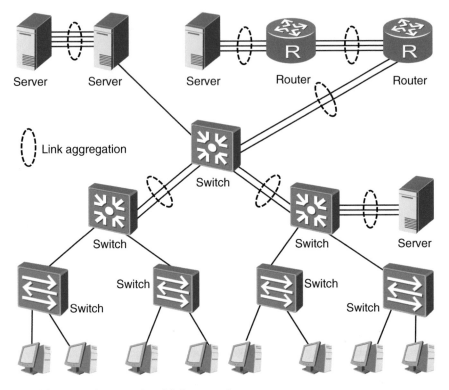

Fig. 10.3 Application scenarios of link aggregation

and a router, between a switch and a server, between a router and a server, between routers, and between servers (see Fig. 10.3). In theory, link aggregation can also be implemented between personal computers (PCs), but this would be unreasonable due to the high cost. Servers are high-performance computers in a way, but they have an important status from the perspective of network application. Reliable connections between servers and other devices must be ensured. Therefore, link aggregation is often applied to servers.

10.1.4 Working Principles

This section explains the working principles of link aggregation implemented between two switches. Figure 10.4 shows an example deployment in which n physical links are bundled into one logical link. Typically, logical links created based on link aggregation are known as aggregate links, and the physical links that compose an aggregate link are known as member links. Accordingly, logical ports created during this process are called aggregate ports, and the physical ports that

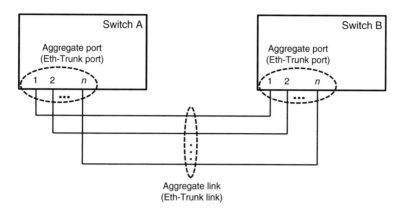

Fig. 10.4 Link aggregation between two switches

compose an aggregate port are called member ports. Aggregate links are also known as Eth-Trunk links, and aggregate ports are also known as Eth-Trunk ports. (Eth is short for Ethernet.)

Let's look at how switch A uses its Eth-Trunk port to send frames to switch B.

1. Frames from other ports on switch A enter the frame sending queue of the Eth-Trunk port.
2. The frame distributor (FD) of the Eth-Trunk port distributes frames in sequence (first frame a, then frame b, then frame c, and so on) to member ports based on an algorithm.
3. Each member port sends the frames that were distributed to it to its physical link.

Figure 10.5 provides a graphical representation of this process. Note that Fig. 10.5 does not show the frame collector (FC) and frame receiving queue of the Eth-Trunk port. If an FD evenly distributes frames to member ports, the bandwidth of an Eth-Trunk port is equal to the sum of the bandwidth provided by each member port. Accordingly, the bandwidth of the Eth-Trunk link will be equal to the total bandwidth provided by all member links. However, in actual implementation, FDs are unable to evenly distribute frames. Therefore, the maximum bandwidth provided by an Eth-Trunk link is typically lower than the total bandwidth provided by all member links.

Next, let's learn about how switch B uses its Eth-Trunk port to receive frames from the Eth-Trunk port on switch A.

1. Each member port receives frames from physical links.
2. All received frames are sent to the FC of the Eth-Trunk port. The FC sends a frame to the frame receiving queue of the Eth-Trunk port immediately after the

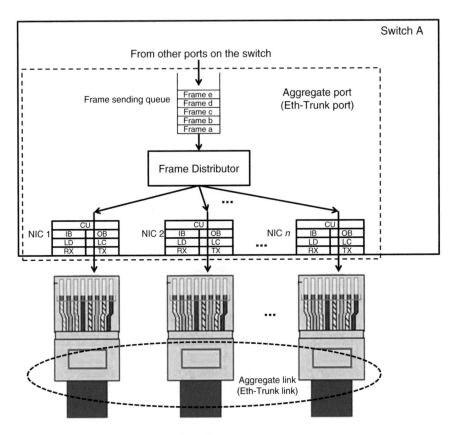

Fig. 10.5 Switch A sending frames through an aggregate port

frame has completely entered the FC. In Fig. 10.6, frame a is the first frame to completely enter the FC, followed by frame b and then frame c.

3. Frames in the frame receiving queue of the Eth-Trunk port are sent in sequence to other ports on switch B.

Figure 10.6 provides a graphical representation of this process. Note that Fig. 10.6 does not show the FD and frame sending queue of the Eth-Trunk port.

The basic principle of link aggregation is sharing the load transmitted over an aggregate link among multiple member links. In addition, if a member link of an aggregate link goes down, other member links continue to share the total traffic load being transmitted over the aggregate link. In this case, the FD transfers the load that would have been sent to the broken link to other member links.

Although link aggregation appears at first to be quite simple, it is more complex than it seems. The major problem that can occur with link aggregation is out-of-order delivery. The problem is described as follows.

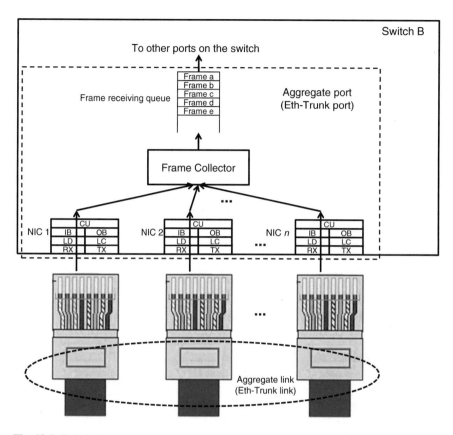

Fig. 10.6 Switch B receiving frames through an aggregate port

As shown in Fig. 10.7, the frame order in the frame sending queue on switch A is a, b, c, d, and then e. Assume that the FD distributes frame a to member link 1, frame b to member link 2, frame c to member link 3, frame d to member link 1, and frame e to member link 1. Frame a is a long frame. Frames b and c are short frames. Therefore, the transmission of frames b and c takes a short time, but the transmission of frame a takes a relatively long time. As a result, the following situation may occur: Frame b is the first frame that completely enters the FC of switch B, followed by frames c, a, d, and finally e. Therefore, the frame order in the frame receiving queue on switch B is b, c, a, d, and e, which is different from the order in the frame sending queue on switch A. This phenomenon is called out-of-order delivery.

Out-of-order delivery can be harmful or harmless depending on the situation.

Figure 10.8 shows an example of harmful out-of-order delivery. PC 1 and PC 3 are running network program X, which uses UDP as the transport layer protocol.

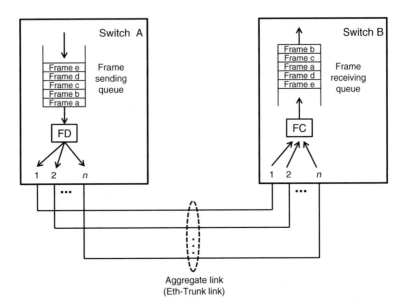

Fig. 10.7 Out-of-order delivery in link aggregation

PC 1 sends unicast frames X1 and X2 in sequence to PC 3. PC 2 and PC 4 are running network program Y, which also uses UDP as the transport layer protocol. PC 2 sends unicast frames Y1 and Y2 in sequence to PC 4. In the frame sending queue of the Eth-Trunk port on switch A, the frame order is X1, Y1, X2, Y2. Assume that the FD of switch A distributes X1 to member link 1, Y1 to member link 2, X2 to member link 2, and Y2 to member link 2. X1 is a long frame. Y1 and X2 are short frames. Because of this, the frame order in the frame receiving queue on switch B is possibly Y1, X2, X1, Y2. In this case, PC 3 will definitely receive X2 before X1, which is the opposite order from the order in which they were sent. The change in frame order is harmful to network program X. That is to say, out-of-order delivery in this example is harmful.

Figure 10.9 shows an example of harmless out-of-order delivery. In Fig. 10.9, all conditions are the same as those in the example illustrated in Fig. 10.8, except for the frame distribution implemented by the FD of switch A. In Fig. 10.9, the FD distributes frames in the following sequence: X1 to member link 1, Y1 to member link 2, X2 to member link 1, and Y2 to member link 2. It takes a long time to transmit X1 because X1 is a long frame. As a result, frames enter the FC of switch B in the following order: Y1, Y2, X1, X2. (Note that X2 is unlikely to enter the FC before X1 does). The frame order in the frame receiving queue on switch B is different from that in the frame sending queue on switch A. However, this difference does not affect the upper-layer application. PC 3 first receives X1 and then X2, and PC 4 first receives Y1 and then Y2. That is to say, out-of-order delivery in this example is harmless.

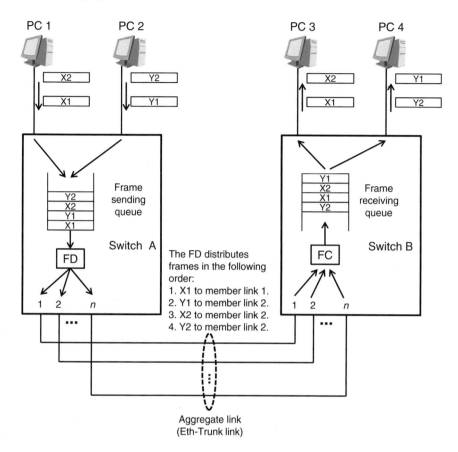

Fig. 10.8 Example of harmful out-of-order delivery

Let's review the concept of out-of-order delivery to reinforce our understanding. Frames vary in length. It takes a shorter time to transmit short frames and a longer time to transmit long frames. Different frames in a frame sending queue may be transmitted over different member links of an aggregate link. Due to these facts, out-of-order delivery is likely to occur. Sometimes, out-of-order delivery is harmless, but sometimes it is harmful. If it is harmful, it must be prevented.

How the FD of an aggregate port distributes frames to member ports determines whether harmful out-of-order delivery can be prevented. To understand how to prevent harmful out-of-order delivery, we must first understand the concept of a conversation. A conversation is a set of frames that must retain the same order in the frame receiving queue of the aggregate port on the receive (Rx) side as the frame order in the frame sending queue of the aggregate port on the transmit (Tx) side. If the frame orders on both sides are the same, harmful out-of-order delivery will not occur. However, if the frame orders are different, harmful out-of-order delivery is

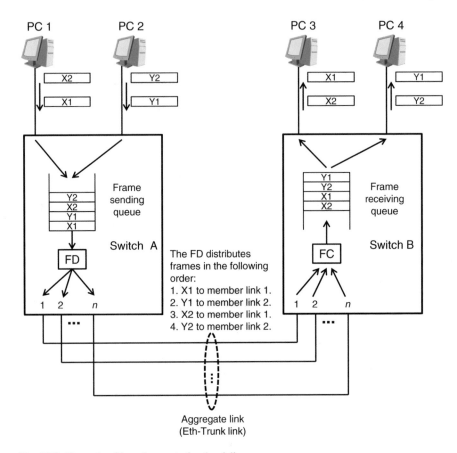

Fig. 10.9 Example of harmless out-of-order delivery

inevitable. Note that each individual frame must belong to a conversation, but cannot belong to multiple conversations.

To prevent harmful out-of-order delivery and implement traffic sharing, the FD of an aggregate port must comply with the following distribution rules:

- Frames that belong to the same conversation must be distributed to the same member link (thereby preventing harmful out-of-order delivery).
- Frames from different conversations can be distributed to the same member link or to different member links (thereby implementing traffic sharing).

These distribution rules ensure that frames from the same conversation will not be out of order, preventing harmful out-of-order delivery. Frames from different conversations may be out of order. However, such out-of-order delivery is harmless.

Figure 10.10 shows the same network as the one in Fig. 10.9 but includes information about the conversations into which the frames are grouped. First, the

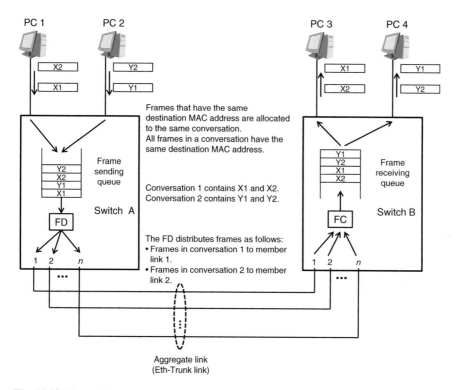

Fig. 10.10 Frames in a conversation being distributed to the same member link

aggregate port on switch A groups frames in the frame sending queue into conversations. To be specific, the aggregate port allocates frames that have the same destination MAC address to the same conversation. This generates conversation 1 and conversation 2. Frames X1 and X2 belong to conversation 1. Frames Y1 and Y2 belong to conversation 2. Based on the distribution rules employed by the FD, conversation 1 can be distributed to member link 1, and conversation 2 to member link 2. Alternatively, conversation 1 can be distributed to member link 2, and conversation 2 to member link 1. Furthermore, both conversations 1 and 2 can be distributed to the same member link; however, this is not the most efficient use of system resources, as traffic is not shared between member links.

The first diagram in Fig. 10.11 shows a more realistic example of how an FD distributes conversations among different member ports of an aggregate port. The second diagram shows what happens in this example if member link 4 is broken. In this case, the FD distributes conversation 5 to member port 2 and conversation 6 to member port 3.

During implementation of link aggregation, the FD of an aggregate link needs to define appropriate conversations based on a hash algorithm and then distribute them. However, it is not easy to define appropriate conversations. In the earlier example that we looked at in Fig. 10.10, the destination MAC address in a frame

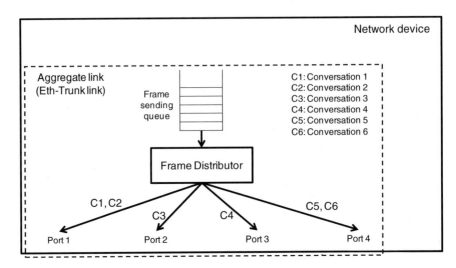

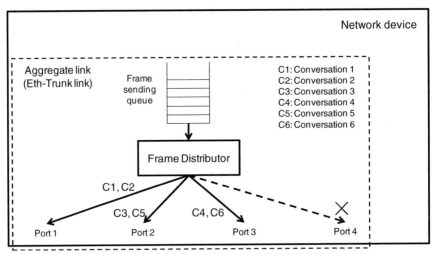

Fig. 10.11 Conversation-based distribution rules employed by an FD

was used as the reference for defining a conversation. However, in a real network
environment, properties of the devices at both ends of an aggregate link (for
example, in link aggregation between switches, between routers, between servers,
between a switch and a router, or between a switch and a server; see Fig. 10.3) and
properties of upper-layer applications also need to act as considerations in defining
conversations. The final reference may be a destination MAC address, a source
MAC address, a destination IP address, a source IP address, a combination of these
types of addresses, or even parameters in the upper-layer protocol.

Fig. 10.12 Link aggregation using LACP

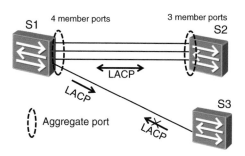

10.1.5 LACP

The Link Aggregation Control Protocol (LACP) is defined in IEEE 802.3ad. This book will not explain LACP in detail, but you should know that LACP is a link aggregation protocol.

Typically, link aggregation can be implemented on a device in two modes: manual load balancing and LACP. LACP increases the complexity of a device but provides a higher degree of automation and avoids misoperation. For example, in Fig. 10.12, if aggregate ports are manually configured on switches S1 and S2, it is possible that four ports are bundled on S1, whereas only three ports are bundled on S2. When not using LACP, it is difficult to discover a mistake such as this. However, if LACP is used, S1 and S2 automatically negotiate with each other by exchanging LACP frames, so the problem is easily discovered.

10.1.6 Configuration Example

In Fig. 10.13, 20 users are connected to switch S1 through FE links. Switches S2 and S1 are interconnected through three GE links. The three GE links need to be bundled into one Eth-Trunk link.

Configuration Roadmap

1. Create Eth-Trunk ports on S1 and S2.
2. (Optional) Configure a link aggregation mode.
3. Add physical ports to Eth-Trunk ports.
4. Configure the connectivity of Layer 2 links (such as VLAN configuration).

Procedure

Create an Eth-Trunk port numbered 1 (Eth-Trunk1) on S1.

```
<Quidway> system-view
[Quidway] sysname S1
[S1] interface Eth-Trunk1
[S1-Eth-Trunk1]
```

Fig. 10.13 Eth-Trunk
configuration example

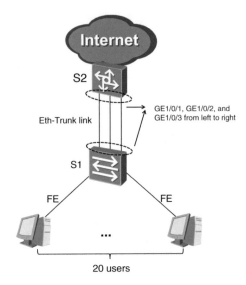

Eth-Trunk link

GE1/0/1, GE1/0/2, and
GE1/0/3 from left to right

20 users

Create an Eth-Trunk port numbered 1 (Eth-Trunk1) on S2. Note that the
Eth-Trunk ports created on both sides must be assigned the same number.

```
<Quidway> system-view
[Quidway] sysname S2
[S2] interface Eth-Trunk1
[S2-Eth-Trunk1]
```

(Optional) On S1, set the working mode of Eth-Trunk1 to manual load balancing.

```
[S1-Eth-Trunk1] mode manual load-balance
```

(Optional) On S2, set the working mode of Eth-Trunk1 to manual load balancing.

```
[S2-Eth-Trunk1] mode manual load-balance
```

The working mode of an Eth-Trunk port can be set to manual load balancing or
LACP by running the **mode {lacp|manual load-balance}** command. By default, an
Eth-Trunk port works in manual load balancing mode. The same working mode
must be set for Eth-Trunk ports on both sides. Before adding member ports to an
Eth-Trunk port, you must set its working mode as required.
On S1, add physical ports GE1/0/1, GE1/0/2, and GE1/0/3 to Eth-Trunk1.

```
[S1-Eth-Trunk1] trunkport gigabitethernet 1/0/1 to 1/0/3
[S1-Eth-Trunk1] quit
```

On S2, add physical ports GE1/0/1, GE1/0/2, and GE1/0/3 to Eth-Trunk1.

```
[S2-Eth-Trunk1] trunkport gigabitethernet 1/0/1 to 1/0/3
[S2-Eth-Trunk1] quit
```

Only physical ports of the same type can be added to an Eth-Trunk port, and they must have the same properties, such as belonging to the same VLAN.

\# Enable Eth-Trunk1 on S1 to allow frames that belong to VLAN 1000 to pass.

```
[S1] interface Eth-Trunk1
[S1-Eth-Trunk1] port link-type trunk
[S1-Eth-Trunk1] port trunk allow-pass vlan 1000
```

\# Enable Eth-Trunk1 on S2 to allow frames that belong to VLAN 1000 to pass.

```
[S2] interface Eth-Trunk1
[S2-Eth-Trunk1] port link-type trunk
[S2-Eth-Trunk1] port trunk allow-pass vlan 1000
```

Run the **display eth-trunk** [*trunk-id* [**interface** *interface-type interface-number*| **verbose**]] command to query and verify the configuration of an Eth-Trunk port. The following is an example:

\# On S1, query the configuration of Eth-Trunk1.

```
[S1] display eth-trunk 1 verbose
Eth-Trunk1's state information is:
WorkingMode: NORMAL        Hash arithmetic: According to SIP-XOR-DIP
Least Active-linknumber: 1 Max Bandwidth-affected-linknumber: 8
Operate status: up         Number Of Up Port In Trunk: 0
--------------------------------------------------------------------------------
PortName                   Status      Weight
GigabitEthernet1/0/1       Up          1
GigabitEthernet1/0/2       Up          1
GigabitEthernet1/0/3       Up          1

Flow statistic
Interface GigabitEthernet1/0/1
    Last 300 seconds input rate 32 bits/sec, 0 packets/sec
    Last 300 seconds output rate 32 bits/sec, 0 packets/sec
    148 packets input, 18944 bytes, 0 drops
    246 packets output, 31488 bytes, 0 drops
 Interface GigabitEthernet1/0/2
    Last 300 seconds input rate 32 bits/sec, 0 packets/sec
    Last 300 seconds output rate 32 bits/sec, 0 packets/sec
    147 packets input, 18816 bytes, 0 drops
    246 packets output, 31488 bytes, 0 drops
 Interface GigabitEthernet1/0/3
    Last 300 seconds input rate 56 bits/sec, 0 packets/sec
    Last 300 seconds output rate 48 bits/sec, 0 packets/sec
    144 packets input, 18432 bytes, 0 drops
    174 packets output, 22272 bytes, 0 drops
 Interface Eth-Trunk1
    Last 300 seconds input rate 96 bits/sec, 0 packets/sec
    Last 300 seconds output rate 96 bits/sec, 0 packets/sec
    439 packets input, 56192 bytes, 0 drops
666 packets output, 85248 bytes, 0 drops
```

In the preceding command output, "WorkingMode: NORMAL" indicates that the working mode of Eth-Trunk1 is manual load balancing. ("WorkingMode: LACP" indicates that the working mode is LACP.) "Least Active-linknumber: 1" indicates that the minimum number of member links in the Up state must be 1. "Operate status: up" indicates that Eth-Trunk1 is in the Up state. The information under "Flow statistic" indicates that Eth-Trunk1 contains three member ports: GigabitEthernet1/0/1, GigabitEthernet1/0/2, and GigabitEthernet1/0/3. The information also shows the amount of traffic forwarded by each port. The traffic forwarded by Eth-Trunk1 is the sum of the traffic forwarded by all member ports.

10.2   Smart Link

10.2.1   Working Principles

In Fig. 10.14, *n* user terminals are connected to access switch S4, and S4 is connected to aggregation switches S2 and S3 through uplinks Link2-4 and Link3-4 respectively. S2 and S3 are connected to core switch S1 through links Link1-2 and Link1-3 respectively. S1 is connected to the Internet through a router. Each switch is running the STP protocol to prevent loops. Assume that the STP tree contains Link1-2, Link1-3, and Link2-4. If Link2-4 is interrupted, Link3-4 will be added to the STP tree, thereby ensuring network connectivity.

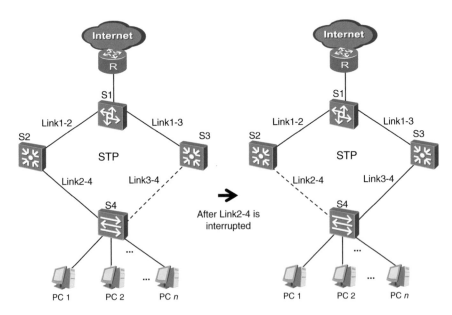

Fig. 10.14 Using STP to eliminate loops

However, STP convergence is slow, typically taking seconds. If high-speed links are used on the network, a large amount of data will be lost when STP is switching links. As a result, services sensitive to packet loss will be greatly affected.

To resolve this problem, Huawei has designed and implemented a proprietary protocol named Smart Link. This protocol is sometimes used to replace STP and switch links in one or a few milliseconds.

A Smart Link group consists of a master port and a slave port. Normally, the master port is active, and the slave port is blocked and therefore inactive. If the master port is faulty, the Smart Link group automatically blocks it and immediately changes the status of the slave port from inactive to active. Smart Link is typically used in a dual-uplink network environment.

In Fig. 10.15, a Smart Link group is configured on switch S4, where GE1/0/1 is the master port and GE1/0/2 is the slave port. Normally, GE1/0/1 is active and GE1/0/2 is blocked, which means that Link1-3, Link1-2, and Link2-4 are working, whereas Link3-4 is interrupted to prevent a loop from forming. If GE1/0/1 becomes faulty or senses that Link2-4 is interrupted, the Smart Link group immediately blocks GE1/0/1 and activates GE1/0/2. In this case, Link1-3, Link1-2, and Link3-4 are working, and Link2-4 is interrupted. Network connectivity is protected without forming a loop.

Smart Link and STP are mutually exclusive. Therefore, STP is not running on the network shown in Fig. 10.15.

The basic working principles of Smart Link are quite simple. However, the way it works in reality is complicated by the way in which MAC address tables are

Fig. 10.15 Example smart link configuration

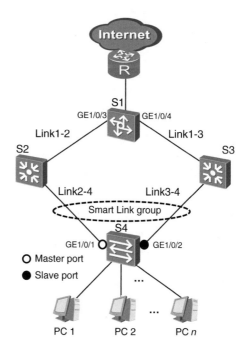

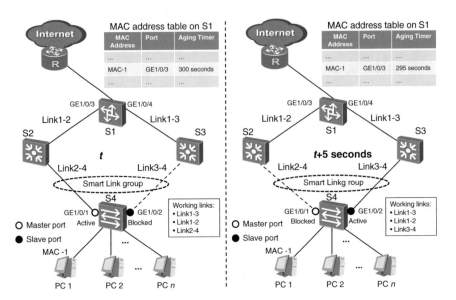

Fig. 10.16 Situations at t and $t + 5$ s

updated. The following example illustrates this issue, after which we will look at how Smart Link resolves it.

In the diagram on the left hand side of Fig. 10.16, a Smart Link group is configured on switch S4, with GE1/0/1 as the master port and GE1/0/2 as the slave port. The network is working properly. That is, Link3-4 is interrupted, whereas Link1-3, Link1-2, and Link2-4 are working properly. The MAC address of the network port on PC 1 is MAC-1.

If PC 1 sends a frame to the Internet at time t, the frame passes through Link2-4 and Link1-2 and enters S1 through port GE1/0/3. S1 then forwards the frame to the router. Based on the MAC address learning mechanism, S1 adds an entry for MAC-1, in which the corresponding port is GE1/0/3 and the value of the aging timer is 300 s (the default value), at nearly time t (ignoring the time spent in transmitting the frame from PC 1 to S1).

However, at $t + 5$ s, Link2-4 is interrupted. This is shown in the diagram on the right hand side of Fig. 10.16. Master port GE1/0/1 on S4 is immediately blocked and slave port GE1/0/2 is activated. Then, the working links become Link1-3, Link1-2, and Link3-4. On S1, the port listed in the entry for MAC-1 remains GE1/0/3, and the value of the aging timer is now 295 s.

In Fig. 10.17, the time is $t + 10$ s. PC 1 did not send any frames between $t + 5$ and $t + 10$. The entry for MAC-1 still exists in the MAC address table on S1. The port is still GE1/0/3, and the value of the aging timer is now 290 s. Assume that at $t + 10$ s, S1 received from the router a frame with the destination MAC address MAC-1. After querying the local MAC address table, S1 forwards the frame through GE1/0/3 rather than GE1/0/4. However, Link2-4 is interrupted. Therefore, the frame cannot be delivered to PC 1, leading to frame loss.

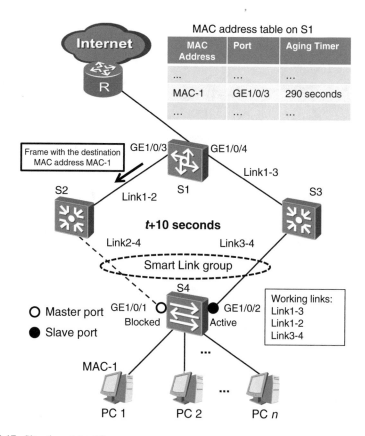

Fig. 10.17 Situation at $t + 10$ s

In a more serious case, if PC 1 does not send any frames between $t + 10$ s and $t + 300$ s, the port corresponding to MAC-1 in the MAC address table on S1 remains GE1/0/3, and all frames with the destination MAC address MAC-1 sent from the router to S1 within that entire time period of 290 s are lost.

How does Smart Link prevent this type of frame loss? Smart Link defines a type of protocol frame named flush frame with the destination MAC address 01-0f-e2-00-00-04, a multicast MAC address. Flush frames are used to instruct a switch to immediately clear an incorrect entry in the MAC address table.

Figure 10.18 provides an example to illustrate how this works. The time is $t + 5$ s. Link2-4 is interrupted. Master port GE1/0/1 on S4 is blocked and slave port GE1/0/2 is activated. Link1-3, Link1-2, and Link3-4 are working. The entry for MAC-1 on S1 is as follows: The port is GE1/0/3, and the value of the aging timer is 295 s. Smart Link enables S4 to instruct its slave port GE1/0/2 to immediately send a flush frame. Upon receiving the flush frame, S1 analyzes it and immediately clears the entry related to MAC-1 in the MAC address table.

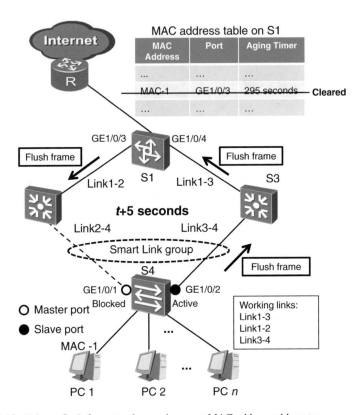

Fig. 10.18 Using a flush frame to clear an incorrect MAC address table entry

In Fig. 10.19, the time is $t + 10$ s. PC 1 did not send any frames between $t + 5$ and $t + 10$. Because of this, there is no entry for MAC-1 in the MAC address table on S1. At $t + 10$, S1 receives a frame with the destination MAC address MAC-1 from the router. S1 cannot find an entry related to MAC-1 in its MAC address table. Therefore, S1 floods the frame through GE1/0/3 and GE1/0/4. The frame forwarded through GE1/0/3 on S1 cannot be delivered to PC 1, because Link2-4 is interrupted. However, the frame forwarded through GE1/0/4 on S1 will be delivered to PC 1 over Link1-3 and Link3-4.

From the preceding example, we can see that flush frames play a critical role in Smart Link. To control the spread of flush frames, Smart Link defines a dedicated VLAN, known as a control VLAN. A control VLAN tag must be added to a flush frame before the flush frame is sent. If a device needs to receive and process flush frames, it must be configured so that it can receive, identify, and process frames that contain control VLAN tags. If not configured in such a way, the device will simply discard frames that contain control VLAN tags when it receives them.

To conclude this section, let's briefly look at the switchback function of Smart Link. Normally, the master port in a Smart Link group is active, and the slave port

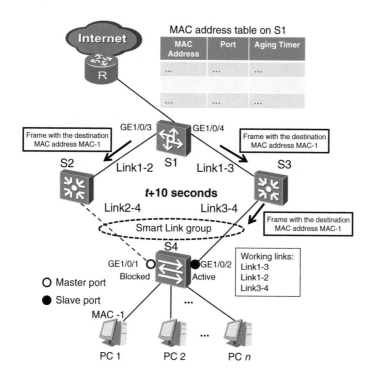

Fig. 10.19 Successful frame delivery

is inactive. If the master port goes down (in other words, the link connected to the master port is interrupted), the master port is blocked and the slave port is activated. However, when the master port recovers, Smart Link will not automatically reactivate the master port or block the slave port. To achieve that, you must configure the switchback function of Smart Link in advance.

When configuring switchback, you must specify the switchback time parameter. The default value is 60 s. When the master port recovers, Smart Link will wait for the period of time specified by the switchback time parameter before performing a switchback. The reason for this is that the master port may be unstable or even intermittently interrupted for a period of time after recovering. Therefore, switchback should not be performed immediately.

10.2.2   Configuration Example

Switches A, B, and C form a loop (see Fig. 10.20). Allocate ports GE1/0/1 and GE1/0/2 on switch A to one Smart Link group. Configure GE1/0/1 as the master port and GE1/0/2 as the slave port.

Fig. 10.20 Smart link
configuration example

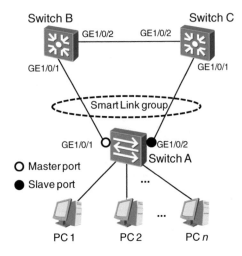

Configuration Roadmap

1. Create a Smart Link group, add the necessary ports to it, and specify the role of each port.
2. Enable the Smart Link group to send flush frames.
3. Enable ports to receive flush frames.
4. Enable the Smart Link switchback function.
5. Enable Smart Link.

Procedure

Smart Link and STP are mutually exclusive. Therefore, before configuring Smart Link, you must enter the corresponding interface view and run the **stp disable** command to disable the STP function.

Configure switch A.

```
[SwitchA] interface gigabitethernet 1/0/1
[SwitchA-GigabitEthernet1/0/1] stp disable
[SwitchA-GigabitEthernet1/0/1] quit
[SwitchA] interface gigabitethernet 1/0/2
[SwitchA-GigabitEthernet1/0/2] stp disable
[SwitchA-GigabitEthernet1/0/2] quit
```

Create Smart Link group 1 on switch A, and run the **port** command to add GE1/0/1 to Smart Link group 1 as the master port and GE1/0/2 to Smart Link group 1 as the slave port.

Configure switch A.

```
[SwitchA] smart-link group 1
[SwitchA-smlk-group1] port gigabitethernet 1/0/1 master
[SwitchA-smlk-group1] port gigabitethernet 1/0/2 slave
```

Run the **flush send** command to enable Smart Link group 1 to send flush frames with control VLAN ID 10 and password 123.

\# Configure switch A.

```
[SwitchA-smlk-group1] flush send control-vlan 10 password
simple 123
```

On switches B and C, run the **smart-link flush receive** command to enable their ports GE1/0/1 and GE1/0/2 to be capable of receiving and processing flush frames that carry control VLAN ID 10.

\# Configure switch B.

```
[SwitchB] interface gigabitethernet 1/0/1
[SwitchB-GigabitEthernet1/0/1]  smart-link  flush  receive
control-vlan 10 password simple 123
[SwitchB-GigabitEthernet1/0/1] quit
[SwitchB] interface gigabitethernet 1/0/2
[SwitchB-GigabitEthernet1/0/2]  smart-link  flush  receive
control-vlan 10 password simple 123
[SwitchB-GigabitEthernet1/0/2] quit
```

\# Configure switch C.

```
[SwitchC] interface gigabitethernet 1/0/1
[SwitchC-GigabitEthernet1/0/1]  smart-link  flush  receive
control-vlan 10 password simple 123
[SwitchC-GigabitEthernet1/0/1] quit
[SwitchC] interface gigabitethernet 1/0/2
[SwitchC-GigabitEthernet1/0/2]  smart-link  flush  receive
control-vlan 10 password simple 123
[SwitchC-GigabitEthernet1/0/2] quit
```

Run the **restore enable** command to configure the switchback function, and run the **timer wtr** command to set the switchback time to 30 s.

\# Configure switch A.

```
[SwitchA-smlk-group1] restore enable
[SwitchA-smlk-group1] timer wtr 30
```

Finally, run the **smart-link enable** command to enable the functions of Smart Link group 1.

\# Configure switch A.

```
[SwitchA-smlk-group1] smart-link enable
```

Verify the configuration of Smart Link group 1 by running the **display smart-link group** command to view information about the Smart Link group. The following command output uses switch A as an example:

```
<SwitchA> display smart-link group 1
Smart Link group 1 information :
  Smart Link group was enabled
  Wtr-time is: 30 sec.
  There is no Load-Balance
  There is no protected-vlan reference-instance
  DeviceID: 0018-2000-0083  Control-vlan ID: 10
  Member               Role   State   ...
  --------------------------------------------
  GigabitEthernet1/0/1     Master Active  ...
  GigabitEthernet1/0/2     Slave  Inactive ...
```

From the preceding command output, we can see that Smart Link group 1 is enabled, GigabitEthernet1/0/1 is the master port in active state, GigabitEthernet1/0/2 is the slave port in inactive state, the control VLAN ID is 10, and the switchback time is 30 s.

10.3   Monitor Link

10.3.1   Working Principles

In Fig. 10.21, a Smart Link group is configured on S4. In this Smart Link group, GE1/0/1 is the master port and is active, and GE1/0/2 is the slave port and is blocked. If GE/1/0/1 on S2 fails, causing Link1-2 to be interrupted, S4 will not detect the failure. Therefore, frames sent from master port GE1/0/1 on S4 will be lost.

To resolve this problem, Huawei has designed and implemented a proprietary protocol named Monitor Link. This protocol is sometimes used with Smart Link to minimize the likelihood of frame loss.

In Fig. 10.21, a Monitor Link group can be configured on S2. The group contains two ports: one is GE1/0/1, which acts as an uplink port, and the other is GE1/0/2, which acts as a downlink port. The working principles of Monitor Link are as follows: A Monitor Link group consists of one uplink port and one or more downlink ports. If the uplink port goes down, all downlink ports are immediately set to the Down state. In other words, downlink ports are linked to the uplink port and have the same state as that of the uplink port.

In Fig. 10.21, Link1-3, Link1-2, and Link2-4 are working under normal conditions. If GE1/0/1 on S2 goes down, Monitor Link enables GE1/0/2 on S2 to enter the Down state. This causes GE1/0/1 on S4 to also enter the Down state. Then, Smart Link on S4 immediately changes the state of slave port GE1/0/2 on S4 from inactive to active. As a result, Link1-3 and Link3-4 become working links, thereby maintaining network connectivity.

To further improve network reliability, we can also configure a Monitor Link group on S3, so that GE1/0/2 and GE1/0/1 on S3 are linked.

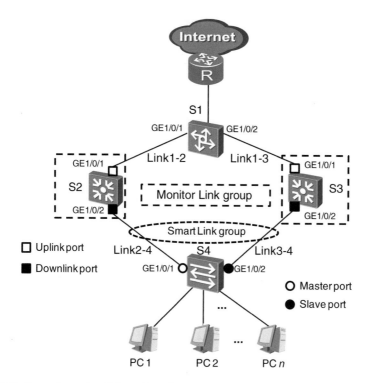

Fig. 10.21 Example monitor link configuration

Figure 10.22 shows Smart Link groups configured on S1, S2, and S3, and Monitor Link groups configured on S2 and S3. Note that the Monitor Link group on S2 considers the Smart Link group on S2 to be the uplink port. The downlink port will be set to the Down state only when both ports in the Smart Link group go down. This is also true for S3.

In Fig. 10.22, if the master port on S2 goes down, the slave port on S2 will be activated immediately, and Monitor Link on S2 will not take effect. Only if both the master and the slave port on S2 go down, will the downlink port on S2 be set to the Down state. In this case, the Smart Link group on S1 will block its master port and activate its slave port. Simultaneous use of Smart Link and Monitor Link can meet certain specialized use cases in complex network environments.

Like Smart Link, Monitor Link also has a switchback function. If the uplink port in a Monitor Link group cannot work, all downlink ports in the group will be set to the Down state. If the uplink port recovers, all the downlink ports also automatically enter the Up state. As with the switchback function of Smart Link, you can also specify a switchback time for the switchback function of Monitor Link.

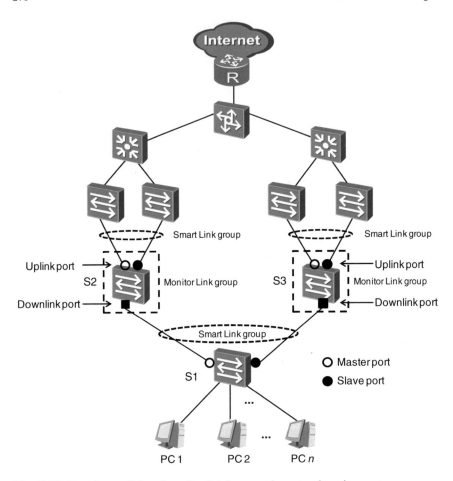

Fig. 10.22 Use of smart link and monitor link in a complex network environment

10.3.2   Configuration Example

In Fig. 10.23, a Smart Link group has been configured on switch A and switch B. You need to configure a Monitor Link group on switch B and switch C.

Configuration Roadmap

1. Create a Monitor Link group on switch B and switch C, and add uplink and downlink ports.
2. Configure the switchback time for the Monitor Link groups configured on switch B and switch C.

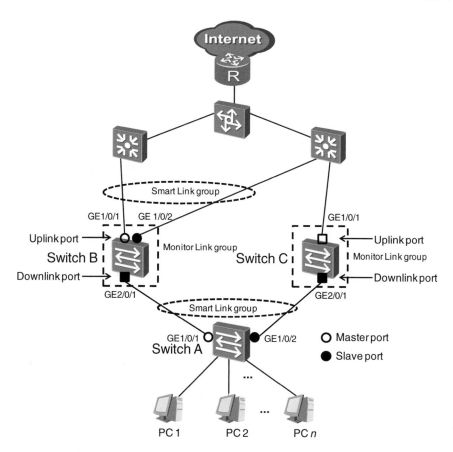

Fig. 10.23 Example monitor link configuration

Procedure

Create Monitor Link group 1 on Switch B, add Smart Link group 1 as the uplink
port to Monitor Link group 1, and add GE2/0/1 as the downlink port to Monitor
Link group 1.

   # Configure switch B.

```
[SwitchB] monitor-link group 1
[SwitchB-mtlk-group1] smart-link group 1 uplink
[SwitchB-mtlk-group1] port gigabitethernet 2/0/1 downlink 1
```

   Create Monitor Link group 2 on switch C, add GE1/0/1 as the uplink port to
Monitor Link group 2, and add GE2/0/1 as the downlink port to Monitor Link
group 2.

Configure switch C.

```
[SwitchC] monitor-link group 2
[SwitchC-mtlk-group2] port gigabitethernet 1/0/1 uplink
[SwitchC-mtlk-group2] port gigabitethernet 2/0/1 downlink 1
```

Run the **timer recover-time** command to set the switchback time to 10 s for both Monitor Link groups.

Configure switch B.

```
[SwitchB-mtlk-group1] timer recover-time 10
```

Configure switch C.

```
[SwitchC-mtlk-group2] timer recover-time 10
```

Verify the configuration by running the **display smart-link group** command to view information about the Smart Link groups, and running the **display monitor-link group** command to view information about the Monitor Link groups. The following command output uses switch B as an example:

```
<SwitchB> display smart-link group 1
Smart Link group 1 information :
  Smart Link group was enabled
  Wtr-time is: 30 sec.
  There is no Load-Balance
  There is no protected-vlan reference-instance
  DeviceID: 0018-2000-0083  Control-vlan ID: 10
  Member              Role    State        ...
  --------------------------------------------------
  GigabitEthernet1/0/1     Master Active        ...
  GigabitEthernet1/0/2     Slave  Inactive      ...

<SwitchB> display monitor-link group 1
Monitor Link group 1 information :
  Recover-timer is 10 sec.
  Member              Role    State    ...
  Smart-link1         UpLk    UP       ...
  GigabitEthernet2/0/1     DwLk[1] UP       ...
```

From the preceding command output, we can see that Smart Link group 1 on switch B is enabled, GE1/0/1 is the master port in active state, GE1/0/2 is the slave port in inactive state, the control VLAN ID is 10, and the switchback time is 30 s. In Monitor Link group 1, the uplink port is Smart Link group 1, the downlink port is GE2/0/1, and the switchback time is 10 s.

10.4 Review Questions

1. Which of the following statements about link aggregation are true? (Choose all that apply)

   A. Link aggregation can be used between two routers.
   B. Link aggregation can be used between two switches.
   C. Link aggregation can be used between two servers.
   D. Link aggregation cannot be used between a switch and a router.
   E. Link aggregation cannot be used between a server and a router.
   F. Link aggregation can be used between a server and a switch.

2. Which of the following statements about link aggregation are true? (Choose all that apply)

   A. Link aggregation can be used to flexibly increase bandwidth between devices.
   B. In the frame receiving queue of the aggregate port on the Rx side, the frame order must be the same as that in the frame sending queue of the aggregate port on the Tx side.
   C. Link aggregation can improve the reliability of connections between devices.
   D. Both Smart Link and LACP are link aggregation standards defined by IEEE.

3. Assume that all ports on a device are GE ports. If an Eth-Trunk port that provides up to 3.5 Gbit/s in bandwidth is needed, which is the minimum number of ports that must be added to the Eth-Trunk port? (Choose one)

   A. 2
   B. 3
   C. 4
   D. 5

4. Which of the following statements about Smart Link are true? (Choose all that apply)

   A. Normally, the master port in a Smart Link group is active, and the slave port is inactive.
   B. Smart Link is defined by Huawei.
   C. STP must be enabled on master and slave ports in a Smart Link group to prevent loops from forming.
   D. If the master port in a Smart Link group is inactive and the slave port is active, the Smart Link configuration is incorrect.

5. Which of the following statements about Monitor Link is true? (Choose one)

    A. The state of the uplink port in a Monitor Link group varies depending on the state of downlink ports.

    B. A Monitor Link group can contain only one downlink port.

    C. A Smart Link group cannot act as the uplink port in a Monitor Link group.

    D. Monitor Link is defined by IETF.

    E. None of above.

Chapter 11
DHCP and NAT

Suppose you are surfing the Internet to learn about new command inputs. You open your Command Line Interface (CLI) and run the **ipconfig** command you just learned about. In the command output, you will see an IP address in use by the network port of your computer. In most cases this IP address is a private address (to review private IP addressing, go back to Sect. 6.4). Two questions now arise. Where does your IP address come from, and because your IP address is a private address, how is your computer accessing the Internet, a public network?

The answers to these two questions come from understanding the Dynamic Host Configuration Protocol (DHCP) and Network Address Translation (NAT), which are discussed in this chapter.

After completing this section, you should be able to understand:

- Basic concepts and functions of DHCP
- How a DHCP client obtains IP addresses for its first and future attempts
- IP address lease and lease duration
- Functions and locations of the DHCP relay agent
- Private and public networks
- NAT definition and functions
- Work principles of the static NAT, dynamic NAT, NAPT, and Easy IP.

11.1 DHCP

11.1.1 Basic Concepts and Functions

Imagine you are working for a renowned company. Every morning when you arrive, you turn on your computer so you can access shared work files from your colleagues, or go through your email. Your computer, or more precisely the network port of your computer, is communicating with other computers on the network through Internet

© Springer Science+Business Media Singapore 2016
Huawei Technologies Co., Ltd., *HCNA Networking Study Guide*,
DOI 10.1007/978-981-10-1554-0_11

Protocol (IP), which has allocated an IP address to serve as the port's identification on the network. Without this identification, your device can't access the network. But how did your computer acquire this IP address in the first place.

To understand this, you also need to understand that, in addition to an IP address, your computer needs access to other information before joining a network. After turning your computer on, it will attempt to obtain a group of necessary parameters and information relevant to the network, such as the gateway address and subnet mask of the home Layer 2 network, and the IP address of the nearby network printer. If the attempt is successful, your computer and the connected networks will function properly. If the attempt is unsuccessful, it means the network has configuration issues.

IETF released the Bootstrap Protocol (BOOTP), which was especially designed to automate network parameter configuration when a device on a network is "booted" up. To remedy defects in the BOOTP protocol, IETF later released another protocol named Dynamic Host Configuration Protocol (DHCP). DHCP dynamically allocates network configuration parameters, and is compatible with BOOTP.

DHCP allocates many diverse parameters, but we will only discuss host IP addresses in this chapter. By the way, when we use the word "host," we mean a network device that requires an IP address, which is often, but not always, a computer. Normally, DHCP is not suitable for assigning IP addresses to routers. The IP addresses of routers are manually configured based on network conditions.

DHCP is a network protocol based on a client/server model. In the example shown in Fig. 11.1, each PC on the network has client software installed on it, and

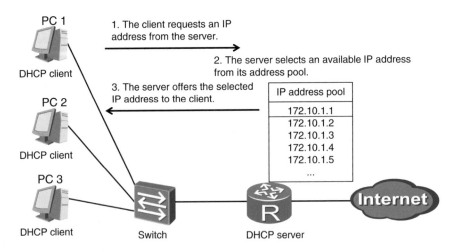

Fig. 11.1 IP address request and assignment using DHCP

the server software installed on the router provides these clients with a resource or service.

Now, let's come back to one of the questions raised at the beginning of this chapter: where does your computer's IP address come from?

You may think you can manually configure an IP address yourself, and this is true in some special cases. However, imagine if all the staff at your company manually configure their own IP addresses at will. If two or more people chose the same IP address, IP address conflicts would occur.

Instead, computers on a network use DHCP to request an IP address. After turning your computer on, it automatically runs the DHCP client. The DHCP client then sends a request to the DHCP server, asking for an IP address. After receiving the request, the DHCP server selects an available IP address from its address pool and offers it to the DHCP client. Finally, your computer applies the IP address to its network port. Figure 11.1 shows how the DHCP protocol works.

11.1.2 Basic Operations

DHCP operations shown in Fig. 11.2 follow four stages: discovery, offer, request, and acknowledgment. Suppose that PC 1, a newly bought computer, has never automatically requested an IP address from a DHCP server. This section will describe how PC 1 acquires an IP address through DHCP for the first time.

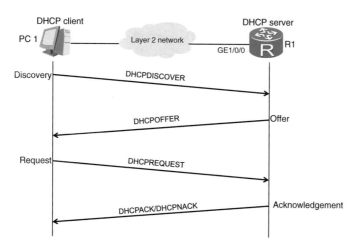

Fig. 11.2 The first time a PC requests an IP address from a DHCP server

DHCP Discovery

In the discovery stage, the DHCP client on PC 1 searches for DHCP servers. After PC 1 is turned on, its local DHCP client sends a broadcast frame. The source MAC address of the broadcast frame is the MAC address of PC 1, the type field is 0x0800, and the payload is the broadcast IP packet. For the IP packet, the destination IP address is 255.255.255.255 (limited broadcast address), the source IP address is 0.0.0.0 (described in Sect. 6.4), the protocol field is 0x11, and the payload is a User Datagram Protocol (UDP) packet. The destination and source port numbers of the UDP packet are 67 and 68 respectively, and the payload is a DHCPDISCOVER message.

DHCP Offer

In this stage, the DHCP server offers an IP address to the DHCP client. In Fig. 11.2, each DHCP server (including the one on R1) that receives the DHCPDISCOVER message will select an appropriate IP address from its available address pool, and send the IP address to the DHCP client through a DHCPOFFER message.

The DHCPOFFER message is encapsulated in a UDP packet with the destination and source port numbers now reversed to 68 and 67, respectively. This is then encapsulated in a broadcast IP packet. The source IP address is the unicast IP address of the DHCP server. The broadcast IP packet is then encapsulated in a broadcast frame, and the source MAC address is the MAC address of the DHCP server.

DHCP Request

After receiving DHCPOFFER messages, the DHCP client on PC 1 determines which offer to accept (in the example, PC 1 accepts the offer from the DHCP client on R1). Usually, the DHCP client will accept the first offer. PC 1 then sends a broadcast frame to R1, requesting the IP address contained in the offer.

The source MAC address of the broadcast frame is the MAC address of PC 1, and the source IP address of the broadcast IP packet inside the frame is 0.0.0.0. The destination and source port numbers of the UDP packet inside the IP packet is 67 and 68 respectively, while the payload of the UDP packet is now a DHCPREQUEST message containing the identifier of the DHCP server on R1.

All DHCP servers on the Layer 2 network will receive the DHCPREQUEST message. R1 analyzes the message, and finds that PC 1 is willing to accept its offer. Other DHCP servers will know that their offers are rejected by PC 1, and will withdraw these offers.

DHCP Acknowledgment

After its offer is accepted, the DHCP server on R1 sends a DHCPACK message to PC 1. The DHCPACK message is encapsulated in a UDP packet with a destination port number of 68 and a source port number of 67. This packet is then encapsulated in a broadcast IP packet. The destination IP address of the broadcast IP packet is the limited broadcast address, and the source IP address is the unicast IP address of the

DHCP server. The broadcast IP packet is then encapsulated in a unicast frame. The type field of the unicast frame is 0x0800. The source MAC address is the MAC address of the DHCP server and the destination MAC address is the MAC address of PC 1.

Once receiving the DHCPACK message from R1, PC 1 acquires its IP address for the first time.

However, the DHCP server on R1 may, for many reasons, send a DHCPNACK (negative acknowledgment) message to the DHCP client on PC 1. If the DHCP client receives a DHCPNACK message, this indicates that the DHCP server denied the request. In this case, PC 1 fails to acquire an IP address and must start again from the discovery stage.

You may ask yourself, "When PC 1 restarts, does it need to perform these four stages again?" Usually the answer is no. PC 1, equipped with its memory storage, remembers the IP address acquired the last time it connected to the network, the identifier of the DHCP server that offered the IP address (the DHCP server on R1), and other information about the DHCP server, such as the unicast IP address and MAC address.

On its next startup, PC 1 will directly enter the third stage: the DHCP request stage. PC 1 will send a DHCPREQUEST message (containing the identifier of the DHCP server on R1), requesting continued use of the IP address it was assigned last time. In response, R1 replies with a DHCPACK message to accept the request of PC 1. However, if the IP address requested by PC 1 is unavailable, the DHCP server on R1 will reply with a DHCPNACK message. PC 1 then has to request a new IP address starting from the DHCP discovery stage (Fig. 11.3).

As defined in DHCP, the IP address offered by a DHCP server is used by a DHCP client, but is owned by the DHCP server itself. Every time a DHCP server offers an IP address to a DHCP client, the DHCP server agrees to an IP address lease with the DHCP client. Every lease has a duration period that cannot be less than one hour, and is usually set to 24 h. The offered IP address is available to the

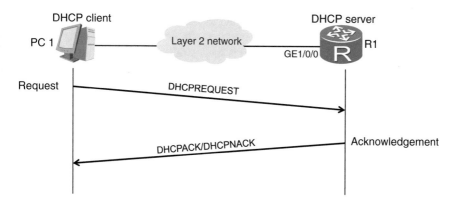

Fig. 11.3 Future IP address request procedure

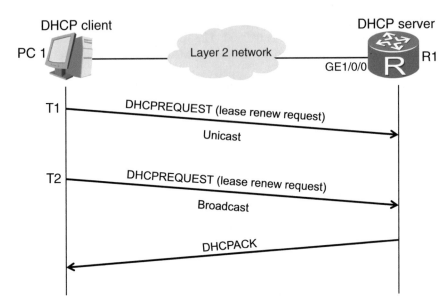

Fig. 11.4 Procedure for extending the duration of lease

DHCP client only during the duration of the lease. Once the lease expires, the right to use the IP address is revoked from the DHCP client. The DHCP client can apply to extend the lease duration before it expires, as shown in Fig. 11.4.

As shown in Fig. 11.4, using defaults specified by DHCP, T1 indicates the time at which the lease has reached its halfway point, and T2 indicates when the client has reached 87.5 % of the duration of its lease. At T1, the DHCP client on PC 1 unicasts a DHCPREQUEST message to the DHCP server on R1 to extend its lease on the IP address. The DHCP server on R1 will reply with a DHCPACK message. If the DHCP client receives the reply message before reaching T2, the IP address lease extension is successful.

If the reply does not arrive before T2, the DHCP client will broadcast a DHCPREQUEST message at T2, yet again requesting an extension of the lease on its IP address. If the DHCP client receives the DHCPACK message before the lease expires, the duration of IP address lease is successfully extended. If the DHCPACK message does not come before the lease expires, PC 1 is denied the right to use the IP address, and has to perform the four DHCP operation stages again to apply for a new IP address.

11.1.3   DHCP Relay Agent

From understanding the DHCP operations described in the previous section, you can see that the DHCP client typically sends the DHCPDISCOVER and

DHCPREQUEST messages using broadcast frames and IP packets. These messages, however, cannot arrive at a DHCP server located on a different Layer 2 network. The DHCP operations mentioned so far are only suitable for when the DHCP server and DHCP client are located on the same Layer 2 network.

So if an enterprise has several Layer 2 networks, should it deploy at least one DHCP server on each network? Theoretically this is possible, but this type of deployment is unnecessary and wasteful. DHCP defines the role of DHCP relay agents, as well as DHCP clients and servers. DHCP relay agents are responsible for transmitting DHCP messages between the clients and servers.

Figure 11.5 shows the process of a DHCP client acquiring configuration parameters (such as an IP address) from the DHCP server using the DHCP relay agent. The DHCP client must reside on the same Layer 2 network as the DHCP relay agent, whereas the server and the relay agent may or may not be on the same Layer 2 network. The DHCP client and relay agent exchange DHCP messages using broadcast, whereas the relay agent and server exchange DHCP messages using unicast. This means that the DHCP relay agent must know the IP address of the DHCP server beforehand.

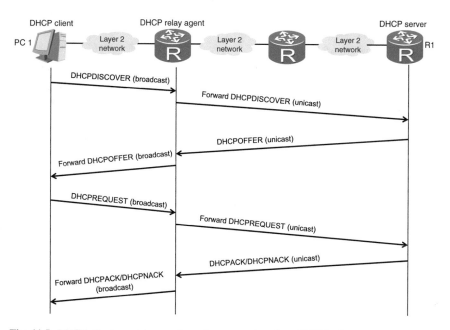

Fig. 11.5 DHCP client receiving configuration parameters from DHCP relay agent

11.1.4 DHCP Server Configuration Example

Figure 11.6 shows the setup of an enterprise that has three departments located on different Layer 2 network segments. Each department has about 50 PCs on each network. The enterprise plans to install a DHCP server on R1, which will provide DHCP configuration services for the PCs in all departments. How should you proceed in this instance?

Configuration Roadmap

1 Enable DHCP on R1.
2. Create three global address pools to offer IP addresses to PCs in three different departments.
3. Configure the attributes of the global address pools.
4. Under the R1 port, configure the global address pool-based service model for the DHCP server to select and offer IP addresses.

To enable DHCP on R1, access the system view and run the **dhcp enable** command.
#Configure R1.

```
<R1> system-view
[R1] dhcp enable
```

From there you can create three global address pools on R1 that will offer IP addresses to PCs in three different departments. The DHCP server can distribute IP addresses using either the **global address pool-based** service model or **interface**

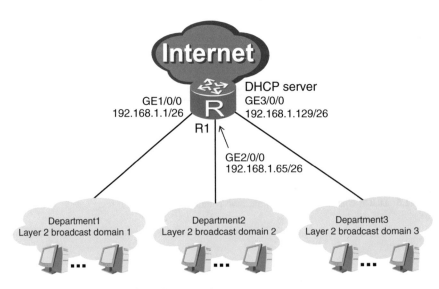

Fig. 11.6 DHCP server configuration example

address pool-based service model. Of the two models, the global address pool-based service model is preferred, as it allows the DHCP client and server to reside on different Layer 2 networks. Using the interface address pool-based service model means the DHCP client can only acquire IP addresses when it resides on the same Layer 2 network as the interface address pool.

To create a global address pool, run the **ip pool** *ip-pool-name* command. In this command, *ip-pool-name* indicates the address pool name, which can be a combination of letters, digits, and underscores.
#Configure R1.

```
<R1> system-view
[R1] ip pool department1
Info: It's successful to create an IP address pool.
[R1-ip-pool-department1] quit
[R1] ip pool department2
Info: It's successful to create an IP address pool.
[R1-ip-pool-department2] quit
[R1] ip pool department3
Info: It's successful to create an IP address pool.
[R1-ip-pool-department3] quit
```

After creating three global address pools named department1, department2, and department3, configure their attributes one by one. Here, department1 is used as an example, and department2 and department3 can be configured in a similar way.

The following shows how to configure the allocable IP address segment for department1. In the system view, run the **ip pool department1** command to display the department1 global address pool view. Then run the **network** *ip-address* [**mask** {*mask*|*mask-length*}] command to configure the allocable IP address segment. In this command, **mask**{*mask*|*mask-length*} indicates the network mask. Considering the fact that each department has about 50 PCs, specify the length of the network mask as 26-bit.
#Configure R1.

```
<R1> system-view
[R1] ip pool department1
[R1-ip-pool-department1] network 192.168.1.0 mask 26
```

As a result, a total of 62 IP addresses from 192.168.1.1 to 192.168.1.62 are available in the department1 address pool. The IP addresses 192.168.1.0 and 192.168.1.63 are non-distributable.

Next, run the **gateway-list** *ip-address* command to specify the gateway IP address from the global address pool that a PC can communicate with after gaining its IP address.
#Configure R1.

```
[R1-ip-pool-department1] gateway-list 192.168.1.1
```

The IP address 192.168.1.1 is specified as the gateway IP address. The system then automatically reserves this address, and will not offer it to any other device. You may have noticed that 192.168.1.1 is actually the IP address of the GE1/0/0 port on R1, and the GE1/0/0 port on R1 is the gateway of department1.

Then, you can run the **lease{day** *day*[**hour** *hour*[**minute** *minute*]]|**unlimited}** command to configure the IP address lease duration. By default, the lease duration is 24 h. In the example, it is set to one hour.
#Configure R1.

```
[R1-ip-pool-department1] lease day 0 hour 1
```

Now you have finished configuring the department1 address pool. Continue by configuring department2 and department3 using the following example.
#Configure R1.

```
<R1> system-view
[R1] ip pool department2
[R1-ip-pool-department2] network 192.168.1.64 mask 26
[R1-ip-pool-department2] gateway-list 192.168.1.65
[R1-ip-pool-department2] lease day 0 hour 1
[R1-ip-pool-department2] quit
[R1] ip pool department3
[R1-ip-pool-department3] network 192.168.1.128 mask 26
[R1-ip-pool-department3] gateway-list 192.168.1.129
[R1-ip-pool-department3] lease day 0 hour 1
```

Now, you need to configure the global address pool-based service model for all ports on R1. Input the command **dhcp select global**.
#Configure R1.

```
<R1> system-view
[R1] interface GigabitEthernet 1/0/0
[R1-GigabitEthernet1/0/0] ip address 192.168.1.1 26
[R1-GigabitEthernet1/0/0] dhcp select global
[R1-GigabitEthernet1/0/0] quit
[R1] interface GigabitEthernet 2/0/0
[R1-GigabitEthernet2/0/0] ip address 192.168.1.65 26
[R1-GigabitEthernet2/0/0] dhcp select global
[R1-GigabitEthernet2/0/0] quit
[R1] interface GigabitEthernet 3/0/0
[R1-GigabitEthernet3/0/0] ip address 192.168.1.129 26
[R1-GigabitEthernet3/0/0] dhcp select global
[R1-GigabitEthernet3/0/0] quit
```

To verify the configurations, access the user view of R1 and run the **display ip pool name** *pool-name* **used** command to view the address pool configuration and offered IP addresses (department1 used in the example here).

```
<R1> display ip pool name department1 used
  Pool-name        : department1
  Pool-No          : 0
  Lease            : 0 Days 1 Hours 0 Minutes
  Domain-name      : -
  DNS-server0      : -
  NBNS-server0     : -
  Netbios-type     : -
  Position           : Local        Status        : Unlocked
  Gateway-0        : 192.168.1.1
  Mask             : 255.255.255.192
  VPN instance     : --
----------------------------------------------------------------------
Start          End           Total Used  Idle(Expired) Conflict Disable
----------------------------------------------------------------------
192.168.1.1  192.168.1.62  61    1       60(0)          0        0
----------------------------------------------------------------------
Network section :
----------------------------------------------------------------------
  Index          IP            MAC          Lease   Status
----------------------------------------------------------------------
    2         192.168.1.3   000B-09CF-B353   60      used
----------------------------------------------------------------------
```

As you can see, the IP address 192.168.1.3 has been offered to a PC whose MAC address is 000B-09CF-B353.

11.1.5 DHCP Relay Agent Configuration Example

In Fig. 11.6 we enabled DHCP on R1, created three global address pools, and configured these pools so the DHCP server can select and allocate IP addresses. Figure 11.7 illustrates the process of configuring the DHCP relay agent on R1.

Configuration Roadmap

1. Enable DHCP on R1.
2. Enable DHCP for all ports on R1 and configure the IP address for the DHCP server.

First, access the system view and run the **dhcp enable** command.
Configure R1.

```
<R1> system-view
[R1] dhcp enable
```

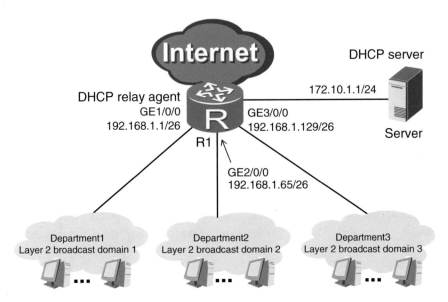

Fig. 11.7 Configuring the DHCP relay agent

Then, enable DHCP for all ports on R1 using the **dhcp select relay** command.
Finally, run the **dhcp relay server-ip** 172.10.1.1 command to configure the IP
address for the DHCP server.
Configure R1.

```
[R1] interface GigabitEthernet 1/0/0
[R1-GigabitEthernet1/0/0] ip address 192.168.1.1 26
[R1-GigabitEthernet1/0/0] dhcp select relay
[R1-GigabitEthernet1/0/0] dhcp relay server-ip 172.10.1.1
[R1-GigabitEthernet1/0/0] quit
[R1] interface GigabitEthernet 2/0/0
[R1-GigabitEthernet2/0/0] ip address 192.168.1.65 26
[R1-GigabitEthernet2/0/0] dhcp select relay
[R1-GigabitEthernet2/0/0] dhcp relay server-ip 172.10.1.1
[R1-GigabitEthernet2/0/0] quit
[R1] interface GigabitEthernet 3/0/0
[R1-GigabitEthernet3/0/0] ip address 192.168.1.129 26
[R1-GigabitEthernet3/0/0] dhcp select relay
[R1-GigabitEthernet3/0/0] dhcp relay server-ip 172.10.1.1
[R1-GigabitEthernet3/0/0] quit
```

To verify the DHCP relay agent configurations for a port on R1, run the **display
this** command. Here, the example shows this command for the GE1/0/0 port.

```
[R1] interface GigabitEthernet 1/0/0
[R1-GigabitEthernet1/0/0] display this
#
interface GigabitEthernet1/0/0
               ip address 192.168.1.0 255.255.255.192
               dhcp select relay
               dhcp relay server-ip 172.10.1.1
#
return
```

11.2 NAT

11.2.1 Basic Concepts

Network address translation (NAT) is a technique used for conversion between private IP addresses and public IP addresses.

As discussed previously, IP addresses fall into three classes: A, B, and C. The following is a list of address ranges in each class that are reserved for private IP addresses:

1. Class A: 10.0.0.0–10.255.255.255
2. Class B: 172.16.0.0–172.31.255.255
3. Class C: 192.168.0.0–192.168.255.255

Outside of these ranges, all other IP addresses are public addresses.

Networks are also classified as either public or private. A network that contains only public IP addresses is a public network. On a public network, all network interfaces use public IP addresses, and the source and destination IP addresses of IP packets transmitted over the network must be public.

On a private network, all network interfaces use private IP addresses. However, under some circumstances, the source or destination IP addresses of IP packets transmitted over a private network can be public (used, for example, to connect to the Internet).

Now that we have some understanding of the concepts of public and private, let's talk about the Internet. The word "Internet" can be used in both a broad and a narrow sense. In the broad sense, it includes both public and private networks. In the narrow sense, it only includes public networks. Figure 11.8 illustrates this distinction. In the case of NAT, we are talking about the Internet in a narrow sense. In other words, when we talk about NAT, the Internet is a collection of public networks that is separate and distinct from private networks.

Network devices on the Internet do not send, receive, or forward any IP packet with a source or destination IP address that is private. In other words, private IP

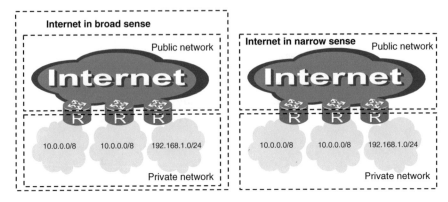

Fig. 11.8 Broad and narrow definitions of the Internet

addresses are forbidden on the Internet. In addition, every IP address on the Internet must be unique.

In the same way, every IP address on a single private network must also be unique. However, duplicate IP addresses may exist on multiple, independent private networks. In Fig. 11.8, the network segment 10.0.0.0/8 is adopted simultaneously by two distinct private networks. Using duplicate IP addresses on different private networks vastly reduces the total number of public IP addresses used, thus slowing the process of public IP address exhaustion.

📖 **NOTE**

IP addresses are 32 bits long, theoretically allowing for about 4.3 billion unique IP addresses. The global population now exceeds 7 billion people. This, combined with the inefficient allocation of addresses with classful networking, the amount of currently available IP addresses is not nearly sufficient to continue to support the rapid expansion of the Internet. This means that the deployment of private networks and the use of private IP addresses are vital to the continued, scalable use of network technology. The diminishing availability of unique IP addresses is known as "IP address exhaustion," a phenomenon that the IPv6 standard has been designed to counteract.

NAT is used for two purposes. The first is to enable private networks to communicate with the Internet, and the second is to enable communication between multiple private networks through the Internet. See Fig. 11.9.

NAT is a methodology that consists of various techniques for mapping the addresses in one address space to a set of corresponding addresses in another. For example, some NAT techniques can only be used to initiate communication requests from private networks to public networks.

In the following sections, we will take a look at the concepts and principles of several basic NAT techniques. Examples are based on the assumption that communication between a private network and a public network is always initiated by

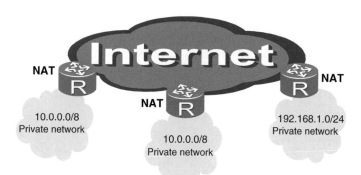

Fig. 11.9 Private networks using NAT to connect to the Internet

the private network. After finishing this chapter, you will be more equipped to perform an in-depth analysis of the operating environment and requirements of a network to determine which NAT technique is best suited to its needs.

11.2.2 Static NAT

Static NAT is based on one-to-one mapping between IP subnets. It is also known as simple NAT.

In Fig. 11.10, a company has deployed a private network and has connected it to the Internet using the router R2. The GE1/0/0 port on R2 is connected to the private

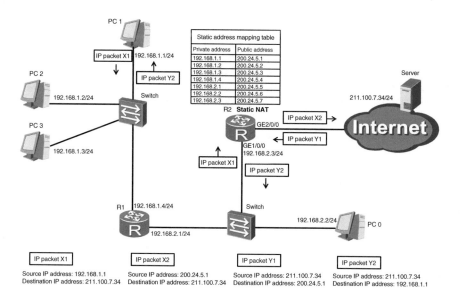

Fig. 11.10 Using static NAT to connect a private network to the Internet

network, and the GE2/0/0 port is connected to the Internet. The private network consists of two network segments (that is, two Layer 2 networks): 192.168.1.0/24 and 192.168.2.0/24. Seven IP addresses have been allocated to devices on these networks:

- 192.168.1.1
- 192.168.1.2
- 192.168.1.3
- 192.168.1.4
- 192.168.2.1
- 192.168.2.2
- 192.168.2.3

The company has also acquired seven public IP addresses in the range 200.24.5.1–200.24.5.7.

You can use static NAT on R2 to enable the private network to communicate with the Internet. Static NAT establishes and maintains a static address mapping table, as shown in Fig. 11.10. This table shows mappings between private and public IP addresses. In this scenario, PC 1 initiates a session by sending IP packet X1 to an Internet server. The source IP address of X1 is 192.168.1.1, which is a private IP address. The destination IP address is 211.100.7.34, which is a public IP address.

When X1 arrives at R2, NAT checks whether the destination IP address of X1 is public. If it is indeed a public IP address, NAT searches its static address mapping table for the public IP address that matches the source IP address of X1. As we can see from the table in Fig. 11.10, 200.24.5.1 is the public IP address that matches the private IP address 192.168.1.1. NAT replaces 192.168.1.1 with 200.24.5.1 to produce a new IP packet, which we will refer to as X2.

X2 is forwarded via the GE2/0/0 port on R2 and reaches the destination server on the Internet. The Internet server responds by sending IP packet Y1 to PC 1. The source and destination IP addresses of Y1 are 211.100.7.34 and 200.24.5.1 respectively, both of which are public IP addresses.

After Y1 arrives at R2, NAT searches the static address mapping table to obtain the private IP address that maps to the destination IP address of Y1. The search result is 192.168.1.1. NAT then replaces 200.24.5.1 with 192.168.1.1, creating a new IP packet named Y2. Y2 enters the private network through the GE1/0/0 port on R2 and ultimately reaches PC 1.

As you can see from this example, the mechanisms behind static NAT are relatively simple, but they require numerous public IP addresses. Therefore, static NAT is rarely used.

Static NAT requires unchanging one-to-one mappings between private IP addresses and public IP addresses. If insufficient public IP addresses are available for mapping private IP addresses, we can use dynamic NAT instead.

11.2.3 Dynamic NAT

As our example company grows in size, the number of private network users increases, while the number of public IP addresses remains the same. In this situation, it is no longer possible to map private IP addresses to public ones on a one-to-one basis.

If the company continues using static NAT on R2, some users will not be able to access the Internet. However, most communication requests initiated by private network users are routed to the private network, rather than to the Internet, so in this situation there would be at most seven concurrent sessions between the private network and the Internet (because the network is allocated seven distinct IP addresses). By taking advantage of this fact, dynamic NAT on R2 can resolve the problem of insufficient public IP addresses.

Dynamic NAT consists of a public IP address resource pool and a dynamic address mapping table. When a private network user attempts to access the Internet, NAT checks the public IP address resource pool to obtain an unassigned address. If all IP addresses are already assigned, NAT will reject the access request. If one or more unassigned addresses are found, NAT will go to the dynamic address mapping table and map the private IP address to a public address.

When the user disconnects from the Internet, NAT deletes the mapping record and places the public IP address back into the address pool. This process allows the same public IP address to be used by different private users at different times. Figure 11.11 illustrates the process of dynamically mapping a private IP address to an available public address in the public IP address resource pool.

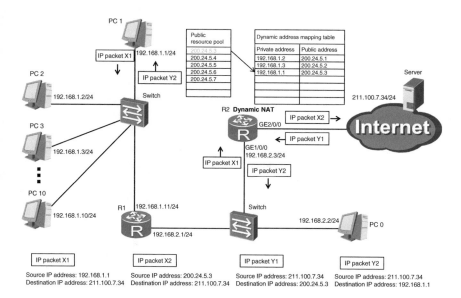

Fig. 11.11 Using dynamic NAT to connect a private network to the Internet

In Fig. 11.11, PC 1 initiates a session by sending IP packet X1 to an Internet server. The source IP address of X1 is 192.168.1.1, which is a private IP address. The destination IP address of X1 is 211.100.7.34, which is a public IP address. When X1 arrives at R2, NAT performs three operations:

1. Selects 200.24.5.3 from the public IP address pool.
2. Opens the dynamic address mapping table.
3. Creates a mapping between 200.24.5.3 and 192.168.1.1.

NAT then replaces 192.168.1.1 with 200.24.5.3 to produce a new IP packet named X2. X2 is forwarded via the GE2/0/0 port on R2 and reaches the destination server on the Internet.

The Internet server responds by sending IP packet Y1 to PC 1. The source and destination IP addresses of Y1 are 211.100.7.34 and 200.24.5.3 respectively, both of which are public IP addresses.

After Y1 arrives at R2, NAT searches the dynamic address mapping table to obtain the private IP address that maps to the destination IP address of Y1. The search result is 192.168.1.1. NAT then replaces 200.24.5.3 with 192.168.1.1, creating a new IP packet named Y2.

Y2 enters the private network through the GE1/0/0 port on R2 and ultimately reaches PC 1. When the session between the Internet server and PC 1 is disconnected, NAT deletes the mapping between 200.24.5.3 and 192.168.1.1 from the dynamic address mapping table, releases 200.24.5.3, and places it back into the address pool.

11.2.4 NAPT

Our example company prospers and hires more than 200 employees. Many of them will require access to the Internet simultaneously. However, the number of concurrent sessions is still limited to seven because only seven public IP addresses are available. In this situation, neither static NAT nor dynamic NAT can fulfill the communication needs of the company, because neither methodology can map a public IP address to more than one private IP address at a time.

If a single public IP address can be mapped to multiple private IP addresses simultaneously, then public IP addresses can be used much more efficiently. Network Address and Port Translation (NAPT) carries out this function. NAPT creates mappings between a combination of a *public* IP address and port number (formatted as "public IP address:port") and a similar combination of a *private* IP address and port number (formatted as "private IP address:port").

Using this methodology, a public IP address can be mapped to several private IP addresses through different port numbers in Transmission Control Protocol (TCP) or User Datagram Protocol (UDP) packets.

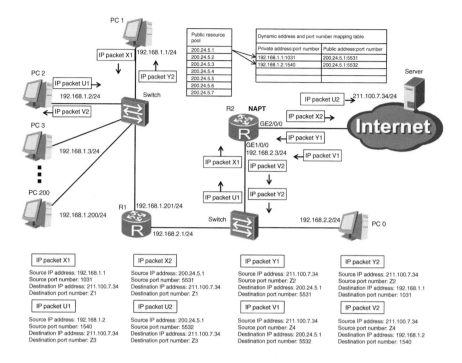

Fig. 11.12   Using NAPT to connect a large private network to the Internet

In Fig. 11.12, NAPT is deployed on R2. For simplicity's sake, we will assume that UDP is adopted.

PC 1 initiates a session by sending IP packet X1 to an Internet server. The source IP address and port number of X1 are 192.168.1.1 (a private address) and 1031 respectively. The destination IP address and port number are 211.100.7.34 (a public address) and Z1 respectively.

When X1 arrives at R2, NAPT selects a public IP address (200.24.5.1) from the address pool and specifies a port number (5531) based on predetermined rules. In the dynamic address and port number mapping table, NAPT creates a mapping between 200.24.5.1:5531 and 192.168.1.1:1031. Based on this mapping, NAPT replaces 192.168.1.1:1031 with 200.24.5.1:5531 to produce a new IP packet named X2. X2 is forwarded via the GE2/0/0 port on R2 and reaches the destination server on the Internet.

The Internet server responds by sending IP packet Y1 to PC 1. The source IP address and port number of Y1 are 211.100.7.34 (a public address) and Z2 respectively. The destination IP address and port number are 200.24.5.1 (also a public address) and 5531 respectively.

After Y1 reaches R2, NAPT searches the dynamic address and port number mapping table for the destination IP address and port number of Y1, that is, 200.24.5.1:5531. It finds that 200.24.5.1:5531 is mapped to 192.168.1.1:1031.

NAPT then replaces 200.24.5.1:5531 with 192.168.1.1:1031, creating a new IP packet named Y2. Y2 enters the private network through the GE1/0/0 port on R2 and ultimately reaches PC 1.

Now let's suppose that when PC 1 is communicating with the Internet server, PC 2 also attempts to access the Internet server. In this scenario, PC 2 sends IP packet U1 to the Internet server. The source IP address and port number of U1 are 192.168.1.2 (a private address) and 1540 respectively. The destination IP address and port number are 211.100.7.34 (a public address) and Z3 respectively.

When U1 arrives at R2, NAPT selects a public IP address (200.24.5.1) from the address pool and specifies a port number (5532) based on predetermined rules. In the dynamic address and port number mapping table, NAPT creates a mapping between 200.24.5.1:5532 and 192.168.1.2:1540. Based on this mapping, NAPT replaces 192.168.1.2:1540 with 200.24.5.1:5532 to produce a new IP packet named U2. U2 is forwarded via the GE2/0/0 port on R2 and reaches the destination server on the Internet.

The Internet server responds by sending IP packet V1 to PC 2. The source IP address and port number of V1 are 211.100.7.34 (a public address) and Z4 respectively. The destination IP address and port number are 200.24.5.1 (also a public address) and 5532 respectively.

After V1 reaches R2, NAPT searches the dynamic address and port number mapping table for the destination IP address and port number of V1, that is, 200.24.5.1:5532. It finds that 200.24.5.1:5532 is mapped to 192.168.1.2:1540. NAPT then replaces 200.24.5.1:5532 with 192.168.1.2:1540, creating a new IP packet named V2. V2 enters the private network through the GE1/0/0 port on R2 and ultimately reaches PC 2.

11.2.5   Easy IP

Easy IP is a simplified version of NAPT. As illustrated in Fig. 11.13, easy IP does not use a public IP address pool. Easy IP requests only one public IP address, that is, the IP address of the GE2/0/0 port on R2. Easy IP also creates and maintains a dynamic address and port number mapping table. In this table, easy IP binds the public IP address to the IP address of the GE2/0/0 port on R2. If the IP address of the GE2/0/0 port on R2 changes, the public IP address in this table also changes. The IP address of the GE2/0/0 interface on R2 can be either manually configured or dynamically allocated.

In all other aspects, easy IP works in the same way as NAPT. In Fig. 11.13, PC 1 and PC 2 communicate with the Internet server in exactly the same way as they did in Fig. 11.12.

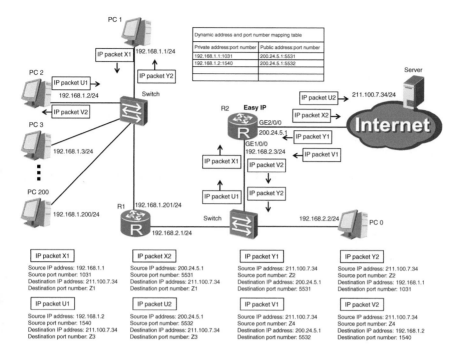

Fig. 11.13 Using Easy IP to connect a large private network to the Internet

11.2.6   Static NAT Configuration Example

In Fig. 11.14, the private network is shown to the left of the router, and the public network is shown to the right of the router. To enable a PC on the private network to communicate with a server on the Internet, we need to configure static NAT on the router and map 192.168.0.2 (private) to 202.10.1.3 (public).

Configuration Roadmap

Configure static NAT on the GE2/0/0 port on the router, and map 192.168.0.2 to 202.10.1.3.

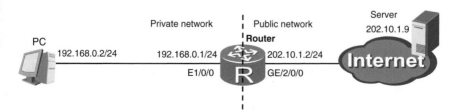

Fig. 11.14 Static NAT configuration example

Procedure

Run the **nat static global** *global-address* **inside** *host-address* command on the router's GE2/0/0 port to bind *global-address* (public IP address) *with host-address* (private IP address).

#Configure the router.

```
[Router] interface gigabitethernet 2/0/0
[Router-GigabitEthernet2/0/0] nat static global 202.10.1.3
inside 192.168.0.2 [Router-GigabitEthernet2/0/0] quit
```

We have finished configuring static NAT. We can now run the **display nat static** command to check whether *global-address* and *host-address* are successfully bound.

```
<Router> display nat static
Static Nat Information:
Interface  : GigabitEthernet2/0/0
Global IP/Port     : 202.10.1.3/----
Inside IP/Port     : 192.168.0.2/----
Protocol : ----
VPN instance-name  : ----
Acl number         : ----
Netmask  : 255.255.255.0
Description : ----

Total :    1
```

From the command output, we can see that 202.10.1.3 has successfully been mapped to 192.168.0.2.

11.3 Review Questions

1. Which of the following statements about the DHCP protocol are true? (Choose all that apply)

   A. The DHCP protocol is the successor to the BOOTP protocol.
   B. Every time a DHCP server offers an IP address to a DHCP client, the DHCP server agrees to an IP address lease with the DHCP client.
   C. The DHCP server, rather than DHCP client, determines the IP address lease duration.
   D. The DHCP relay agent serves as an intermediary for transmitting DHCP messages between the DHCP server and client.
   E. Without the DHCP relay agent, the DHCP server and client cannot transmit DHCP messages.

2. To acquire an IP address from the DHCP server for the first time, the DHCP client goes through four stages. What is the sequence of these four stages? (Choose one)

A. Discovery, request, offer, acknowledgment
B. Discovery, request, acknowledgment, offer
C. Discovery, offer, request, acknowledgment
D. Discovery, acknowledgment, request, offer

3. The DHCP client has acquired an IP address from the DHCP server. The DHCP client has restarted, and wants to use the last offered IP address again. Which stages does the DHCP client need to go through? (Choose all that apply)

A. Discovery
B. Request
C. Acknowledgment
D. Offer

4. Which of the following statements about the DHCP relay agent are true? (Choose all that apply)

A. If the DHCP server and relay agent reside on the same network segment (Layer 2 broadcast domain), but both of them are located on a different network segment from the DHCP client, DHCP protocol will not work correctly.
B. If the DHCP client and relay agent reside on the same network segment (Layer 2 broadcast domain), but both of them are located on a different network segment from the DHCP server, DHCP protocol will work correctly.
C. The DHCP relay agent is mandatory for DHCP protocol. Without the DHCP relay agent, DHCP protocol cannot work.

5. Which of the following statements about NAT are true? (Choose all that apply)

A. NAT is used for communication between public network users.
B. NAT is used for communication between users in the same private network.
C. NAT is used for communication between private and public network users.
D. NAT helps to save public IP address resources.
E. NAT helps to save private IP address resources.
F. Easy IP is a special case of NAPT.

6. Dynamic NAT, static NAT, and NAPT vary in how they make use of public IP addresses. In ascending order from least to most efficient use of public IP addresses, which of the following sequences is correct? (Choose one)

A. Dynamic NAT, static NAT, NAPT
B. NAPT, dynamic NAT, static NAT
C. Static NAT, NAPT, dynamic NAT
D. Static NAT, dynamic NAT, NAPT

Chapter 12
PPP and PPPoE

This chapter discusses the basics of the Point-to-Point Protocol (PPP) and Point-to-Point Protocol over Ethernet (PPPoE), and provides a detailed explanation about the phases involved in each protocol, as well as the many functions provided by these protocols.

After completing this section, you should be able to:

- Understand the basic concepts and functions of both PPP and PPPoE.
- Differentiate between PPP frame and PPPoE packet formats.
- Be familiar with the different phases involved in PPP and PPPoE.

12.1 PPP

12.1.1 Basic Concepts

PPP is a Layer 2 protocol that establishes a direct link between two nodes across different physical layer connections using wide area network (WAN) technology. PPP provides a secure framing mechanism for data encapsulation, including authentication, error detection, and an extensive suite of additional support, such as link aggregation and compression.

PPP involves several key components for transmitting datagrams over physical links; notably the Link Control Protocol (LCP) that establishes and terminates link transmissions once a PPP connection has been established between nodes. One or more Network Control Protocols (NCPs) are also used as optional configuration parameter negotiations for the network layer.

While the Ethernet protocol runs on Ethernet interfaces and links, PPP runs on serial interfaces and links. Within this chapter all references to serial interfaces,

© Springer Science+Business Media Singapore 2016
Huawei Technologies Co., Ltd., *HCNA Networking Study Guide*,
DOI 10.1007/978-981-10-1554-0_12

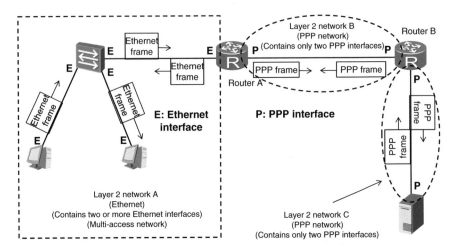

Fig. 12.1 Ethernet (multi-access) and PPP networks

including EIA RS-232-C, EIA RS-422, EIA RS-423, ITU-T V.35 or any serial interface that supports full-duplex communications, will be referenced as PPP interfaces.

A point-to-point network is established when two interfaces enabled with PPP exchange PPP frames over a PPP link. In Fig. 12.1, there are three Layer-2 networks. Network A is an Ethernet network, and networks B and C are PPP networks.

Figure 12.2 shows how Router A is able to extract and encapsulate both Ethernet and PPP frames so that an IP packet can be forwarded across both Ethernet and PPP interfaces.

As shown in Fig. 12.1, Router B has two interfaces, and both of them are PPP interfaces. Figure 12.3 shows the working process of Router B. After receiving a PPP frame from the PPP link, PPP interface Intf-1 of Router B extracts the IP packet from the PPP frame and sends the IP packet to PPP interface Intf-2. Intf-2 encapsulates the IP packet into a PPP frame and sends the PPP frame over the PPP link. After receiving a PPP frame from the PPP link, PPP interface Intf-2 of Router B extracts the IP packet from the PPP frame and sends the IP packet to PPP interface Intf-1. PPP interface Intf-1 encapsulates the IP packet into a PPP frame, and then sends the PPP frame over the PPP link.

12.1.2 PPP Frame Format

Figure 12.4 details the PPP frame format and the individual fields comprising a PPP frame.

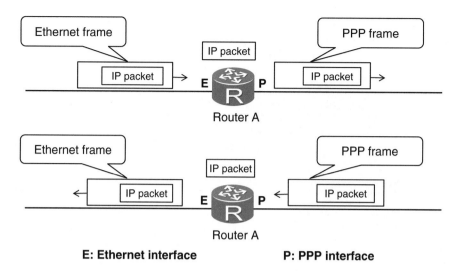

Fig. 12.2 IP packet encapsulation process for Router A

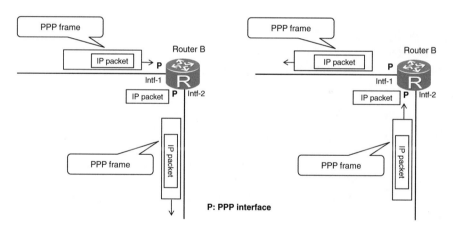

Fig. 12.3 IP packet encapsulation process for Router B

Flag

The Flag field consists of 8 bits and is always set to 0x7e. This field signifies the end of the previous PPP frame and the start of the current PPP frame.

Address

The Address field consists of 8 bits and is always set to 0xff. Note that this field is not a MAC address, but it means all interfaces and is equivalent to a broadcast address.

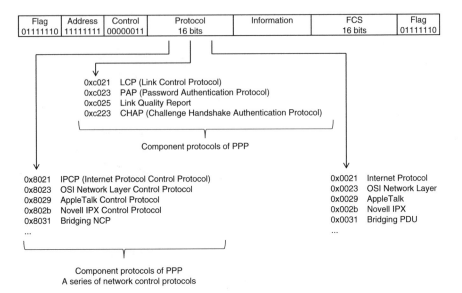

Fig. 12.4 PPP frame format

PPP frames are moved from one point to the other of a PPP link. Therefore, unlike Ethernet frames, PPP frames do not contain the source or destination MAC address. In fact, PPP interfaces do not need MAC addresses.

Control

The Control field consists of 8 bits and is always set to 0x03.

Protocol

The Protocol field consists of 16 bits and its value determines what type of protocol packet is contained in the Information field.

Figure 12.4 shows the protocols represented by the values of the Protocol field.

Information

The Information field is also known as the PPP payload and has a variable length.

FCS

The frame checksum (FCS) field consists of 16 bits and is used for error checking.

12.1.3   Phases in PPP

PPP involves a local interface and a peer interface connected together through a PPP link. As shown in Fig. 12.5, a PPP link goes through five phases in the process

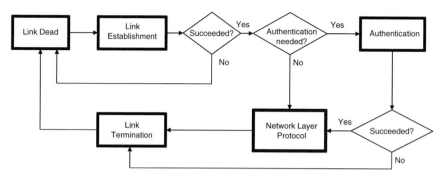

Fig. 12.5 Phases in PPP

of configuring, maintaining and terminating the link: link dead, link establishment, authentication, network layer protocol, and link termination.

The first phase is PPP link dead phase. During this phase, the physical layer functions of PPP interfaces are not ready. Once the physical layer functions of the local and peer interfaces are ready, PPP enters the link establishment phase. In this phase, the interfaces exchange PPP frames carrying LCP packets to negotiate parameters such as the Maximum Receive Unit (MRU) so that PPP can function.

During the link establishment phase, the local and peer interfaces must also negotiate whether to go directly to the network layer protocol phase, or whether the authentication phase is needed prior to the network layer phase. If the authentication phase is required, an authentication protocol must be negotiated. If however the local and peer interfaces agree to bypass the authentication phase, PPP automatically enters the network layer protocol phase. During this phase, the local and peer interfaces use the NCP to negotiate network layer parameters so that PPP frames carrying network layer Protocol Data Units (PDUs) on the PPP link can be sent and received.

PPP link termination occurs in many situations, such as failure in the authentication phase, poor communication on the link, and administrative link shutdown. The PPP link then returns back to the initial link dead phase.

In the following three sections, the link establishment, authentication, and network layer protocol phases will be discussed in detail.

12.1.4 Link Establishment Phase

During the link establishment phase, the local and peer interfaces exchange PPP frames carrying LCP packets. LCP is an integral component within PPP. Figure 12.6 illustrates how an LCP packet is formatted.

The Protocol field value of the PPP frame is 0xc021, indicating that the Information field of the PPP frame is an LCP packet. LCP packets have four fields:

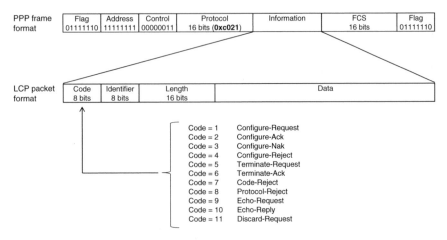

Fig. 12.6 LCP packet format

Code, Identifier, Length, and Data fields. The Code field value determines the LCP packet type.

The Identifier field matches requests sent from the local interface and replies sent from the peer interface. The Length field indicates the total length of an LCP packet (including the Code, Identifier, Length, and Data fields). The Data field is variable in length due to the type of LCP packets used.

From the 11 types of LCP packets, the Configure-Request packet will be used in this example. Figure 12.7 shows how the local and peer interfaces must send at least one Configure-Request packet to each other in the link establishment phase. The Configure-Request packet contains the expected parameter settings of the sender. If the peer replies with a Configure-Ack packet, the peer recognizes and

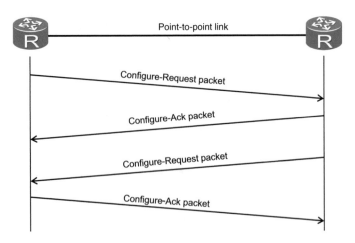

Fig. 12.7 PPP link establishment

accepts all the options in the Configure-Request packet sent from the local interface. If however the peer replies with a Configure-Nak packet, one or many options in the Configure-Request packet are unusable for the peer. In this case, the local device must change the desired options in the Configure-Request packet, send the new Configure-Request packet to the peer, and wait for the reply. This process may repeat multiple times until the local and peer devices reach an agreement on the options in the Configure-Request packets and send a Configure-Ack packet to each other, signifying the success of the link establishment phase.

Figure 12.8 shows the format of the Configure-Request packet within the PPP frame. The Data field of the Configure-Request packet has a maximum of eight options, with each option being a negotiable parameter. Each option contains three fields: Type, Length, and Data.

Figure 12.9 shows the MRU option with the Type field set to 1 and the Length field set to 4, indicating that the total length of the MRU option is four bytes: one byte for the Type field, one for the Length field, and two for the Data field. The value of the Data field is the value of the MRU parameter.

Figure 12.10 shows that for the Authentication Protocol option, while the Type field is set to 3, the Length field can be set to 4 or 5 depending on the Data field. If the first two bytes of the Data field is 0xc023, the Length field is set to 4; if the first two bytes of the Data field is 0xc223, the Length field is set to 5.

If the first two bytes of the Data field is 0xc023, the interface sending the Configure-Request packet expects to use PAP to authenticate the peer interface. However, if the first two bytes of the Data field is 0xc223, the interface expects to use CHAP to authenticate the peer interface. When the first two bytes of the Data field is 0xc023, the total length of the Data field is two bytes. When the first two bytes of the Data field is 0xc223, the total length of the Data field is three bytes. The

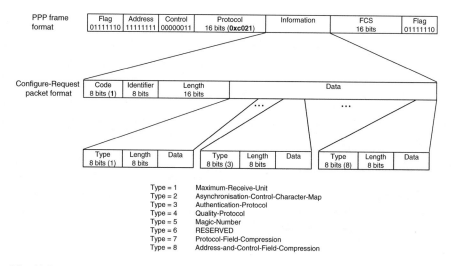

Fig. 12.8 Configure-Request packet format

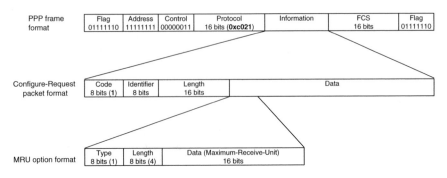

Fig. 12.9 MRU option format

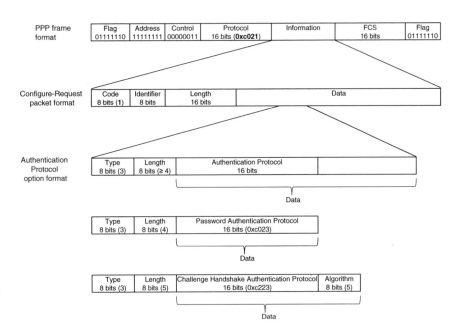

Fig. 12.10 Authentication Protocol option format

last byte of the Data field indicates the encryption algorithm expected to be used in CHAP authentication.

It should be noted that, the negotiated Authentication Protocol options are not necessarily the same on the local and peer interfaces. The negotiation result could be: only one interface authenticates the other, both interfaces authenticate each other; neither interface authenticates the other. When both interfaces authenticate each other, they could use the same or different authentication protocols, such as PAP and CHAP.

All eight options (including Type = 6 Reserved) can be included in one Configure-Request packet. However, if some options are not included in the Configure-Request packet, it means that the default values of the missing options are used.

12.1.5 Authentication Phase

After the link establishment phase, if one or both interfaces request authentication then PPP will enter the authentication phase.

The authentication phase needs to use PAP or CHAP. PAP and CHAP are two component protocols of PPP. The following example will use PAP to describe the authentication process.

In the PAP packet format shown in Fig. 12.11, the Protocol field value of the PPP frame is 0xc023, indicating that the Information field of the PPP frame is a PAP packet. The Code field determines the type of PAP packets. The Code field can be set to 1 for Authenticate-Request packets, 2 for Authenticate-Ack packets, or 3 for Authenticate-Nak packets.

As shown in Fig. 12.12, the Peer-ID field is the user name, and the Password field is the password for the user name.

During the link establishment phase, if interface B sends a Configure-Request packet indicating that interface B expects to use PAP to authenticate interface A, and interface B receives a Configure-Ack from interface A, PPP will enter the

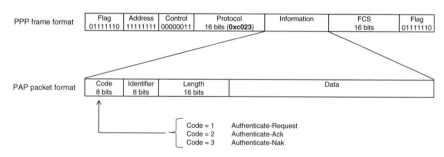

Fig. 12.11 PAP packet format

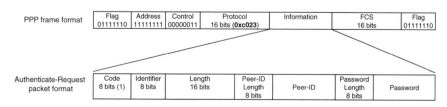

Fig. 12.12 Authenticate-Request packet format

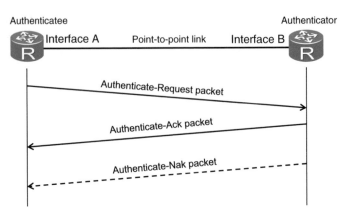

Fig. 12.13 PAP authentication process

authentication phase shown in Fig. 12.13. This makes interface B the authenticator and interface A the authenticatee. During the authentication phase, interface A sends interface B an Authenticate-Request packet containing a user name and password. After receiving the Authenticate-Request packet, interface B checks the user name and password against its user list for a match. If the user name is not included in the user list, or the password does not match the user name, interface B returns an Authenticate-Nak packet to interface A, and authentication fails. If both the user name and password match an entry in the list, interface B returns an Authenticate-Ack packet to interface A, indicating successful authentication.

A severe security risk associated with PAP authentication is that PAP Authenticate-Request packets send user names and passwords in plain text. CHAP is recommended as a more secure authentication protocol because user names and passwords are encrypted.

12.1.6 Network Layer Protocol Phase

If the link establishment phase succeeds, and either interfaces A and B agree to skip the authentication phase, or the authentication phase succeeds, PPP automatically enters the network layer protocol phase.

During the network layer protocol phase, interfaces A and B use the NCP to negotiate network layer parameters so they can send and receive PPP frames carrying network layer PDUs on the PPP link.

Figure 12.4 demonstrates how NCP refers to a range of protocols, and how each network layer protocol has a corresponding NCP to use during negotiations. For example, NCP could refer to Internet Protocol Control Protocol (IPCP) or Novell IPX Control Protocol. If network layer PDUs (such as IP or Novell IPX packets) need to be transmitted on the PPP link, the PPP interfaces must use the corresponding NCP to negotiate. If two types of network layer PDUs, such as

IP and Novell IPX packets, need to be transmitted on the PPP link, the PPP interfaces must use separate NCPs to negotiate the PPP link.

Because IP packets are regarded as some of the most common network layer PDUs, the following example will be discussed using these packets.

Figure 12.14 illustrates the format of an IPCP packet. The Protocol field value of the PPP frame is 0x8021, indicating that the Information field of the PPP frame is an IPCP packet. The Code field determines the type of IPCP packets. In total there are seven different types available.

Figure 12.15 demonstrates how IPCP uses Configure-Request and Configure-Ack packets for IP negotiation. Negotiations must be performed in both directions of the link, meaning each PPP interface must send a Configure-Request packet to the other interface. When both interfaces receive the Configure-Ack packet from the

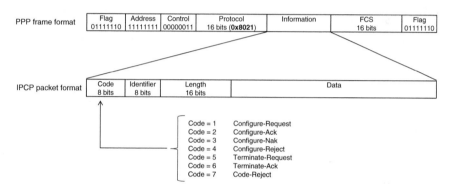

Fig. 12.14 IPCP packet format

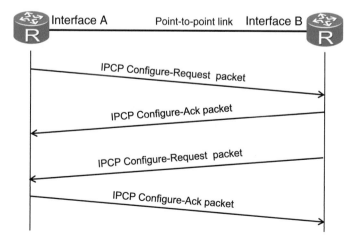

Fig. 12.15 IPCP negotiation

other interface, the negotiation is successful. After the IPCP negotiation succeeds, the PPP link can transfer PPP frames carrying IP packets.

Two IPCP negotiations occur during this phase. One is the IP packet format (standard or compressed) and the other is the interface IP address.

As shown in Fig. 12.16, if the IP address of interface A is IP-A, and interface A wants the other interface to know and recognize its IP address, the Configure-Request packet sent by interface A must contain IP-A. Upon receiving the Configure-Request packet from interface A, interface B checks whether the IP-A contained in the packet is a valid unicast IP address, and whether the IP address is the same as its address. If IP-A is a valid unicast IP address and is different from interface B's IP address, interface B returns a Configure-Ack packet, signifying that it recognizes IP-A as the IP address of interface A. If IP-A is not a valid unicast IP address or is the same as interface B's own IP address, interface B returns a Configure-Nak packet, signifying that it does not recognize IP-A as the IP address of interface A. In this situation, interface A must change its IP address and send a new Configure-Request packet.

Another situation is when no IP address is assigned to interface A, meaning the other interface needs to assign an IP address, as shown in Fig. 12.17. In this case, the Configure-Request packet sent by interface A must contain the IP address 0.0.0.0. After receiving the Configure-Request packet from interface A, interface B checks the IP address in the packet. When interface B discovers that the IP address is 0.0.0.0, interface B knows that interface A is requesting an IP address. Interface B returns a Configure-Nak packet containing the IP address to be assigned (for example, IP-A). After receiving the Configure-Nak packet, interface A extracts IP address IP-A and sends interface B a Configure-Request packet containing IP-A.

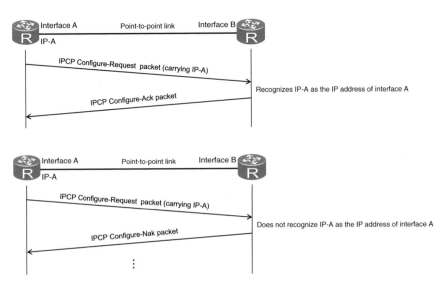

Fig. 12.16 Interface IP address negotiation

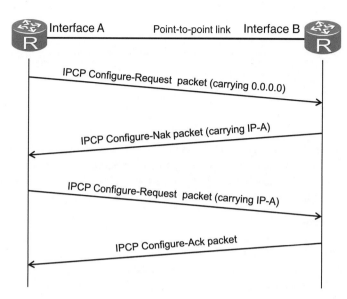

Fig. 12.17 IP address request

Interface B then checks whether the IP address (IP-A) in the packet is a valid unicast IP address, and whether the IP address is the same as its own IP address. If IP-A is a valid and different unicast IP address, interface B returns a Configure-Ack packet.

Similar to LCP negotiation, NCP negotiation happens through the exchange of Configure-Request, Configure-Ack, and Configure-Nak packets, with all defined options contained in one Configure-Request packet during the negotiation. If some defined options are missing in the Configure-Request packet, it means that the default values of these options are used.

12.1.7 Basic PPP Configuration Examples

As shown in Fig. 12.18, routers R1 and R2 are connected through a PPP link. The network administrator wants to set the IP address of Serial 0/0/1 on R1 to 10.0.0.1/30, and Serial 0/0/1 on R2 to 10.0.0.2/30 so that IP packets can be transmitted through the PPP link.

Configuration Roadmap

1. Set the link layer protocol to PPP on interface Serial 0/0/1 of R1 and R2.
2. Assign an IP address to interface Serial 0/0/1 of R1 and R2.

Fig. 12.18 Basic PPP configuration example 1

Procedure

Step 1   To set the link layer protocol to PPP on a router interface, enter the system
         view and run the **interface** *interface-type interface-number* command to
         enter the interface view. Then, in the interface view, run the **link-protocol
         ppp** command to set the link layer protocol to PPP.

```
# Configure R1.
<R1> system-view
[R1] interface serial 0/0/1
[R1-Serial0/0/1] link-protocol ppp
# Configure R2.
<R2> system-view
[R2] interface serial 0/0/1
[R2-Serial0/0/1] link-protocol ppp
```

Step 2   Run the **ip address** *ip-address* {*mask*|*mask-length*} command to configure
         the IP address for the interface.

```
# Configure R1.
[R1-Serial0/0/1] ip address 10.0.0.1 30
# Configure R2.
[R2-Serial0/0/1] ip address 10.0.0.2 30
```

Step 3   Verify the PPP configurations (R1 is used as the example).

```
[R1] display interface serial 0/0/1
Serial0/0/1 current state : UP
Line protocol current state : UP
...
Internet Address is 10.0.0.1/30
Link layer protocol is PPP
LCP opened, IPCP opened
...
```

In the output, "Internet Address is 10.0.0.1/30" indicates that the IP
address of Serial 0/0/1 on R1 is 10.0.0.1/30; "Link layer protocol is PPP"
indicates that the data link layer protocol on Serial 0/0/1 on R1 is PPP and

"LCP opened, IPCP opened" indicates that LCP and IPCP negotiation is successful. Since the Network Control Protocol is IPCP, the PPP link can transmit IP packets.

Step 4   Run the **ping** command to verify that IP packets can be transmitted.

```
<R1> ping 10.0.0.2
  PING 10.0.0.2: 56 data bytes, press CTRL_C to break
    Reply from 10.0.0.2: bytes=56 Sequence=1 ttl=255 time=50 ms
    Reply from 10.0.0.2: bytes=56 Sequence=2 ttl=255 time=50 ms
    Reply from 10.0.0.2: bytes=56 Sequence=3 ttl=255 time=50 ms
    Reply from 10.0.0.2: bytes=56 Sequence=4 ttl=255 time=60 ms
    Reply from 10.0.0.2: bytes=56 Sequence=5 ttl=255 time=30 ms

  --- 10.0.0.2 ping statistics ---
  5 packet(s) transmitted
  5 packet(s) received
  0.00% packet loss
round-trip min/avg/max = 30/48/60 ms
```

The displayed output indicates that IP packets can be transmitted.

Figure 12.19 demonstrates another configuration example in which routers R1 and R2 are again connected through a PPP link, however the network administrator now wants to set the IP address of Serial 0/0/1 on R1 to 10.0.0.1/30 and allow R1 to assign IP address 10.0.0.2 to Serial 0/0/1 on R2, enabling the link between R1 and R2 to transmit IP packets.

Configuration Roadmap

1. Set the link layer protocol to PPP on Serial 0/0/1 of R1 and R2.
2. Set the IP address of Serial 0/0/1 on R1 to 10.0.0.1, and configure R1 to assign IP address 10.0.0.2 to R2.
3. Configure R2 to obtain an IP address from R1 for Serial 0/0/1.

Fig. 12.19 Basic PPP configuration example 2

Procedure

Step 1   Set the link layer protocol to PPP on interface Serial 0/0/1 of R1 and R2.

```
# Configure R1.
<R1> system-view
[R1] interface serial 0/0/1
[R1-Serial0/0/1] link-protocol ppp
# Configure R2.
<R2> system-view
[R2] interface serial 0/0/1
[R2-Serial0/0/1] link-protocol ppp
```

Step 2   Set the IP address of Serial 0/0/1 on R1 to 10.0.0.1/30, and run the **remote address** *ip-address* command to assign IP address 10.0.0.2 to Serial 0/0/1 on R2.

```
# Configure R1.
[R1-Serial0/0/1] ip address 10.0.0.1 30
[R1-Serial0/0/1] remote address 10.0.0.2
```

Step 3   In the Serial 0/0/1 interface view on R2, run the **ip address ppp-negotiate** command to indicate that the interface wants the peer to assign an IP address to it.

```
# Configure R2.
[R2-Serial0/0/1] ip address ppp-negotiate
```

Step 4   Verify the configurations (R2 is used as the example).

```
[R2] display interface serial 0/0/1
Serial0/0/1 current state : UP
Line protocol current state : UP
...
Internet Address is negotiated, 10.0.0.2/32
Link layer protocol is PPP
LCP opened, IPCP opened
...
```

In the output, "Internet Address is negotiated, 10.0.0.2/32" indicates that the IP address of Serial 0/0/1 on R2 is 10.0.0.2/32, which is obtained from R1 through negotiation.

Step 5   Run the **ping** command to verify that the PPP link can transmit IP packets.

```
<R1> ping 10.0.0.2
  PING 10.0.0.2: 56 data bytes, press CTRL_C to break
    Reply from 10.0.0.2: bytes=56 Sequence=1 ttl=255 time=130 ms
    Reply from 10.0.0.2: bytes=56 Sequence=2 ttl=255 time=10 ms
    Reply from 10.0.0.2: bytes=56 Sequence=3 ttl=255 time=30 ms
    Reply from 10.0.0.2: bytes=56 Sequence=4 ttl=255 time=20 ms
    Reply from 10.0.0.2: bytes=56 Sequence=5 ttl=255 time=30 ms

  --- 10.0.0.2 ping statistics ---
    5 packet(s) transmitted
    5 packet(s) received
    0.00% packet loss
round-trip min/avg/max = 10/44/130 ms
```

The displayed output indicates that IP packets can be transmitted.

12.2   PPPoE

12.2.1   Basic Concepts

A typical network for connecting home users to the Internet involves connecting PCs to the home gateway through Ethernet or fast Ethernet (FE) links. As shown in Fig. 12.20, HG-1, HG-2, and HG-3 are the routers (or gateways) of home networks 1, 2, and 3, respectively. HG-1 uses Asymmetric Digital Subscriber Line (ADSL) technology to convert Ethernet frames into transmittable signals on telephone lines. The IP Digital Subscriber Line Access Multiplexer (IP-DSLAM) of the carrier receives the ADSL signals from the different HGs, demodulates the ADSL signals into Ethernet frames, and sends the frames to the Access Concentrator (AC) through a Gigabit Ethernet (GE) link. The IP-DSLAM is equivalent to a Layer-2 Ethernet aggregation switch.

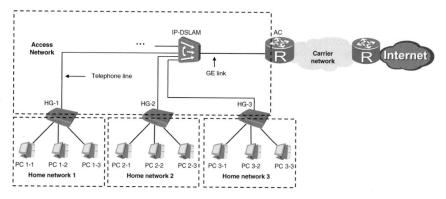

Fig. 12.20 Typical network for connecting home users to the Internet

   Carriers need to charge home users for Internet access. However, Ethernet frames have no field to carry user name and password information, nor are frames forwarded from HG-1 and HG-2 from the IP-DSLAM to the AC distinguishable. If a carrier cannot distinguish the traffic from different home users, the carrier is unable to charge users for Internet access.

   While Ethernet frames cannot carry user name or password information, the PPP can authenticate users through a user name and password. PPP over Ethernet (PPPoE) was developed so that PPP networks, such as those found in Fig. 12.20, can operate similar to a multi-access network and allow two Ethernet interfaces in a broadcast domain to create a point-to-point tunnel and encapsulate PPP frames into Ethernet frames. Figure 12.21 shows how a typical network operates from the point of PPPoE application.

   From Fig. 12.21 you can see how home gateways can set up a virtual (logical) PPP link with the AC using PPPoE and exchange PPP frames. These PPP frames are encapsulated into Ethernet frames to allow exchanges over Ethernet links.

   Figure 12.22 shows the basic architecture of the PPPoE protocol. PPPoE uses a client/server (C/S) architecture. The device running the PPPoE client program is called a host, and the device running the PPPoE server program is called an AC.

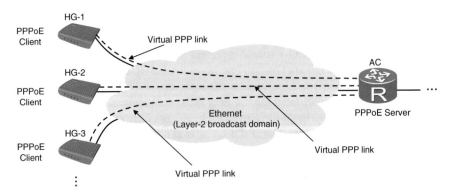

Fig. 12.21 PPPoE access network

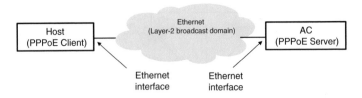

Fig. 12.22 Basic PPPoE architecture

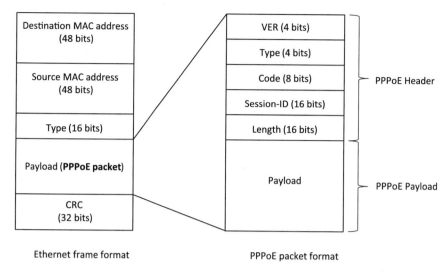

Fig. 12.23 PPPoE packet format

12.2.2 PPPoE Packet Format

Figure 12.23 shows the format of PPPoE packets. If the value of the Type field of an Ethernet frame is 0x8863 or 0x8864, the payload of the Ethernet frame is a PPPoE packet.

PPPoE packets consist of a PPPoE header and a PPPoE payload. In the PPPoE header, the VER (version) and Type fields are always set to 0x1, the Code field indicates the PPPoE packet type, the Length field indicates the length of the PPPoE packets, and the Session-ID field identifies PPPoE sessions.

The PPP frame is in PPPoE payload.

12.2.3 Phases in PPPoE

PPPoE involves two phases: Discovery and PPP Session.

Discovery Phase

Figure 12.24 illustrates how during the PPPoE Discovery phase, the host and AC exchange four types of PPPoE packets:

- PPPoE Active Discovery Initiation (PADI), with the Code field in the header being set to 0x09;
- PPPoE Active Discovery Offer (PADO), with the Code field being set to 0x07;

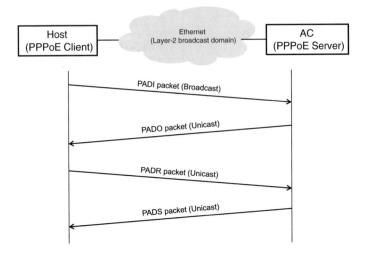

Fig. 12.24 PPPoE Discovery phase

- PPPoE Active Discovery Request (PADR), with the Code field being set to 0x19;
- PPPoE Active Discovery Session-Confirmation (PADS), with the Code field being set to 0x65.

During the Discovery phase seen in Fig. 12.25, the host broadcasts a PADI to search the network for the AC and tell the AC the desired service type. The payload of the PADI packet contains several Type-Length-Value tags, which indicate the desired service types.

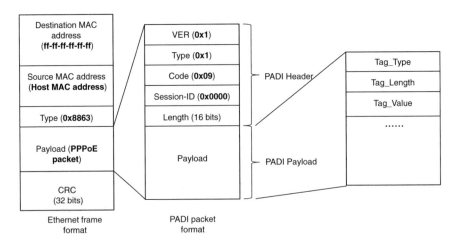

Fig. 12.25 PADI packet format

Upon receiving the PADI packet, the AC compares the requested service types in the PADI packet with the services it can provide. If the AC can provide the services requested by the host, the AC will reply with a unicast PADO packet. If the AC cannot provide the requested service, the AC does not reply. Figure 12.26 shows the format of PADO packets.

If there are multiple ACs on the network, the host may receive multiple PADO packets. Generally the host selects the AC whose PADO packet is the first to arrive on the host as the PPPoE server, and unicasts a PADR packet to that AC. Figure 12.27 shows the format of PADR packets.

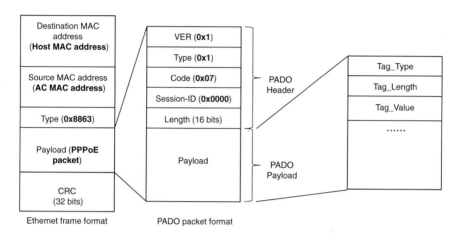

Fig. 12.26 PADO packet format

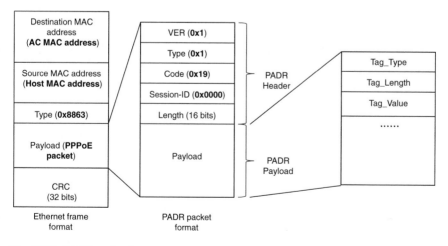

Fig. 12.27 PADR packet format

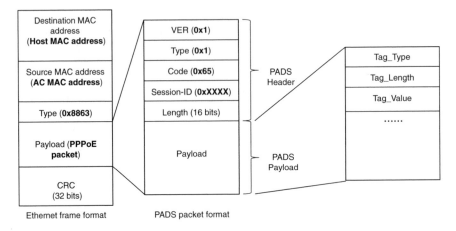

Fig. 12.28 PADS packet format

After receiving the PADR packet, the AC determines the PPPoE session ID, and sends a unicast PADS packet containing the PPPoE session ID in the PPPoE Session_ID field. Figure 12.28 shows the format of PADS packets.

After the host receives the PADS and obtains the PPPoE session ID, the PPPoE session between the host and AC is established. The host and AC then enter the PPP Session phase.

PPP Session Phase

In the PPP Session phase, the host and AC exchange Ethernet frames containing PPP frames. Figure 12.29 shows how the Type field of the Ethernet frame is set to 0x8864 (in the Discovery phase, the field is always set to 0x8863), indicating that the payload of the Ethernet frame is a PPPoE frame. In PPPoE frames, the Code field is set to 0x00, and the Session-ID field is the value determined during the Discovery phase. Now the payload of the PPPoE packet is a PPP frame. However, the PPP frame is incomplete and contains only the Protocol and Information fields of the PPP frame, because other fields of PPP frames are unnecessary on virtual PPP links.

By using PPPoE, the host and AC can exchange PPP frames during the PPP Session phase. The exchange of PPP frames allows the host and AC to go through the Link Establishment, Authentication, and Network Layer Protocol phases, and will enable the host and AC to exchange IP packets.

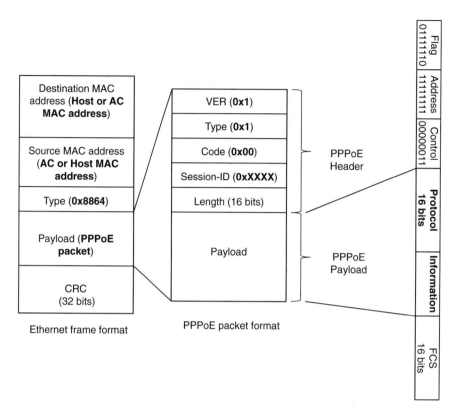

Fig. 12.29 Ethernet frame carrying a PPP frame

12.3 Review Questions

1. Which of the following statements about PPP are correct? (Choose all that apply)

   A. LCP is a component protocol of PPP.
   B. PAP is a component protocol of PPP.
   C. IPCP is a component protocol of PPP.
   D. IPCP is a type of NCP.

2. Which of the following statements about PPP are correct? (Choose all that apply)

   A. PPP consists of the Link Dead, Link Establishment, Authentication (optional), Network Layer Protocol, and Link Termination phases.
   B. During the Link Establishment phase of PPP, the PPP interfaces negotiate the parameters of the PPP link by exchanging NCP packets.

 C. During the Link Establishment phase of PPP, the PPP link can transmit IP packets.

 D. The IPCP negotiation must be successful to allow the PPP link to transmit IP packets.

3. Which two phases does PPPoE have? (Choose one)

 A. PPPoE Discovery and PPP Link Establishment phases.

 B. PPPoE Discovery and PPP Session phases.

 C. PPPoE Discovery and PPPoE Authentication phases.

4. Which four types of PPPoE packets are exchanged during the PPPoE Discovery phase? (Choose one)

 A. PADI, PADO, PADR, and PADT packets.

 B. PADI, PADO, PADR, and PADS packets.

 C. PADI, PADO, PADS, and PADT packets.

5. Which of the following statements about PPPoE is correct? (Choose one)

 A. During the PPP Session phase of PPPoE, IP packets are encapsulated in PPP frames, PPP frames are encapsulated in Ethernet frames, and Ethernet frames are encapsulated in PPPoE packets.

 B. During the PPP Discovery phase of PPPoE, IP packets are encapsulated in PPP frames, PPP frames are encapsulated in PPPoE packets, and PPPoE packets are encapsulated in Ethernet frames.

 C. During the PPP Discovery phase of PPPoE, IP packets are encapsulated in PPP frames, PPP frames are encapsulated in Ethernet frames, and Ethernet frames are encapsulated in PPPoE packets.

 D. During the PPP Session phase of PPPoE, IP packets are encapsulated in PPP frames, PPP frames are encapsulated in PPPoE packets, and PPPoE packets are encapsulated in Ethernet frames.

Chapter 13
Network Management and Security

In this chapter, we will focus on three basic protocols involved in network management: Simple Network Management Protocol (SNMP), Structure of Management Information (SMI), and Management Information Base (MIB).

One important part of network management is network security. When we think about network security, the first thing that usually comes to mind is passwords. As we will see in this chapter, network security is not that simple. Network security involves all network technologies. It has developed into an industry and field with its own technologies and methods. Describing the entirety of network security is beyond the scope of this chapter. Instead, we will look at a common security technique: access control list (ACL).

After completing this chapter, you will be able to understand:

- Fundamental concepts of network management
- The three main protocols used by network management systems (NMS)
- The basic architecture of Simple Network Management Protocol (SNMP)
- The fundamentals and functions of ACL
- The differences between basic and advanced ACLs
- The structure and matching sequences of ACL rules
- Wildcard characters in ACLs.

13.1 Network Management

13.1.1 Basic Concepts in Network Management

A network administrator faces many problems throughout the day. They may need to identify the location of routers, deal with switching issues, ensure that network segments are properly connected, and monitor the traffic on network devices.

© Springer Science+Business Media Singapore 2016
Huawei Technologies Co., Ltd., *HCNA Networking Study Guide*,
DOI 10.1007/978-981-10-1554-0_13

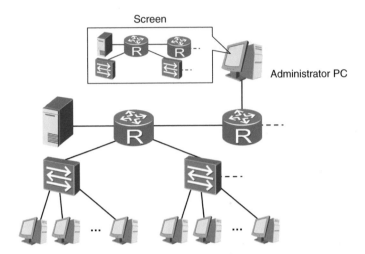

Fig. 13.1 Screen of the administrator PC

In this section, we will look at how we can diagnose and fix these problems.

Simply speaking, network management is to gain visibility into the network structure and status and then take action when necessary. Network management is vital to ensure reliable network operation.

Figure 13.1 gives an example of what a network administrator sees when monitoring a network. The icons on the screen of administrator PC represent real network devices, such as routers, switches, and servers.

If you click an icon, the name and the location of the device will be displayed. If a device has a problem, the device icon changes color. If you click the icon of a router and check the detailed information, you can see the number of IP packets received on some interface in a 24-h period.

13.1.2 Network Management System

eSight is Huawei's next generation network management system (NMS) for enterprise networks and data centers. Once installed on a network administrator's computer, it can:

1. Display network topology
2. Monitor and analyze network port status
3. Monitor and analyze network performance data
4. Create fault alarms and perform diagnosis
5. Allow remote configuration

After installation and configuration, an NMS can communicate with managed devices. The NMS collects, analyzes, and processes information from those

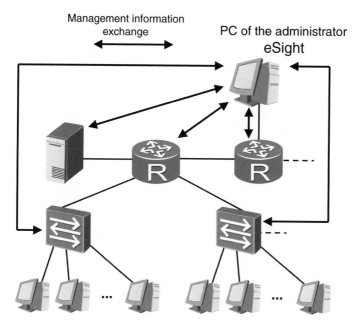

Fig. 13.2 Management information exchange

managed devices. It also provides visibility to the network administration in the form of figures, tables, text, and even voice (Fig. 13.2).

To communicate with each other, the NMS and managed devices use Simple Network Management Protocol (SNMP). Like Dynamic Host Configuration Protocol (DHCP), SNMP uses a Client/Server (CS) model.

As we can see in Fig. 13.3, the SNMP client runs on the NMS computer while the SNMP server runs on managed devices. Management information is carried in the SNMP protocol data units (PDUs).

For networks that use the TCP/IP suite of protocols, NMS requires three protocols: SNMP, Structure of Management Information (SMI), and Management Information Base (MIB). SNMP is the core protocol, but requires the other two protocols to define sets of related managed objects and describe the structure of management data.

13.1.3 SMI

In the network management, a managed object can be a router, a switch, a board on a router, a port on a board, or the number of IP packets received by a port. Managed objects are large in number and vary in type and level.

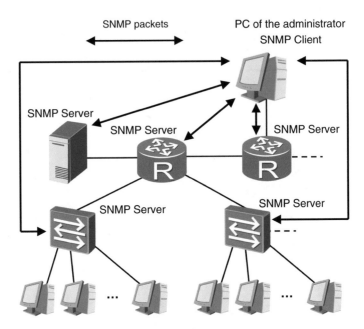

Fig. 13.3 SNMP management information exchange

SMI provides rules to organize managed objects. SMI rules are classified into three types. These rules determine:

- How managed objects are named
- How types of managed objects are defined
- How objects related information is coded

In SMI, the object identifier is used to distinguish the type of the managed object. SMI uses a tree structure to define object identifiers, as shown in Fig. 13.4.

As shown in Fig. 13.4, each box represents a managed object with its own parent and child objects. The structure is hierarchical. For the "internet" object, the object identifier is 1.3.6.1 (iso.org.dod.internet); for the "interface" object, the object identifier is 1.3.6.1.2.1.2 (iso.org.dod.internet.mgmt.mib-2.interface).

13.1.4   MIB

While SMI defines the rules, Management Information Base (MIB) is the application of the rules on the managed devices. MIB must identify the managed objects on a managed device and determine the name and type of each managed object.

The function of MIB is to create a database on a managed device. The database includes the managed objects and their names, types, and contents, all of which must comply with SMI rules. In this database, each managed object is equivalent to

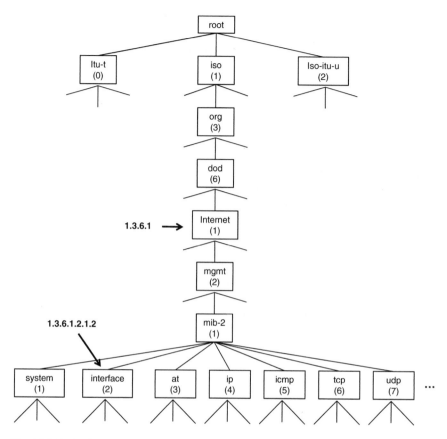

Fig. 13.4 Rules for naming managed objects

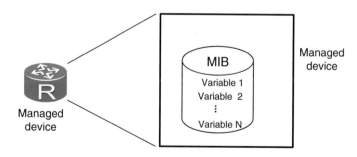

Fig. 13.5 MIB

a variable, each object name a variable name, each object type a variable type, and each object content a variable value.

Figure 13.5 shows an MIB database on a managed device. It is a mathematical representation of the managed objects. For example, when the internal temperature of a device drops, the value of the variable associated with temperature in the MIB will decrease. When an interface of a device receives an IP packet, the value of the variable associated with number of received IP packets in the MIB will increase by 1.

13.1.5   SNMP

SNMP consists of two parts:

- Manager (SNMP client)—software that runs on the administrator's computer
- Agent (SNMP server)—software that runs on managed devices

SNMP has at eight types of PDUs:

- GetRequest
  A manager-to-agent request for the value of a variable or list of variables.
- GetNextRequest
  A manager-to-agent request for subsequent variables and their values.
- GetBulkRequest
  A manager-to-agent request for multiple GetNextRequest. This is an optimized version of GetNextRequests.
- SetRequest
  A manager-to-agent request to change the value of a variable or list of variables.
- Response
  An agent-to-manager response that includes variables and acknowledgement.
- Trap
  An agent-to-manager notification that enables an agent to notify the manager of significant events.
- InformRequest
  An agent-to-manager and manager-to-manager notification acknowledging receipt.
- Report
  An agent-to-manager notification reporting that information requested is not available.

SNMP PDUs are encapsulated in UDP packets. SNMP manager-to-agent PDUs are sent to agent UDP port 161. Agent-to-manager PDUs are sent to manager UDP port 162.

As shown in Fig. 13.6, the manager can send a GetRequest PDU to the agent to request information about a managed object on a managed device. Upon receiving the GetRequest PDU, the agent extracts the information about the managed object from the MIB, encapsulates the information into a Response PDU, and sends it to the manager.

If the manager needs to configure or change the information about a managed object, the manager can send a SetRequest PDU to the agent. Upon receiving the

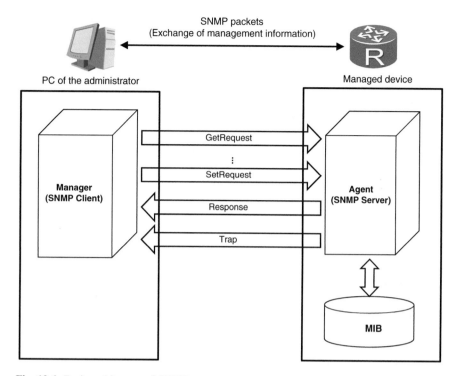

Fig. 13.6 Basic architecture of SNMP

SetRequest PDU, the agent configures or changes the information about the managed object in the MIB.

The following example describes how a manager can control a managed object remotely.

The value of a countdown timer on a server is determined by a variable in the MIB. When the value of the countdown timer reaches 0, the server shuts down automatically. If the administrator wants to immediately shut down the server, the administrator can send a SetRequest PDU to the server agent.

This example PDU sets the value of the variable (corresponding to the countdown timer) in the MIB to 0. The server immediately shuts down. If the administrator wants to shut down the server in two hours, the administrator can send a SetRequest PDU to the server agent that sets the value of the variable (corresponding to the countdown timer) in the MIB to 7200 s.

To sum up, the manager can send the agents PDUs, such as GetRequest and SetRequest PDUs, to check or change the information about managed objects. The agents can also send Trap PDUs to managers, carrying significant event and alarm information.

SNMP is hierarchical. As shown in Fig. 13.7, a manager can also be an agent of a higher-level manager.

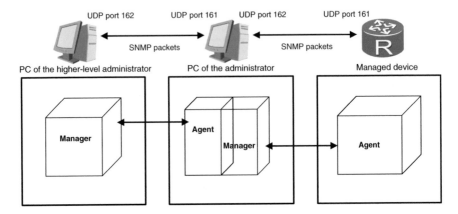

Fig. 13.7 Hierarchical architecture of SNMP

13.2 Network Security

13.2.1 Access Control List Fundamentals

An access control list (ACL) is a widely used network technology that defines which source and destination IP addresses or subnets, protocols, and applications ports can access different areas of a network. As we will see, ACLs can offer great flexibility in controlling access on a network and are often implemented with other technologies, such as firewalls, routing policies, Quality of Service (QoS), and traffic filtering.

In this book, we will look at ACLs from the perspective of network security as it is implemented on Huawei network devices. Please note that implementation varies with different vendors.

ACLs are divided into different types: basic, advanced, Layer-2, and user-defined. The most widely used are basic and advanced. Each ACL configured on a network device has an ACL number. The range of possible ACL numbers is different depending on ACL type:

- Basic—2000 to 2999
- Advanced—3000 to 3999
- Layer-2—4000 to 4999
- User-defined—5000 to 5999

When configuring an ACL, the number must fall in the correct range for the ACL type.

An ACL consists of multiple deny|permit statements. Note that the meaning of deny or permit will vary depending on what technologies ACL is working with. For example, when ACL is implemented with traffic filtering, deny mean access denied while permit mean access permitted.

When an ACL is configured on a device, the device compares received packets against the ACL rules one by one. If a packet matches an ACL rule, the device performs the action (permit or deny) as defined in the rule. When the packet matches a rule, the device stops the comparison process. If the packet does not match a rule, the packet is compared against the next rule. If the packet does not match any rule in the ACL, the device allows the packet, by default. This is known as an implicit permit.

Each ACL rule has rule ID. By default, packets are matched against the rules in ascending order of rule IDs. By default, devices automatically assign an ID incrementally as they are created. For example, if the increment is 5 (Huawei device default), the automatically assigned rules will be 5, 10, 15, and so on. Likewise, if the rule ID increment is set to 2, the automatically assigned rule IDs will be 2, 4, 6, and so on. The larger the increment, the more rules that can be inserted between two adjacent rules.

13.2.2 Basic ACL

In a basic ACL rule, only the source IP address, IP fragment, and time range can be defined.

The command syntax of a basic ACL is:

rule [*rule-id*] {**deny|permit**} [**source**{*source-address source-wildcard*|**any**}|
fragment|logging|time-range *time-name*]

The elements of the command are:

- **rule**: Creates a rule
- *rule-id*: Rule ID number
- **deny|permit**: The rule either denies or permits as specified
- **source**: Specifies the source IP address.
- *source-address*: Source IP address.
- *source-wildcard*: A wildcard in the source IP address. *source-wildcard* and *source-address* can be used together to determine a set of IP addresses or a single IP address. The usage of *source-wildcard* is the same as the usage of *wildcard-mask* described in Sect. 8.3.11.
- **any**: Indicates that the source IP address can be any IP address.
- **fragment**: Specifies that only non-first IP fragments can match this rule.
- **logging**: Specifies that IP packets matching this rule will be logged.
- **time-range** *time-name*: Specifies that the rule is effective only during the period of *time-name*.

As shown in Fig. 13.8, a company network includes the Research and Development (R&D), Human Resources, and Financial Department areas. In the R&D area, an intern is using a PC (IP address: 172.16.10.100/24).

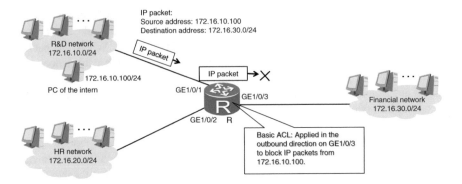

Fig. 13.8 Basic ACL

For security reasons, we need to prevent the intern from sending packets to the Financial Department area. To do this, we can create a basic ACL on router R. The basic ACL will match IP packets sent from the intern's IP address. The ACL will be configured on GE1/0/3 and applied in the outbound direction.

Now let's see how to configure router R. First, we need to create an ACL numbered 2000 in the system view of router R.

```
[R] acl 2000
[R-acl-basic-2000]
```

Then, in the ACL view, we create the following rule:

```
[R-acl-basic-2000] rule deny source 172.16.10.100 0.0.0.0
[R-acl-basic-2000]
```

This rule will deny the IP packets from 172.16.10.100.

Finally, we use the **traffic-filter** command to apply ACL 2000 on the GE1/0/3 interface of router R in the outbound direction.

```
[R-acl-basic-2000] quit
[R] interface gigabitethernet 1/0/3
[R-GigabitEthernet1/0/3] traffic-filter outbound acl 2000
[R-GigabitEthernet1/0/3]
```

Now, IP packets from 172.16.10.100 cannot pass through the GE1/0/3 interface of router R.

13.2.3 Advanced ACL

In advanced ACLs, you can define the source IP address, destination IP address, protocol, packet priority, packet length, TCP/UDP source port, and TCP/UDP destination port. Advanced ACLs allow for more accurate, narrow, and flexible rules.

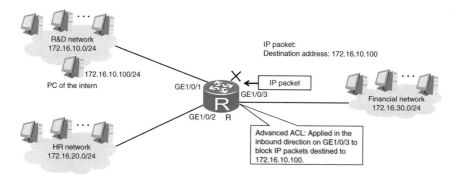

Fig. 13.9 Advanced ACL

The syntax of advanced ACLs varies according to how IP packets are encapsulated. The following syntax is a simplified version for all IP packets.

rule [*rule-id*] {**deny**|**permit**} **ip** [**destination** {*destination-address destination-wildcard*|**any**}] [**source** {*source-address source-wildcard*|**any**}]

Figure 13.9 shows the same network as Fig. 13.8. This time, however, we need to prevent the intern from receiving IP packets from the Financial Department network. To do this, we can configure an advanced ACL on router R. The advanced ACL will be configured on GE1/0/3, applied in the inbound direction, and match IP packets destined to the IP address of the intern.

Now let's see how to configure router R. First, we need to create an ACL numbered 3000 in the system view of router R.

```
[R] acl 3000
[R-acl-adv-3000]
```

Then, in the ACL view, create the following rule:

```
[R-acl-adv-3000]  rule  deny  destination  172.16.10.100
0.0.0.0
[R-acl-adv-3000]
```

This rule denies the IP packets destined to 172.16.10.100.

Finally, use the **traffic-filter** command to apply ACL 3000 on GE1/0/3 of router R in the inbound direction.

```
[R-acl-adv-3000] quit
[R] interface gigabitethernet 1/0/3
[R-GigabitEthernet1/0/3] traffic-filter inbound acl 3000
[R-GigabitEthernet1/0/3]
```

Now, IP packets destined to 172.16.10.100 cannot pass through GE1/0/3 of router R.

13.2.4   Basic ACL Configuration Example

Figure 13.10 shows a company network. For security reasons, we need to allow only the PC of the network administrator Telnet access to router R while denying all other PCs Telnet access.

Configuration Roadmap

1. Create a basic ACL on router R.
2. Create rules in the basic ACL to distinguish IP packets from the network administrator and IP packets from other PCs.
3. Apply the basic ACL on the Virtual Type Terminal (VTY) line.

Procedure

Assume that the IP address of the network administrator's PC is 172.16.0.2 and the administrator used Telnet to connect to router R from the PC.

1. To create the ACL on router R, enter the system view and run the **acl** *acl-number* command.

```
<Router> system-view
[Router] acl 2000
[Router-acl-basic-2000]
```

2. Use the **rule** command to create a rule. First, create a rule to permit IP packets from 172.16.0.2.

```
[Router-acl-basic-2000] rule permit source 172.16.0.2 0
```

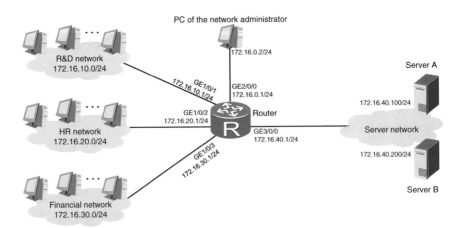

Fig. 13.10 Basic ACL configuration example

3. Then, create a rule to deny IP packets from all other IP addresses.

```
[Router-acl-basic-2000] rule deny source any
```

4. Run the **display acl 2000** command to check the configuration of ACL 2000.

```
[Router-acl-basic-2000] quit
[Router] quit
<Router> display acl 2000
Basic ACL 2000, 2 rules
ACL's step is 5
  rule 5 permit source 172.16.0.2 0 (0 times matched)
  rule 10 deny (0 times matched)
```

From the output, we can see that ACL 2000 has two rules, which are automatically numbered 5 and 10. Here "step" refers to the increment in ACL numbering. "Times matched" refers the number of times packets have matched this rule. In this output it is zero because we have not applied on the router yet.

5. Then, apply ACL 2000 on the VTY line.

```
<Router> system-view
[Router] user-interface vty 0 4
[Router-ui-vty0-4]
[Router-ui-vty0-4] acl 2000 inbound
```

6. To verify whether the configuration has taken effect, log out the administrator and telnet to the router as the administrator again.

```
<PC> telnet 172.16.0.1
Trying 172.16.0.1...
Press CTRL+K to abort
Connected to 172.16.0.1...
Info: The max number of VTY users is 10, and the number of
current VTY users on line is 1.
The current login time is 2014-10-03 02:06:00.
<Router>
```

7. Display the ACL 2000 configuration on the router.

```
<Router> display acl 2000
Basic ACL 2000, 2 rules
ACL's step is 5
  rule 5 permit source 172.16.0.2 0 (1 times matched)
  rule 10 deny (0 times matched)
```

From the output, we can see that the first rule has been matched once, meaning that the IP packet sent from the PC of the administrator has matched the rule.

8. Then, try to telnet to the router from other PCs.

```
<PC> telnet 172.16.10.1
Trying 172.16.10.1...
Press CTRL+K to abort
Error: Failed to connect to the remote host.
```

9. Display the ACL 2000 configuration on the router.

```
<Router> display acl 2000
Basic ACL 2000, 2 rules
ACL's step is 5
  rule 5 permit source 172.16.0.2 0 (1 times matched)
  rule 10 deny (1 times matched)
```

From the output, we can see that the second rule has been matched once, meaning that the IP packet sent from the PC of a non-administrator has matched the rule.

13.3   Review Questions

1. Which three protocols are used by a network management system? (Choose one)

   A. SMTP, SMI, and MIB
   B. SNMP, SMI, and RIP
   C. SNMP, SMI, and MIB

2. In SNMP, what is the destination port of trap packets? (Choose one)

   A. 161
   B. 162
   C. 163

3. Which one of the following ACL rules is a valid basic ACL rule? (Choose one)

   A. rule permit ip
   B. rule deny ip
   C. rule permit source any
   D. rule permit tcp source any

4. To permit the IP packets from network 172.16.10.0/24, which of the following basic ACL rules should be used? (Choose one)

   A. rule permit source 172.16.10.0 0.0.0.0
   B. rule permit source 172.16.10.0 255.255.255.255
   C. rule permit source 172.16.10.0 0.0.255.255
   D. rule permit source 172.16.10.0 0.0.0.255

5. To deny IP packets destined from network 172.16.10.1 to network 172.16.20.0/24, which of the following advanced ACL rules should be used? (Choose one)

   A. rule deny source 172.16.10.1 0.0.0.0
   B. rule deny source 172.16.10.1 0.0.0.0 destination 172.16.20.0 0.0.0.255
   C. rule deny tcp source 172.16.10.1 0.0.0.0 destination 172.16.20.0 0.0.0.255
   D. rule deny ip source 172.16.10.1 0.0.0.0 destination 172.16.20.0 0.0.0.255

6. Which of the following statements about advanced ACL rules are correct? (Choose all that apply)

   A. TCP destination ports can be specified in advanced ACL rules.
   B. TCP source ports can be specified in advanced ACL rules.
   C. UDP destination ports can be specified in advanced ACL rules.
   D. UDP source ports can be specified in advanced ACL rules.
   E. Destination IP addresses can be specified in advanced ACL rules.

Chapter 14
Appendix-Answers to Review Questions

1.1.4

1. Answer: ABC
2. Answer: BC

1.2.4

1. Answer: ABEF
2. Answer: D
3. Answer: B
4. Answer: ABCE

1.3.3

1. Answer: AD
2. Answer: C
3. Answer: E
4. Answer: C

1.4.3

1. Answer: BC
2. Answer: B
3. Answer: B
4. Answer: B
5. Answer: A

2.9

1. Answer: ABD
2. Answer: C
3. Answer: B
4. Answer: C
5. Answer: ABCD

© Springer Science+Business Media Singapore 2016
Huawei Technologies Co., Ltd., *HCNA Networking Study Guide*,
DOI 10.1007/978-981-10-1554-0_14

3.1.3

1. Answer: BD
2. Answer: AC
3. Answer: ABD
4. Answer: BC

3.2.3

1. Answer: B
2. Answer: B
3. Answer: BD
4. Answer: BC

3.3.6

1. Answer: B
2. Answer: C
3. Answer: AD
4. Answer: BC
5. Answer: B

3.4.3

1. Answer: BD
2. Answer: C
3. Answer: A
4. Answer: B
5. Answer: B

4.7

1. Answer: A
2. Answer: B
3. Answer: BC
4. Answer: D
5. Answer: AD
6. Answer: ABC
7. Answer: A

5.10

1. Answer: AC
2. Answer: ABC
3. Answer: ABC
4. Answer: A
5. Answer: BC

6.7

1. Answer: ABD
2. Answer: CEG
3. Answer: A
4. Answer: C
5. Answer: D
6. Answer: AB
7. Answer: ABC

7.4

1. Answer: C
2. Answer: C
3. Answer: ABC
4. Answer: DE
5. Answer: CD
6. Answer: C

8.1.9

1. Answer: C
2. Answer: ABC
3. Answer: A
4. Answer: B
5. Answer: D
6. Answer: A

8.2.9

1. Answer: CD
2. Answer: C
3. Answer: D
4. Answer: D
5. Answer: ABD
6. Answer: AB

8.3.12

1. Answer: B
2. Answer: ABCG
3. Answer: AB
4. Answer: C
5. Answer: CFH
6. Answer: AC
7. Answer: D

9.5

1. Answer: AC
2. Answer: BCD
3. Answer: AC
4. Answer: BCEFG

10.4

1. Answer: ABCF
2. Answer: AC
3. Answer: C
4. Answer: AB
5. Answer: E

11.3

1. Answer: ABCD
2. Answer: C
3. Answer: BC
4. Answer: AB
5. Answer: CDF
6. Answer: D

12.3

1. Answer: ABCD
2. Answer: AD
3. Answer: B
4. Answer: B
5. Answer: D

13.3

1. Answer: C
2. Answer: B
3. Answer: C
4. Answer: D
5. Answer: D
6. Answer: ABCDE

Printed in the United States
By Bookmasters